# Berlitz

# Latin American
# **Spanish**
## *phrase book*

**Berlitz Publishing Company, Inc.**

Princeton   Mexico City   London   Eschborn   Singapore

# HOW TO USE THIS BOOK

We suggest that you start with the Pronunciation section (pp. 6-9), then turn to Basic Expressions (pp. 10-19). These sections give you some useful words, phrases, and short dialogs and help you get used to pronouncing and using the language.

Consult the Contents pages (pp. 3-5) for the section you need. In each chapter you'll find travel facts, hints, and useful information. Sample phrases are followed by translations and pronunciation.

Look for special YOU MAY HEAR and YOU MAY SEE boxes that highlight phrases that someone may say to you or signs you may see during your travels.

Read along with the dialog boxes (e.g. IN A CAFÉ) that present short, useful conversations. An audio recording of the dialogs in this book can be heard in the Cassette Pack and CD Pack versions.

If you want to know the meaning of a word, your fastest look-up is via the Dictionary section (pp. 168-214).

If you wish to learn about constructing sentences, check the Grammar in the Reference section (pp. 215-218).

Note the color margins are indexed to help you quickly locate the section you need.

If you have difficulty speaking and understanding the language, you can hand the phrase book to the Spanish speaker to encourage pointing to the appropriate sentence.

Copyright © 2001 Berlitz Publishing Company, Inc.
400 Alexander Park, Princeton, NJ, 08540 USA
9-13 Grosvenor St., London, W1X 9FB UK

Berlitz Trademark Reg. U.S. Patent Office and other countries
Marca Registrada

Cover Photo:     © Steve Lucas/International Stock
Layout:          Media Content Marketing, Inc.

ISBN 2-8315-7846-9
Printed in Spain

# TABLE OF CONTENTS

# PRONUNCIATION

This section is designed to make you familiar with the sounds of Spanish using our simplified phonetic transcription. You'll find the pronunciation of the Spanish letters and sounds explained below, together with their "imitated" equivalents. This system is used throughout the phrase book: simply read the pronunciation as if it were English, noting any special rules below.

## THE SPANISH LANGUAGE

There are almost 350 million speakers of Spanish worldwide – it is the third most widely spoken language after Chinese and English. These are the countries where you can expect to hear Spanish spoken (figures are approximate):

### México  Mexico

Spanish is spoken by most of the 98 m. population. Other languages: 6 m. speak Indian languages, esp. *Nahuatl* (1.5 m.), *Maya* (1 m.) in Yucatán.

### América del Sur  South America

Spanish is spoken by the great majority in **Argentina** (34 m.); **Bolivia** (less than half the 7.5 m. population), other languages: *Quechua* (2 m.), *Aymara* (1.5 m.); **Colombia** (35 m.), other: *Arawak*, *Carib*; **Ecuador** (11 m.), other: *Quechua* (0.5 m.); **Paraguay** – three quarters the 5.5 m. population, other: *Guarani* (3 m.); **Peru** (24 m.), other: *Quechua* (5 m.), *Aymara* (0.5 m.); **Uruguay** (3.5 m.); **Venezuela** (22 m.), other: *Arawak*, *Carib*.

### América Central  Central America

Spanish is spoken in **Costa Rica** (3.5 m.); **Cuba** (11 m.); **Dominican Republic** (8 m.); **Puerto Rico** (4 m.); **El Salvador** (6 m.); **Guatemala** (10 m.), other: *Quiché* (1 m.), *Cakchiquel* (0.5 m.); **Honduras** (5.5 m.), other: *Lenca*, *Carib*; **Nicaragua** (4 m.); **Panama** (3 m.).

### Estados Unidos  United States

Spanish is spoken by approx. 18 m. people, especially in Texas, New Mexico, Arizona, California, southern Florida, and New York City.

### España  Spain

Spanish is spoken by most of the population (40 m.). Other languages: *Catalan* in northeastern Spain (6 m.), *Galician* – a dialect of Portuguese – in northwestern Spain (3 m.) and *Basque* (almost 1 m.).

### África  Africa

Spanish is the official language of **Equatorial Guinea** (4.5 m.), other: *Fang*. Spanish is also spoken in the Spanish zone of **Morocco**.

The Spanish alphabet is the same as English, with the addition of the letter **ñ**. The acute accent (´) indicates stress, not a change in sound.

Some Spanish words have been incorporated into English, for example **bonanza, canyon, patio, plaza, siesta**.

Until recently in Spanish, **ch** and **ll** were treated as separate letters, alphabetically ordered after **c** and **l** respectively. Look out for this when looking up old telephone directories or dictionaries.

There are some differences in vocabulary and pronunciation between the Spanish spoken in Spain and that in the Americas – although each is easily understood by the other. This phrase book and dictionary is specifically geared to travelers in Spanish-speaking Americas.

## CONSONANTS

| Letter | Approximate pronunciation | Symbol | Example | Pronunciation |
|--------|---------------------------|--------|---------|---------------|
| b | 1. as in English | b | **bueno** | _bweno_ |
| | 2. between vowels as in English, but softer | b | **bebida** | _bebeeda_ |
| c | 1. before **e** and **i**, like _s_ in _sit_ | s | **centro** | _sentro_ |
| | 2. otherwise like _k_ in _kit_ | k | **como** | _komo_ |
| ch | as in English | ch | **mucho** | _moocho_ |
| d | 1. as in English _dog_, but less decisive | d | **donde** | _dondeh_ |
| | 2. at the end of a word, like _th_ in _this_ | th | **usted** | _oosteth_ |
| g | 1. before **e** and **i**, like _ch_ in Scottish lo_ch_ (except in Caribbean and Central America where pronounced like _h_ in _hat_) | kh | **urgente** | _oorkhenteh_ |
| | 2. otherwise, like _g_ in _get_ | g | **ninguno** | _neengoono_ |
| h | always silent | | **hombre** | _ombreh_ |
| j | like _ch_ in Scottish lo_ch_ | kh | **bajo** | _bakho_ |
| ll | like _lli_ in mi_lli_on; in some parts like _y_ in _yet_ or _s_ in plea_s_ure | l-y | **lleno** | _l-yeno_ |
| ñ | like _ni_ in o_ni_on | ñ | **señor** | _señor_ |
| qu | like _k_ in _kick_ | k | **quince** | _keenseh_ |

| r | more strongly trilled (like a Scottish *r*), especially at the beginning of a word | r | **río** | _reeo_ |
| rr | strongly trilled | rr | **arriba** | _arreeba_ |
| s | like *s* in *s*it often with a slight lisp | s | **vista** | _beesta_ |
| v | like *b* in *b*ad, but softer | b | **viejo** | _beeyekho_ |
| x | 1. usually like *x* in ta*x*i | ks | **examen** | _eksamen_ |
| | 2. before a consonant, like *s* in *s*it | s | **extraño** | _estraño_ |
| | 3. in several Indian words in Mexico, Central and South America, like *ch* in Scottish lo*ch* | kh | **México** | _mekheeko_ |
| z | like *s* in *s*it | s | **zumo** | _soomo_ |

Letters **ch, f, k, l, m, n, p, t, w,** and **y** are pronounced as in English

## VOWELS

| Letter | Approximate pronunciation | Symbol | Example | Pronunciation |
|--------|---------------------------|--------|---------|---------------|
| a | in length, between *a* in English p*a*t, and *a* in English b*a*r | a | **gracias** | _graseeas_ |
| e | 1. like *e* in g*e*t | e | **puedo** | _pwedo_ |
| | 2. in a syllable ending in a vowel like *e* in th*e*y | eh | **me** | _meh_ |
| i | 1. like *ee* in f*ee*t | ee | **sí** | _see_ |
| | 2. shorter, like *i* in s*i*t | | **gracias** | _graseeas_ |
| o | like *o* in g*o*t | o | **dos** | _dos_ |
| u | 1. like *oo* in f*oo*d | oo | **una** | _oona_ |
| | 2. like *w* in *w*ell | w | **cuanto** | _kwanto_ |
| | 3. silent after *g* in words like **guerra**, except where marked *ü* as in **antigüedad** | w | | |
| y | only a vowel when alone or at the end of a word, like *ee* in f*ee*t | ee | **y** | _ee_ |

Note: to aid pronunciation the phonetic transcription uses *y* where applicable between groups of vowels to indicate the sound value of *y* in yes.

## STRESS

Stress has been indicated in the phonetic transcription: underlined letters should be pronounced with more stress (i.e. louder) than the others.

In words ending with a vowel, **-n** or **-s**, the next to last syllable is stressed, e.g. **mañana** (*mañana*); in words ending in a consonant, the last syllable is stressed, e.g. **señor** (*señor*); the acute accent (´) is used in Spanish to indicate that a syllable is stressed, e.g. **río** (*reeo*).

Some Spanish words have more than one meaning; the accent mark is employed to distinguish between them, e.g.: **él** (he) and **el** (the); **sí** (yes) and **si** (if); **tú** (you) and **tu** (your).

---

### PRONUNCIATION OF THE SPANISH ALPHABET

| | | | |
|---|---|---|---|
| **A** | *ah* | **Ñ** | *enyeh* |
| **B** | *beh* | **O** | *oh* |
| **C** | *seh* | **P** | *peh* |
| **D** | *deh* | **Q** | *koo* |
| **E** | *eh* | **R** | *erreh* |
| **F** | *ehfeh* | **S** | *ehseh* |
| **G** | *kheh* | **T** | *teh* |
| **H** | *acheh* | **U** | *oo* |
| **I** | *ee* | **V** | *beh* |
| **J** | *khota* | **W** | *dobleh beh* |
| **K** | *ka* | **X** | *ekees* |
| **L** | *ehleh* | **Y** | *ee greeyega* |
| **M** | *emeh* | **Z** | *seta* |
| **N** | *aynneh* | | |

# BASIC EXPRESSIONS

## GREETINGS/APOLOGIES

| ESSENTIAL | |
|---|---|
| Yes./No. | **Sí./No.** *see / no* |
| Okay. | **De acuerdo [Bueno].** |
| | *deh akwerdo [bweno]* |
| Please. | **Por favor.** *por fabor* |
| Thank you (very much). | **(Muchas) gracias.** |
| | *(moochas) graseeas* |

| | |
|---|---|
| Hello./Hi! | **Hola./¡Qué tal!** *ola/keh tal* |
| Nice to meet you. | **Encantado de conocerlo (a).** |
| | *encantado de konoserlo (a)* |
| Good morning/afternoon. | **Buenos días/Buenas tardes.** |
| | *bwenos deeyas/bwenas tardes* |
| Good evening. | **Buenas noches.** |
| | *bwenas noches* |
| Good night. | **Buenas noches. [Hasta mañana.]** |
| | *bwenas noches [asta mañana]* |
| Good-bye. | **Adiós.** *adeeyos* |
| Excuse me! | **¡Disculpe!** |
| *(getting attention)* | *deeskoolpeh* |
| Excuse me!/Sorry! | **¡Lo siento!** |
| | *lo seeyento* |
| It was an accident. | **Fue un accidente.** |
| | *fweh oon akseedenteh* |
| Don't mention it. | **No fue nada. [No hay de qué.]** |
| | *no fweh nada [no eye deh keh]* |

| ON THE STREET |
|---|
| **¡Hola! ¿Cómo está?** *ola komo esta* (*Hi. How are you?*) |
| **Bien gracias. ¿Y usted?** *beeyen gratheeyas ee oosteth* |
| (*Fine. And yourself?*) |
| **Bien gracias.** *beeyen gratheeyas* (*Fine. Thanks.*) |

## COMMUNICATION DIFFICULTIES

Do you speak English? **¿Habla usted inglés?**
*abla oosteth eengles*

Does anyone here speak English? **¿Hay alguien aquí que hable inglés?**
*eye algeeyen akeeh keh ableh eengles*

I don't speak (much) Spanish. **No hablo (mucho) español.**
*no ablo (moocho) español*

Could you speak more slowly? **¿Podría hablar más despacio, por favor?** *podreea ablar mas despaseeyo por fabor*

Could you repeat that? **¿Podría repetírmelo, por favor?**
*podreea repeteermelo por fabor*

Excuse me? [Pardon?] **¿Perdón?** *perdon*

Could you spell it? **¿Podría deletreármelo?**
*podreea deletrearmelo*

Please write it down. **Escríbalo, por favor.**
*eskreebalo por fabor*

Can you translate this for me? **¿Puede traducirme esto, por favor?**
*pwedeh tradooseermeh esto por fabor*

What does this/that mean? **¿Qué significa esto/eso? [¿Qué quiere decir esto/eso?]** *keh seegneefeeka esto/eso [keh keeyereh deseer esto/eso]*

Please point to the phrase in the book. **Muéstreme la frase en el libro, por favor.** *mwestrameh la fraseh en el leebro por fabor*

I understand. **Entiendo.** *enteeyendo*

I don't understand. **No entiendo.** *no enteeyendo*

Do you understand? **¿Entiende? [¿Comprende?]** *enteeyendeh [komprendeh]*

Where can I find a translator? **¿Dónde puedo encontrar a un traductor?** *donde pooedo enkontrar a oon tradooctor*

Where can I find an English-speaking tour guide? **¿Dónde puedo encontrar a un guía de turistas que hable Inglés?** *donde pooedo enkontrar a oon ghia de tooristas keh ableh eengles*

## QUESTIONS
### Where?

| | |
|---|---|
| Where is it? | **¿Dónde está?** _dondeh esta_ |
| Where are you going? | **¿Adónde va usted?** _adondeh ba oosteth_ |
| to the meeting place [point] | **al sitio de reunión** _al seeteeyo deh reooneeyon_ |
| away from me | **lejos de mí** _lekhos deh mee_ |
| downstairs | **abajo** _abakho_ |
| from the U.S. | **de los Estados Unidos** _deh los estados ooneedos_ |
| here | **aquí** _akee_ |
| in the car | **en el carro** _en el karro_ |
| inside | **adentro** _adentro_ |
| outside | **afuera** _afooera_ |
| over there | **allá** _al-ya_ |
| near the bank | **cerca del banco** _serka del banko_ |
| opposite the market | **enfrente del mercado** _enfrenteh del merkado_ |
| on the right/left | **a la derecha/a la izquierda** _a la derecha/a la eeskeeyerda_ |
| outside the café | **fuera del café/de la cafetería** _fwera del kafeh/deh la kafetereeya_ |
| shopping | **de compras** _deh kompras_ |
| there | **allá** _al-ya_ |
| to breakfast/lunch/dinner | **al desayunar/comer/cenar** _a desal-yioonar/komer/senar_ |
| to the hotel | **al hotel** _al otel_ |
| to the mountains | **a las montañas** _a las montanyas_ |
| to the ocean | **al mar** _al mar_ |
| to the ship | **al barco/crucero** _al barko/croosero_ |
| toward Bogota | **en dirección a Bogotá** _en deerekseeyon a Bogotah_ |
| upstairs | **arriba** _arreeba_ |

## When?

| | |
|---|---|
| When does the museum open? | **¿A qué hora abre el museo?** *a keh ora abreh el mooseo* |
| When does the train arrive? | **¿A qué hora llega el tren?** *a keh ora l-yega el tren* |
| 10 minutes ago | **hace diez minutos** *aseh deeyes meenootos* |
| after lunch | **después de la comida [el almuerzo]** *despwes deh la komeeda [el almwerso]* |
| always | **siempre** *seeyempreh* |
| at 7 p.m. | **a las siete de la noche** *a las seeyeteh deh la nocheh* |
| on weekends | **los fines de semana** *los feenes deh semana* |
| before Friday | **antes del viernes** *antes del beeyernes* |
| by tomorrow | **para mañana** *para mañana* |
| early | **temprano** *temprano* |
| every week | **todas las semanas** *todas las semanas* |
| frequently | **frecuentemente** *frekwentementeh* |
| from 9 a.m. to 6 p.m. | **de nueve de la mañana a seis de la tarde** *deh nwebeh deh la mañana a seys deh la tardeh* |
| immediately | **inmediatamente** *eenmedeeyatamenteh* |
| in 20 minutes | **dentro de veinte minutos** *dentro deh beynteh meenootos* |
| never | **nunca** *noonka* |
| not yet | **todavía no** *todabeeya no* |
| now | **ahora** *aora* |
| often | **a menudo** *a menoodo* |
| on March 8 | **el ocho de marzo** *el ocho deh marso* |
| on weekdays | **los días de la semana** *los deeyas deh la semana* |
| sometimes | **algunas veces** *algoonas beses* |
| soon | **pronto** *pronto* |
| then | **luego** *lwego* |

## What kind of ...?

| | |
|---|---|
| I'd like something ... | **Quisiera algo ...** *keeseeyera algo* |
| It's ... | **Es ...** *es* |
| beautiful/ugly | **hermoso(-a)/feo(-a)** *ermoso(-a)/feo(-a)* |
| big/small | **grande/pequeño(-a)** *grandeh/pekeño(-a)* |
| cheap/expensive | **barato(-a)/caro(-a)** *barato(-a)/karo(-a)* |
| clean/dirty | **limpio(-a)/sucio(-a)** *leempeeyo(-a)/sooseeyo(-a)* |
| dark/light | **oscuro(-a)/claro(-a)** *oskooro(-a)/klaro(-a)* |
| delicious/revolting | **delicioso(-a)/repugnante** *deleeseeyoso(-a)/repooknanteh* |
| easy/difficult | **fácil/difícil** *faseel/deefeeseel* |
| empty/full | **vacío(-a)/lleno(-a)** *baseeoh/l-yeno(-a)* |
| good/bad | **bueno(-a)/malo(-a)** *bweno(-a)/malo(-a)* |
| heavy/light | **pesado(-a)/liviano(-a)** *pesado(-a)/leebeeyano(-a)* |
| hot/warm/cold | **muy caliente/caliente/frío(-a)** *mwee kaleeyenteh/kaleeyenteh/freeyo(-a)* |
| narrow/wide | **angosto(-a)/ancho(-a)** *angosto(-a)/ancho(-a)* |
| old/new | **viejo(-a)/nuevo(-a)** *beeyekho(-a)/nwebo(-a)* |
| open/shut | **abierto(-a)/cerrado(-a)** *abeeyerto(-a)/serado(-a)* |
| pleasant, nice/unpleasant | **agradable/desagradable** *agradableh/desagradableh* |
| quick/slow | **rápido(-a)/lento(-a)** *rapeedo(-a)/lento(-a)* |

## How much/many?

| | |
|---|---|
| How much is that? | **¿Cuánto cuesta eso?/¿Cuánto es?** <br> *kwanto kwesta eso/kwanto es* |
| How many are there? | **¿Cuántos hay?** <br> *kwantos eye* |
| 1/2/3 | **uno/dos/tres** <br> *oono/dos/tres* |
| 4/5 | **cuatro/cinco** <br> *kwatro/seenko* |
| none | **ninguno(-a)** <br> *neengoono(-a)* |
| about 100 pesos | **alrededor de cien pesos** <br> *alrededor deh seeyen pesos* |
| a little | **un poquito** <br> *oon pokeeto* |
| a lot (of) | **mucho** *moocho* |
| enough | **suficiente** <br> *soofeeseeyenteh* |
| few/a few of them | **pocos(-as)/unos(-as) pocos(-as)** <br> *pokos(-as)/oonos(-as) pokos(-as)* |
| more than that | **más que eso** *mas keh eso* |
| less than that | **menos que eso** *menos keh eso* |
| much more | **mucho más** <br> *moocho mas* |
| nothing else | **nada más** *nada mas* |
| too much | **demasiado(-a)** <br> *demaseeyado(-a)* |

## Why?

| | |
|---|---|
| Why is that? | **Y eso, ¿por qué?** *ee eso por keh* |
| Why not? | **¿Por qué no?** *por keh no* |
| because of the weather | **por el clima** *por el kleema* |
| because I'm in a hurry | **porque tengo prisa [estoy de prisa]** <br> *porkeh tengo preesa [estoy deh preesa]* |
| I don't know why. | **Yo no sé por qué.** *yo no seh por keh* |

### Who?/Which?

| | |
|---|---|
| Who's there? | **¿Quién es?** *keeyen es* |
| It's me! | **¡Soy yo!** *soy yo* |
| It's us! | **¡Somos nosotros!** *somos nosotros* |
| someone | **alguien** *algeeyen* |
| no one | **nadie** *nadeeyeh* |
| Which one do you want? | **¿Cuál desea usted? [¿Cuál quiere?]** *kwal deseya oosteth [kwal keeyereh]* |
| one like that | **uno(-a) como ése(-a)** *oono(-a) komo eseh(-a)* |
| that one/this one | **ése(-a)/éste(-a)** *ese(-a)/este(-a)* |
| not that one | **ése(-a) no** *ese(-a) no* |
| something/nothing | **algo/nada** *algo/nada* |
| none | **ninguno(-a)** *neengoono(-a)* |

### Whose?

| | |
|---|---|
| Whose is that? | **¿De quién es eso?** *Deh keeyen es eso* |
| It's ... | **Es ...** *es* |
| mine/ours | **mío/nuestro** *meeyo/nwestro* |
| yours *(sing. polite/familiar)* | **suyo/tuyo** *sooyo/tooyo* |
| yours *(plur. polite/familiar)* | **de ustedes/vuestro** *deh oostedes/vwestro* |
| his/hers/theirs | **de él/de ella/de ellos(-as)** *deh el/deh el-ya /deh el-yos(-as)* |
| It's ... turn. | **Es ... turno.** *es ... toorno* |
| my/our/your *(sing.)* | **mi/nuestro/su\*** *mee/nwestro/soo* |
| his/her/your *(plur.)*/their | **su\*** *soo* |

Note: adjectives agree in number and gender with the noun they describe. Here adjectives describe the noun **turno** – masculine, singular.

16

## Is it …?/Are there …?

| | |
|---|---|
| Is it …? | **¿Está …?** *esta* |
| Is it free of charge? | **¿Esto es gratis?** *esto es gratees* |
| It isn't ready. | **Esto no está listo.** *esto no esta leesto* |
| Is there …? | **¿Hay …?** *eye* |
| Are there …? | **¿Hay …?** *eye* |
| Are there any buses into town? | **¿Hay buses a la ciudad?** *eye booses a la seeoodath* |
| Here it is/they are. | **Aquí está/están.** *akee esta/estan* |
| There it is/they are. | **Allá está/están.** *al-ya esta/estan* |

## How?

| | |
|---|---|
| How would you like to pay? | **¿Cómo desea pagar?** *komo deseea pagar* |
| by cash | **en efectivo** *en efekteebo* |
| by credit card | **con tarjeta de crédito** *kon tarkheta deh kretheeto* |
| How are you getting here? | **¿En qué se viene?** *en keh seh beeyeneh* |
| by car | **en carro** *en karro* |
| on foot | **a pie** *a peeyeh* |
| equally | **por partes iguales** *por partes eegwales* |
| extremely | **demasiado [extremadamente]** *demaseeyado [ekstremadamenteh]* |
| quickly | **rápidamente** *rapeedamenteh* |
| slowly | **lentamente** *lentamenteh* |
| too fast | **demasiado rápido(-a)** *demaseeyado rapeedo(-a)* |
| totally | **totalmente** *totalmenteh* |
| very | **muy** *mwee* |
| with a friend | **con un(a) amigo(-a)** *kon oon(a) ameego(-a)* |
| quiet/noisy | **tranquilo(-a)/ruidoso(-a)** *trankeelo(-a)/rooeedoso(-a)* |

| right/wrong | **correcto(-a)/incorrecto(-a)** |
| | *korekto(-a)/eenkorekto(-a)* |
| tall/short | **alto(-a)/bajo(-a)** *alto(-a)/bakho(-a)* |
| vacant/occupied | **desocupado [libre]/ocupado(-a)** |
| | *desokoopado [leebreh]/okoopado(-a)* |

## Can … ?

| Can I have …? | **¿Me puede traer …?** |
| | *meh pwedeh trayer* |
| Can you tell me? | **¿Puede decirme?** |
| | *pwedeh deseermeh* |
| Can you help me? | **¿Puede ayudarme?** |
| | *pwedeh ayoodarmeh* |
| Can I help you? | **¿Puedo ayudarlo?** *pwedo ayoodarlo* |
| Can you direct me to …? | **¿Puede decirme cómo llegar a …?** |
| | *pwedeh deseermeh komo l-yegar a* |

## What do you want?

| I'd like … | **Quisiera …** *keeseeyera* |
| Could I have …? | **¿Podría traerme …?** |
| | *podreeya trayermeh* |
| We'd like … | **Quisiéramos …** *keeseeyeramos* |
| Give me … | **Tráigame …** *traeegameh* |
| I'm looking for … | **Estoy buscando …** *estoy booskando* |
| I need to … | **Necesito …** *neseseeto* |
| go … | **ir …** *eer* |
| find … | **encontrar …** *enkontrar* |
| see … | **ver …** *behr* |
| speak to … | **hablar con …** *ablar kon* |

### IN THE POST OFFICE

**¿De quién es este bolso?** *deh keeyehn es este bolso*
*(Whose handbag is that?)*
**Es el mío. Gracias.** *es el meeyo gratseeyas (It's
mine. Thanks.)*
**No hay de qué.** *no eye deh keh (You're welcome.)*

18

## OTHER USEFUL WORDS

| | | |
|---|---|---|
| fortunately | **afortunadamente** | *afortoonada<u>men</u>teh* |
| hopefully | **ojalá** | *okh<u>a</u>la* |
| of course | **por supuesto [claro que sí]** | |
| | *por soopw<u>e</u>sto [<u>kla</u>ro keh see]* | |
| perhaps/possibly | **tal vez/es posible** | *tal bes/es po<u>see</u>bleh* |
| probably | **probablemente** | *probable<u>men</u>teh* |
| unfortunately | **desafortunadamente** | |
| | *desafortoonada<u>men</u>teh* | |

## EXCLAMATIONS

| | | |
|---|---|---|
| At last! | **¡Por fin!** | *por feen* |
| Go on. | **Continúa. [Adelante.]** | *kontee<u>noo</u>a [athe<u>lan</u>teh]* |
| Damn! | **¡Maldición! [¡Maldita sea!]** | |
| | *maldeesee<u>yon</u> [mal<u>dee</u>ta seh-a]* | |
| Good God! | **¡Santo Dios!** | *<u>san</u>to dee<u>yos</u>* |
| I don't mind. | **Me da igual. [No hay cuidado.]** | |
| | *meh da ee<u>gwal</u> [no eye kwee<u>da</u>do]* | |
| No way! | **¡Ni hablar! [¡De ninguna manera!]** | |
| | *nee a<u>blar</u> [deh neen<u>goo</u>na ma<u>ne</u>ra]* | |
| Really? | **¿De verdad? [¿De veras?]** | |
| | *de ber<u>dath</u> [deh <u>be</u>ras]* | |
| Rubbish. | **Mentiras. [Tonterías.]** | |
| | *men<u>tee</u>ras [tonte<u>ree</u>as]* | |
| That's enough. | **Es suficiente.** | *es soofeesee<u>yen</u>teh* |
| That's true. | **Es cierto.** | *es seey<u>er</u>to* |
| I can't believe it! | **¡No te creo! [¡No lo puedo creer!]** | |
| | *no teh <u>kre</u>o [no lo <u>pwe</u>do krey<u>er</u> ]* | |
| How are things? | **¿Qué tal?** | *keh tal* |
| Fine, thank you. | **Bien, gracias.** | *bee<u>yen</u> <u>gra</u>seeyas* |
| great/terrific | **excelente/de maravilla** | |
| | *exe<u>len</u>teh/deh mara<u>bee</u>l-ya* | |
| fine/not bad/okay | **bien** | *bee<u>yen</u>* |
| not good | **no muy bien** | *no mwee bee<u>yen</u>* |
| terrible | **terrible** | *ter<u>ree</u>bleh* |

# ACCOMMODATIONS

Early reservation and confirmation are essential in most major tourist centers,. The tourist information office can help if you're having difficulty finding a room. Prices charged are generally per room; a single (**sencillo**) is therefore cheaper than a large family room with several beds. Rooms with air conditioning generally cost more, though a ceiling fan (**ventilador**) is often sufficient.

### Hotel  _otel_
Prices and facilities vary according to the six categories: **gran turismo**, five, four, three, two, and one star.

### Motel  _motel_
Local automobile associations (e.g. **AMA** in Mexico) have lists of recommended motels.

### Apartamento amueblado/sin amueblar
_apartamento amweblado/seen amweblar_
Furnished and unfurnished apartment; consult a real estate agent.

### Casa de huéspedes  _kassa deh wespedes_
Guest house, usually for stays of several days or even months. The choice is between **pensión completa** (full board) and **media pensión** (bed and breakfast plus one other meal). Generally provides a friendly, relaxed atmosphere.

### Hospedajes  _ospedakhes_
A large family home that has an extra bedroom rented out with shared bathroom; provides inexpensive accommodations and local hospitality.

### Pensión  _penseeyon_
The equivalent of a boarding house, often offering **pensión completa** or **media pensión**. May have permanent lodgers.

### Residencial  _reseedenseeal_
Modest short-term budget accommodations. Facilities are usually shared with other guests.

### Albergue juvenil  _albergeh deh khoobeneel_
Youth hostels can generally be found in most major towns in Central and South America.

## RESERVATIONS
### In advance

Can you recommend a hotel in ...?
**¿Puede recomendarme un hotel en ...?**
_pwedeh rekomendarmeh oon otel en_

Is it near the center of town?
**¿Está cerca del centro?**
_esta serka del sentro_

How much is it per night?
**¿Cuánto cuesta por noche?**
_kwanto kwesta por nocheh_

Is there anything cheaper?
**¿Hay algo más barato?**
_eye algo mas barato_

Could you book me a room there, please?
**¿Podría reservarme una habitación en ese hotel, por favor?** _podreea reserbarmeh oona abeetaseeyon en eseh otel por fabor_

How do I get there?
**¿Cómo se llega allá?**
_komo seh lyega al-ya_

### At the hotel

Do you have a room?
**¿Tiene habitaciones disponibles?**
_teeyeneh abeetaseeyones deesponeebles_

Is there another hotel nearby?
**¿Hay algún otro hotel por aquí?**
_eye algoon otro otel por akee_

I'd like a single/ double room.
**Quisiera una habitación sencilla/doble.**
_keeseeyera oona abeetaseeyon senseelyah/dobleh_

I'd like a room with ...
**Quisiera una habitación con ...**
_keeseeyera oona abeetaseeyon kon ..._

a double bed/twin beds
**cama matrimonial [doble]/dos camas** _kama matreemoneeal [dobleh]/dos kamas_

a bath/shower
**baño/ducha** _baño/doocha_

### AT THE HOTEL RECEPTION

**¿Tiene habitaciones disponibles?** _teeyeneh abeetaseeyones deesponeebles (Do you have any vacancies?)_
**Lo siento.** _lo seeyento (I'm sorry.)_
**Gracias. Adiós.** _graseeyas adyos (Thank you. Good bye.)_

## RECEPTION

| | |
|---|---|
| I have a reservation. | **Tengo una habitación reservada.** *tengo oona abeetaseeyon reserbada* |
| My name is … | **Me llamo…** *meh l-yamo* |
| We've reserved a double and a single room. | **Hemos reservado una habitación doble [cuarto doble] y una sencilla.** *emos reserbado oona abeetaseeyon dobleh [kwarto dobleh] ee oona senseel-ya.* |
| I confirmed by mail. | **Confirmé por escrito.** *konfeermeh por eskreeto* |
| Could we have adjoining rooms? | **¿Podríamos tener habitaciones contiguas [cuartos contiguos]?** *podreeamos tener abeetaseeyones konteegwas [kwartos konteegwos]* |

## AMENITIES AND FACILITIES

| | |
|---|---|
| Is there (a) … in the room? | **¿Hay … en la habitación [el cuarto]?** *eye … en la abeetaseeyon [el kwarto]* |
| air conditioning | **aire acondicionado** *ayreh akondeeseeyonado* |
| TV/telephone | **televisión/teléfono** *telebeeseeyon/telefono* |
| Does the hotel have (a) …? | **¿El hotel tiene …?** *el otel teeyeneh* |
| satellite TV | **televisión satélite** *telebeeseeyon sateleeteh* |
| laundry service | **servicio de lavandería** *serbeeseeyo deh labandereea* |
| swimming pool | **piscina** *peeseena* |
| Could you put … in the room? | **¿Podría poner … en la habitación [el cuarto]?** *podreea poner … en la abeetaseeyon [el kwarto]* |
| an extra bed | **una cama adicional** *oona kama adeeseeonal* |
| a crib [child's cot] | **una cuna para bebé** *oona koona para bebeh* |

| | |
|---|---|
| Do you have facilities for children/the disabled? | **¿Hay servicios especiales para niños/ personas incapacitadas?** *eye serbeeseeyos espeseeyales para neeños/personas eenkapaseetadas* |

## HOW LONG?

| | |
|---|---|
| We'll be staying … | **Pensamos quedarnos …** *pensamos kedarnos* |
| overnight only | **solamente esta noche** *solamenteh esta nocheh* |
| a few days | **unos pocos días** *oonos pokos deeas* |
| a week (at least) | **(por lo menos) una semana** *(por lo menos) oona semana* |
| I'd like to stay an extra night. | **Quisiera quedarme una noche más.** *keeseeyera kedarmeh oona nocheh mas* |

## PRICE

| | |
|---|---|
| How much is it …? | **¿Cuánto cuesta …?** *kwanto kwesta* |
| per night/week | **la noche/la semana** *la noche/la semana* |
| for bed and breakfast | **la noche con desayuno incluido** *la noche kon desayoono eenklooeedo* |
| excluding meals | **la noche sin las comidas** *la noche seen las komeedas* |
| for full board (American Plan [A.P.]) | **la pensión completa** *la penseeyon kompleta* |
| for half board (Modified American Plan [M.A.P.]) | **la media pensión** *la medeea penseeyon* |
| Does the price include …? | **¿El precio incluye …?** *el preseeo eenklooyeh* |
| breakfast | **el desayuno** *el desayoono* |
| sales tax [VAT] | **el IVA** *el eeba* |
| Do I have to leave a deposit? | **¿Tengo que dejar un depósito?** *tengo keh dekhar oon deposeeto* |
| Is there a discount for children? | **¿Hay algún descuento especial para niños?** *eye algoon deskwento espeseeyal para neeños* |

## DECISIONS

| | |
|---|---|
| May I see the room? | **¿Puedo ver la habitación [el cuarto]?** _pwedo ber la abeetaseeyon [el kwarto]_ |
| That's fine. I'll take it. | **Está bien. La tomo.** _esta beeyen. la tomo_ |
| It's too … | **Es demasiado …** _es demaseeyado_ |
| dark/small | **oscura/pequeña** _oskoora/pekeña_ |
| noisy | **ruidosa** _rooeedosa_ |
| Do you have anything …? | **¿Tiene algo …?** _teeyeneh algo_ |
| bigger/cheaper | **más grande/más barato** _mas grandeh/mas barato_ |
| quieter/warmer | **más tranquilo/más caliente** _mas trankeelo/mas kaleeyenteh_ |
| No, I won't take it. | **No. No la tomo.** _no. no la tomo_ |

### AT THE HOTEL RECEPTION

**¿Puedo ver la habitación?** _pwedo ber la abeetaseeyon_ (May I see the room?)

**Por supuesto.** _por soopwesto_ (Of course.)

**Está bien. La tomo.** _esta beeyen. la tomo_ (That's fine. I'll take it.)

### YOU MAY SEE

| | |
|---|---|
| **HABITACIÓN P…** | room only … pesos |
| **DESAYUNO INCLUIDO** | breakfast included |
| **SERVICIO DE RESTAURANTE** | meals available |
| **NOMBRE/APELLIDO** | first name/last name |
| **DOMICILIO/CALLE/NÚMERO** | home address/street/number |
| **NACIONALIDAD/PROFESIÓN** | nationality/profession |
| **FECHA/LUGAR DE NACIMIENTO** | date/place of birth |
| **PROCEDENCIA/DESTINO** | coming from/going to |
| **NÚMERO DE PASAPORTE** | passport number |
| **LUGAR/FECHA** | place/date |
| **FIRMA** | signature |

## PROBLEMS

| The … doesn't work. | **… no funciona.** … *no foonseeona* |
|---|---|
| air conditioning | **El aire acondicionado** *el ayreh akondeeseeonado* |
| fan | **El ventilador** *el benteelador* |
| heat [heating] | **La calefacción** *la kalefakseeyon* |
| light | **La luz** *la loos* |
| I can't turn the heat [heating] on/off | **No puedo encender/apagar la calefacción.** *.no pwedo ensender/apagar la kalefakseeyon* |
| There is no hot water/toilet paper. | **No hay agua caliente/papel higiénico.** *no eye agwa kaleeyenteh/papel eekheeyeneeko* |
| The faucet [tap] . is dripping | **El grifo [La llave] está goteando.** *el greefo [la l-yabeh] esta goteando* |
| The sink/toilet is blocked. | **El lavamanos/inodoro está tapado.** *el labamanos/inodoro esta tapado* |
| The window/door is jammed. | **La ventana/puerta está atascada.** *la bentana/pwerta esta ataskada.* |
| My room has not been made up. | **No han ordenado mi cuarto.** *no an ordenado mee kwarto* |
| The … is broken. | **… está roto(-a).** … *esta roto(-a)* |
| blind | **La persiana** *la perseeana* |
| lock | **La cerradura** *la seradoora* |
| There are insects in our room. | **Hay insectos en nuestra habitación.** *eye eensektos en nwestra abeetaseeyon* |

## ACTION

| Could you have that seen to? | **¿Podría hacer revisar eso también?** *podreea asehr rebeesar eso tambeeyen* |
|---|---|
| I'd like to move to another room. | **Quisiera trasladarme a otra habitación [otro cuarto].** *keeseeyera trasladarmeh a otra abeetaseeyon [otro kwarto]* |
| I'd like to speak to the manager. | **Quisiera hablar con el gerente del the hotel.** *keeseeyera ablar kon el kherenteh del otel* |

## REQUIREMENTS

The 110-volt, 60-cycle AC is the norm throughout Mexico, Central America, Colombia, and Venezuela. Further south, the 220-volt, 50-cycle operates in Peru, Bolivia (except La Paz), Paraguay, Uruguay, Chile, and Argentina. If you bring your own electrical appliances to Latin America, you may need to buy an adaptor to fit the various types of electrical sockets.

### About the hotel

| | |
|---|---|
| Where's the …? | **¿Dónde está …?** _dondeh esta_ |
| bar | **el bar** _el bar_ |
| dining room | **el comedor** _el komedor_ |
| elevator [lift] | **el ascensor** _el asensor_ |
| parking lot [car park] | **el estacionamiento [el parqueadero]** _el estaseeonameeyento [el parkeadero]_ |
| shower | **la ducha** _la doocha_ |
| swimming pool | **la piscina** _la peeseena_ |
| tour operator's bulletin board | **la cartelera de anuncios del operador de viajes** _la kartelera deh anoonseeos del operador deh beeyakhes_ |
| Where are the bathrooms [toilets]? | **¿Dónde están los baños?** _dondeh estan los baños_ |
| What time is the front door locked? | **¿A qué hora se cierra con llave la puerta principal?** _a keh ora seh seeyera la pwerta preenseepal_ |
| What time is breakfast served? | **¿A qué hora se sirve el desayuno?** _a keh ora seh seerbeh el desayoono_ |
| Is there room service? | **¿Ofrecen servicio a la habitación?** _ofresen serbeesyo a la abeetaseeyon_ |

## Personal needs

| | |
|---|---|
| The key to room …, please. | **La llave de la habitación …, por favor.** *la l-yabeh deh la abeetaseeyon … por fabor.* |
| I've lost my key. | **Se me perdió mi llave.** *se meh perdeeyo mee l-yabeh* |
| I've locked myself out of my room. | **Me he quedado fuera de la habitación.** *meh eh kedado fwera deh la abeetaseeyon.* |
| Could you wake me at …? | **¿Podría despertarme a las …?** *podreea despertarmeh a las* |
| I'd like breakfast in my room. | **Quisiera tomar el desayuno en la habitación.** *keeseeyera tomar el desayoono en la abeetaseeyon* |
| Can I leave this in the safe? | **¿Puedo dejar esto en la caja de seguridad [caja fuerte]?** *pwedo dekhar esto en la kakha deh segooreedath [kakha fwerteh]* |
| May I have (an) extra …? | **¿Me puede traer … adicional?** *meh pwedeh trayer … adeeseeonal* |
| bath towel | **una toalla** *oona toal-ya* |
| blanket | **una manta** *oona manta* |
| hangers | **una percha** *oona percha* |
| pillow | **una almohada** *oona almoada* |
| Is there any mail for me? | **¿Hay alguna carta para mí?** *eye algoona karta para mee* |
| Are there any messages for me? | **¿Hay algún recado para mí?** *eye algoon rekado para mee* |

---

### YOU MAY SEE

| | |
|---|---|
| **MARQUE EL NÚMERO … PARA** | dial … for |
| **LLAMADAS FUERA DEL HOTEL/ LLAMADAS EXTERNAS** | an outside line |
| **NO INTERRUMPIR** | do not disturb |
| **PUERTA CONTRA INCENDIOS** | fire door |
| **SALIDA DE EMERGENCIA** | emergency exit |
| **SÓLO PARA MÁQUINAS DE AFEITAR** | razors [shavers] only |

## RENTING

| | |
|---|---|
| We've reserved an apartment/cottage in the name of … | **Hemos reservado un departamento/ cabaña a nombre de …** _emos reserbado oon departamento/kabañaa nombre deh_ |
| Where do we pick up the keys? | **¿Dónde recogemos las llaves?** _dondeh rekohemos las l-yabes_ |
| Which is the front door key? | **¿Cuál es la llave de la puerta principal?** _kwal es la l-yabeh deh la pwerta preenseepal_ |
| Where is the …? | **¿Dónde está …?** _dondeh esta_ |
| electric meter | **el medidor [contador] eléctrico** _el medeedor [kontador] elektreeko_ |
| valve | **la llave de cierre** _la l-yabeh deh seeyereh_ |
| water heater | **el calentador de agua** _el kalentador de agwa_ |
| Are there any spare …? | **¿Tiene … de repuesto?** _teeyeneh …de repwesto_ |
| fuses | **algunos fusibles** _algoonos fooseebles_ |
| gas bottles | **algunos cilindros de gas** _algoonos seeleendros deh gas_ |
| sheets | **algunas sábanas** _algoonas sabanas_ |
| Which day does the maid come? | **¿Qué día viene la aseadora?** _keh deeya beeyeneh la aseadora_ |
| Where/When do I put out the trash [rubbish]? | **¿Dónde/Cuándo se saca la basura?** _dondeh/kwando seh saka la basoora]_ |

**Problems?**

| | |
|---|---|
| Where can I contact you? | **¿Dónde puedo localizarlo(-la)?** _dondeh pwedo lokaleesarlo(-la)_ |
| How does the stove/ water heater work? | **¿Cómo funciona la estufa/el calentador?** _komo foonseeyona la estoofa/el kalentador_ |
| The … is/are dirty. | **El/la … está sucio(-a).** _el/la … esta sooseeo(-a)_ |
| We accidentally broke/ lost … | **Se nos rompió/perdió … por accidente.** _se nos rompeeo/perdeeo … por akseedenteh_ |
| That was already damaged when we arrived. | **Eso no funcionaba cuando nosotros llegamos.** _eso no foonseeyonaba kwando nosotros l-yegamos_ |

**Useful terms**

| boiler | **la caldera** *la kaldera* |
| dishes [crockery] | **la loza [vajilla]** *la losa [bakheel-ya]* |
| freezer | **el congelador** *el konkhelador* |
| frying pan | **la sartén** *la sarten* |
| kettle | **la tetera** *la tetera* |
| lamp | **la lámpara** *la lampara* |
| refrigerator | **la nevera** *la nebera* |
| saucepan | **la cacerola** *la kaserola* |
| stove [cooker] | **la estufa** *la estoofa* |
| toilet paper | **el papel higiénico** *el papel eekheeyeneeko* |
| utensils [cutlery] | **los cubiertos** *los koobeeye tos* |
| washing machine | **la lavadora** *la labadora* |

**Rooms**

| balcony | **el balcón** *el balkon* |
| bathroom | **el baño** *el baño* |
| bedroom | **la alcoba [el dormitorio]** *la alkoba [el dormeetoreeyo]* |
| dining room | **el comedor** *el komedor* |
| kitchen | **la cocina** *la koseena* |
| living room | **la sala** *la sala* |
| toilet | **el baño** *el baño* |

## YOUTH HOSTEL

| Do you have any places left for tonight? | **¿Tiene cupo disponible para esta noche?** *teeyeneh koopo deesponeeble para esta nocheh* |
| Do you rent out bedding? | **¿Alquila usted la ropa de cama?** *alkeela oosteth la ropa deh kama* |
| What time are the doors locked? | **¿A qué hora se cierra con llave la puerta?** *a keh ora seh seeyera kon l-yabeh la pwerta* |
| I have an International Student Card. | **Tengo credencial internacional de estudiante.** *tengo kredenseeal eenternaseeonal deh estoodeeanteh* |

## CAMPING

In some parts of Latin America, camping isn't allowed without a permit. However, there are many authorized campsites with excellent facilities. In Argentina, most cities have sites where tents can be pitched. Camping and sleeping on the beach is allowed in Mexico, but isn't recommended, for safety reasons.

### Booking

Is there a campsite near here?
**¿Hay alguna zona de campamento por aquí?** *eye algoona sona deh kampamento por akee*

Do you have space for a tent/trailer [caravan]?
**¿Tiene sitio para una tienda de campaña/casa móvil?** *teeyeneh seeteeyo para oona teeyenda deh kampaña/kasa mobeel*

What is the charge …?
**¿Cuál es el precio …?** *kwal es el preseeo*

per day/week
**por día/por semana** *por deeya/por semana*

for a tent/car
**por tienda/por carro** *por teeyenda/por karro*

for a trailer [caravan]
**por casa móvil** *por kasa mobeel*

### Facilities

Are there cooking facilities on site?
**¿Se puede cocinar en la zona de campamento?** *se pwedeh koseenar en la sona deh kampamento*

Are there any electric outlets [power points]?
**¿Hay alguna toma de corriente?** *eye algoona toma deh koreeyenteh*

Where is/are the …?
**¿Dónde está(n) …?** *dondeh esta(n)*

laundry facilities
**el servicio de lavandería** *el serbeeseeo deh labandereeya*

showers
**las duchas** *las doochas*

trash cans [dustbins]
**los botes de la basura [las canecas]** *los botes deh la basoora [las kanekas]*

---

## YOU MAY SEE

| | |
|---|---|
| **PROHIBIDO ACAMPAR** | no camping |
| **AGUA POTABLE** | drinking water |

## Complaints

It's too sunny/shady here. **Hace demasiado sol/demasiada sombra aquí.** *aseh demaseeyado sol/ demaseeyada sombra akee*

It's too crowded here. **Hay demasiada gente aquí.** *eye demaseeyada khenteh akee*

The ground's too hard/ uneven. **El terreno está demasiado duro/ irregular.** *el terreno esta demaseeyado dooro/eeregoolar*

Do you have a more level spot? **¿Hay algún sitio más plano?** *eye algoon seeteeyo mas plano*

I can't camp here. **No puedo acampar aquí.** *no pwedo akampar akee*

## Camping equipment

| | | |
|---|---|---|
| butane gas | **el gas butano** *el gas bootano* | |
| cot [campbed] | **la cama plegable** *la kama plegableh* | |
| charcoal | **el carbón vegetal** *el karbon bekhetal* | |
| flashlight [torch] | **la linterna** *la leenternah* | |
| groundcloth [groundsheet] | **la tela impermeable** *la tela impermeableh* | |
| guy rope | **la cuerda** *la kwerda* | |
| hammer | **el martillo** *el marteel-yo* | |
| kerosene [primus] stove | **la cocineta** *la koseeneta* | |
| knapsack | **la mochila** *la mocheela* | |
| mallet | **el mazo** *el maso* | |
| matches | **los fósforos** *los fosforos* | |
| (air) mattress | **el colchón (inflable)** *el kolchon (eenflableh)* | |
| paraffin | **la parafina** *la parafeena* | |
| sleeping bag | **el saco de dormir [el sleeping]** *el sako de dormeer [el sleepeen]* | |
| tent | **la tienda [la carpa]** *la teeyenda [la karpa]* | |
| tent pegs | **las estacas de la tienda [la carpa]** *las estakas deh la teeyenda [la karpa]* | |
| tent pole | **el poste de la tienda [la carpa]** *el posteh deh la teeyenda [karpa]* | |

## CHECKING OUT

What time do we have to check out?
**¿A qué hora debemos desocupar el cuarto?**
*a keh ora debemos desokoopar el kwarto*

Could we leave our baggage here until ...?
**¿Podemos dejar nuestro equipaje aquí hasta ...?** *podemos dekhar nwestro ekeepakheh akee asta ...*

Could you order us a taxi, please?
**¿Podría pedirnos un taxi, por favor?**
*podreea pedeernos oon taxi por fabor*

## PAYING

A service charge is generally included in hotel and restaurant bills. However, if the service has been particularly good, you may want to leave an extra tip.

The bill, please.
**La cuenta, por favor.**
*la kwenta por fabor*

I think there's a mistake in this bill.
**Creo que hay un error en esta cuenta.**
*kreo keh eye oon error en esta kwenta*

I've made ... telephone calls.
**Hice ... llamadas.**
*eeseh ... l-yamadas.*

I've taken ... from the mini-bar.
**Tomé ... del mini-bar.** *tomeh ... del mini-bar*

Can I have an itemized bill?
**¿Me puede dar una factura detallada?**
*meh pwedeh dar oona faktoora detal-yada*

Could I have a receipt?
**¿Me podría dar un recibo?**
*meh podreea dar oon reseebo*

Is the tip inlcuded in the bill?
**¿Está incluída la propina en la cuenta?**
*esta inklooida la propina en la kooenta*

Do you take credit cards?
**¿Acepta tarjetas de crédito?**
*asepta tarhetas de kredito*

# EATING OUT

## RESTAURANTS

### Cafetería  *kafetereeya*

A small café serving both alcoholic and non-alcoholic drinks; varied menus. Sit at the counter or – for a little more money – choose a table. The **menú del día** (set menu) may be very good.

### Cantina  *kanteena*

Roughly equivalent to an English pub or an American tavern; standards vary; always a wide variety of appetizers on hand. A cantina is a great place for meeting friends and discussing the world. But one thing: cantinas are for men only.

### Fonda  *fonda*

Similar to an inn; food is plentiful and service usually good.

### Fresquería  *freskereeya*

Serves refreshments and drinks. It may also be called **refresquería**.

### Hacienda  *asseeyenda*

Some old **haciendas** (big ranches), dating back to colonial times in Mexico, have been transformed into first class, luxury restaurants. You will find fountains, gardens, tropical flowers, and exotic birds in what may be compared with a real museum of old furniture and paintings. Regional and international dishes are served; music is played by **mariachi** orchestras.

### Hostería  *ostereeya*

Restaurant, often specializing in regional dishes.

### Lonchería  *lonchereeya*

Bar serving snacks and light meals.

### Pastelería  *pastelereeya*

A pastry shop, also called **confitería**. Some serve coffee, tea, and non-alcoholic drinks.

### Posada  *possada*

Similar to **fondas**, these inns specialize in local cuisine.

### Restaurante  *restoranteh*

Classified according to the standard of cuisine and service: **de lujo** (deluxe), **de primera**, **de segunda**, and **de tercera** (first, second and third class).

**Salón de té** *salon deh teh*
Smart, expensive tea shop.

**Snack-bar** *"snack bar"*
The English word has been taken over to describe fast-food establishments.

### Meal times

#### el desayuno *el dessayoono*
Breakfast: generally served from 8 to 10 a.m. Traditionally a light meal, usually consisting of a selection of sweet breads and coffee with milk (**café con leche**) or hot chocolate (**chocolate caliente**); hotels are now offering more filling fare for tourists, serving a buffet breakfast.

#### el almuerzo *el almwerso*
Lunch is generally served between 1 and 4 p.m. In Latin America people like to linger over a meal, so service may seem on the leisurely side. If you are in a hurry, go for fast-food outlets, pizzerias or cafés.

#### la cena *la sena*
Dinner is usually served later than at home, starting around 8 p.m. and continuing until late. However, in tourist areas you can get a meal at most places just about any time of day.

## LATIN-AMERICAN CUISINE

Latin-American cuisine in all its rich variety arose from a collision of two cooking worlds, that of the natives and the conquerors. Avocado, chocolate, peanuts, potatoes, tomatoes, and turkeys are some of the culinary gifts that Latin America has presented to the world.

Sweet corn (**maíz**) and chilies form the basis of the cooking in all Latin-American countries. Here are some of the dishes using these two ingredients: **tacos** (Mexico), **tamales** (Colombia), **hallacas** (Venezuela).

Many delicious dishes are prepared with seafood; for example, **cazuela de mariscos** (fish in white sauce), **ceviche** (fish marinated in lemon juice).

| ESSENTIAL | |
|---|---|
| A table for … | **Una mesa para …** *oona mesa para* |
| 1/2/3/4 | **uno/dos/tres/cuatro** *oono/dos/tres/kwatro* |
| Thank you. | **Gracias.** *graseeas* |
| The bill, please. | **La cuenta, por favor.** *la kwenta por fabor* |

## FINDING A PLACE TO EAT

| | |
|---|---|
| Can you recommend a good restaurant? | **¿Puede recomendarme un buen restaurante?** *pwedeh rekomendarmeh oon bwen restoranteh* |
| Is there a(n) ... near here? | **¿Hay ... cerca de aquí?** *eye ... serka deh akee* |
| traditional local restaurant | **un restaurante típico de la región** *oon restoranteh teepeeko deh la rekheeyon* |
| Chinese restaurant | **un restaurante chino** *oon restoranteh cheeno* |
| fish restaurant | **un restaurante con especialidad en pescado** *oon restoranteh kon espeseeyaleedath en peskado* |
| inexpensive restaurant | **un restaurante barato** *oon restoranteh barato* |
| steak house | **un restaurante especializado en carnes** *oon restoranteh espeseeyaleesado en karnes* |
| vegetarian restaurant | **un restaurante vegetariano** *oon restoranteh begetareeyano* |
| Where can I find a(n) ...? | **¿Dónde puedo encontrar ...?** *dondeh pwedo enkontrar ...* |
| café | **un café [una cafetería]** *oon kafeh [oona kafetereeya]* |
| café/restaurant with outdoor tables | **un café/un restaurante con mesas al aire libre** *oon kafeh/oon restoranteh kon mesas al ayreh leebreh* |
| fast-food restaurant | **un restaurante de comidas rápidas** *oon restoranteh deh komeedas rapeedas* |
| ice cream parlor | **una heladería** *oona eladereeya* |
| pizzeria | **una pizzería** *oona peesereeya* |

## RESERVATIONS

| | |
|---|---|
| I'd like to reserve a table for two. | **Quisiera reservar una mesa para dos.** <br> *keeseeyera reserbar oona mesa para dos* |
| For this evening/ tomorrow at … | **Para esta noche/mañana a las …** <br> *para esta nocheh/mañana a las* |
| We'll come at 8:00. | **Llegaremos a las 8:00.** *lyegaremos a las ocho* |
| A table for two, please. | **Una mesa para dos, por favor.** <br> *oona mesa para dos por fabor* |
| We have a reservation. | **Tenemos una reservación.** <br> *tenemos oona reserbaseeyon* |

### YOU MAY HEAR

| | |
|---|---|
| **¿A nombre de quién, por favor?** | What's the name, please? |
| **Lo siento. Todo está reservado.** | I'm sorry. We're very busy/full. |
| **Tendremos una mesa disponible/ libre en … minutos.** | We'll have a free table in … minutes. |
| **Va(n) a tener que regresar en … minutos.** | You'll have to come back in … minutes. |

## WHERE TO SIT

| | |
|---|---|
| Could we sit …? | **¿Podemos sentarnos …?** <br> *podemos sentarnos* |
| over there/outside | **allá/afuera** *al-ya/afwera* |
| in a non-smoking area | **en la sección de no fumadores** <br> *en la sekseeyon deh no foomadores* |
| by the window | **cerca de la ventana** *serka deh la bentana* |
| Smoking or non-smoking? | **¿Fumadores o no fumadores?** <br> *foomadores o no foomadores* |

### IN A RESTAURANT

**¿Tiene una mesa afuera?** *teeyeneh oona mesa afwera*
*(Do you have a table outside?)*
**Por supuesto.** *por soopwesto (Of course.)*
**Muchas gracias.** *moochas graseeyas (Thank you very much.)*

## YOU MAY HEAR

| | |
|---|---|
| ¿Desean ordenar? | Are you ready to order? |
| ¿Qué desea(n) comer? | What would you like? |
| ¿Desea(n) pedir las bebidas primero? | Would you like to order drinks first? |
| Le(s) recomiendo … | I recommend … |
| No tenemos … | We don't have … |
| Eso demorará … minutos. | That will take … minutes. |
| Buen provecho. Espero que disfruten la comida. | Enjoy your meal. |

## ORDERING

Waiter!/Waitress!
**¡Mesero!/¡Mesera!** me*sero*/me*sera*

May I see the wine list?
**¿Puedo ver la lista de vinos?**
*pwedoh bear la leesta deh beenos*

Do you have a set menu?
**¿Tienen el menú del día?**
*teeyenen el menoo del deeya*

Can you recommend some typical local dishes?
**¿Puede recomendarme algunos platos típicos de la región?** *pwedeh rekomendarmeh algoonos platos teepeekos deh la rekheeyon*

Could you tell me what … is?
**¿Podría explicarme qué es …?**
*podreea espleekarmeh keh es*

What is in it?
**¿Qué ingredientes tiene?**
*keh eengredeeyentes teeyeneh*

What kind of … do you have?
**¿Qué clase de … tiene?**
*keh klaseh deh … teeyeneh*

I'd like a bottle/glass/carafe of …
**Quisiera una botella/un vaso/una jarra de …** *keeseeyera oona botel-ya/oon baso/oona kharra deh*

## IN A RESTAURANT

**¡Mesero!** me*sero* (Waiter!)
**Sí, señora.** see sen*yohra* (Yes, m'am.)
**El menú, por favor.** el me*noo* por fa*bor* (The menu, please.)
**Sí, cómo no.** see *komo* no (Sure.)

## Side dishes

| | |
|---|---|
| Could I have … without …? | **¿Podría traerme … sin …?** *podreea trayermeh…seen* |
| With a side order of … | **Con una porción adicional de …** *kon oona porseeyon adeeseeyonal deh* |
| Could I have salad instead of vegetables, please? | **¿Podría traerme ensalada en vez de verduras, por favor?** *podreea trayermeh ensalada en bes deh berdooras por fabor* |
| Does the meal come with vegetables/potatoes? | **¿La carne viene con verduras/papas?** *la karneh beeyeneh kon berdooras/papas* |
| Do you have any sauces? | **¿Tiene salsas?** *teeyeneh salsas* |
| I'd like … with that. | **Quisiera … con eso.** *keeseeyera … kon eso* |
| vegetables/salad | **verduras/ensalada** *berdooras/ensalada* |
| potatoes/fries [chips] | **papas/papas fritas (papas a la francesa)** *papas/papas freetas (papas a la fransesa)* |
| sauce | **salsa** *salsa* |
| ice | **hielo** *eeyelo* |
| May I have some …? | **¿Podría traerme un poco de …?** *podreea trayermeh oon poko deh* |
| bread | **pan** *pan* |
| butter | **mantequilla** *mantekeel-ya* |
| lemon | **limón** *leemon* |
| mustard | **mostaza** *mostasa* |
| pepper | **pimienta** *peemeeyenta* |
| salt | **sal** *sal* |
| seasoning | **aderezo** *adereso* |
| sugar | **azúcar** *asookar* |
| artificial sweetener | **endulzador** *endoolsador* |
| vinaigrette | **salsa vinagreta** *salsa beenagreta* |

### General questions

Could I have a(n) (clean) …, please?
**¿Podría traerme un(-a) … limpio(-a), por favor?** _podreea trayermeh oon(-a) … leempeeyo(-a) por fabor_

ashtray
**un cenicero** _oon seneesero_

cup/glass
**una taza/un vaso** _oona tasa/oon baso_

fork/knife/spoon
**un tenedor/cuchillo/una cuchara** _oon tenedor/koocheel-yo/oona koochara_

napkin
**una servilleta** _oona serbeel-yeta_

plate
**un plato** _oon plato_

I'd like some more …, please.
**Quisiera un poco más de …, por favor.** _keeseeyera oon poko mas deh… por fabor_

Nothing more, thanks.
**Nada más. Gracias.** _nada mas. graseeas_

Where are the bathrooms [toilets]?
**¿Dónde están los baños?** _dondeh estan los baños_

### Special requirements

I can't eat food containing …
**No puedo consumir alimentos que contengan …** _no pwedo konsoomeer aleementos keh kontengan_

salt/sugar
**sal/azúcar** _sal/asookar_

Do you have meals/drinks for diabetics?
**¿Tiene comidas/bebidas especiales para diabéticos?** _teeyeneh komeedas/bebeedas espeseeyales para deeabeteekos_

Do you have vegetarian meals?
**¿Tiene comida vegetariana?** _teeyeneh komeeda bekhetareeyana_

### For the children

Do you have children's portions?
**¿Tiene porciones especiales para niños?** _teeyeneh porseeyones espeseeyales para neeños_

Could we have a child's seat?
**¿Podría traernos un asiento para niños?** _podreea trayernos oon aseeyento para neeños_

Where can I feed/ change the baby?
**¿Dónde puedo alimentar/cambiar al bebé?** _dondeh pwedo aleementar/kambeeyar al bebeh_

## FAST FOOD/CAFÉ

### Something to drink

| | |
|---|---|
| I'd like (a cup of) … | **Quisiera …** *keeseeyera* |
| coffee/tea | **un café/un té** *oon kafeh/oon teh* |
| black/with milk | **un café negro [tinto]/un café con leche** *oon kafeh negro [teento]/oon kafeh kon lecheh* |
| I'd like a … of red/white wine. | **Quisiera un(-a) … de vino tinto/blanco.** *keeseeyera oon(-a) … deh beeno teento/blanko.* |
| carafe/bottle/glass | **garafa/botella/vaso** *kharafa/botel-ya/baso* |
| Do you have … beer? | **¿Tiene … cerveza?** *teeyeneh … serbesa* |
| bottled/draft [draught] | **en botella/de barril** *en botel-ya/deh barreel* |

### And to eat …

| | |
|---|---|
| A piece of …, please. | **Un pedazo de…, por favor.** *oon pedaso deh… por fabor* |
| cake | **un pastel** *oon pastel* |
| I'd like (a/an) …, please. | **Quiero…, por favor.** *keeyero … por fabor* |
| two of those | **dos de ésos** *dos deh esos* |
| burger | **una hamburguesa** *oona amboorgesa* |
| fries [chips] | **papas fritas (papas a la francesa)** *papas freetas (papas a la fransesa)* |
| sandwich | **un sandwich** *oon sandweech* |
| ice cream | **un helado de …** *oon elado deh …* |
| vanilla/chocolate/strawberry | **vainilla/chocolate/fresa** *bayneel-ya/chokolateh/fresa* |
| A … portion, please. | **Una porción …, por favor.** *oona porseeyon … por fabor* |
| small | **pequeña** *pekeña* |
| regular [medium] | **mediana** *medeeyana* |
| large | **grande** *grandeh* |
| It's to go [take away]. | **Es para llevar.** *es para l-yebar* |
| That's all, thanks. | **Eso es todo, gracias.** *eso es todo, graseeyas* |

## IN A CAFÉ

**Dos cafés, por favor.** *dos kafehs por fabor*
*(Two coffees, please.)*
**¿Algo más?** *algo mas (Anything else?)*
**Eso es todo. Gracias.** *eso es todo graseeyas*
*(That's all, thanks.)*

## COMPLAINTS

| | |
|---|---|
| I have no knife/fork/spoon. | **No tengo cuchillo/tenedor/cuchara.** *no tengo koocheel-yo/tenedor/koochara* |
| There must be some mistake. | **Debe haber una equivocación [un error].** *debeh aber oona ekeebokaseeyon [oon error]* |
| That's not what I ordered. | **Esto no es lo que yo pedí.** *esto no es lo keh yo pedee* |
| I asked for … | **Yo pedí …** *yo pedee* |
| The meat is … | **La carne está …** *la karne esta* |
| overdone | **demasiado cocinada** *demaseeyado koseenada* |
| underdone | **poco cocinada** *poko koseenada* |
| too tough | **demasiado dura** *demaseeyado doora* |
| This is too … | **Esto está demasiado …** *esto esta demaseeyado* |
| bitter/sour | **amargo/ácido** *amargo/aseedo* |
| The food is cold. | **La comida está fría.** *la komeeda esta freea* |
| This isn't fresh. | **Esto no está fresco.** *esto no esta fresko* |
| How much longer will our food be? | **¿Cuánto tiempo más va a tardar nuestra comida?** *kwanto teeyempo mas ba a tardar nwestra komeeda* |
| We can't wait any longer. We're leaving. | **No podemos esperar más. Nos vamos.** *no podemos esperar mas. nos bamos* |
| This isn't clean. | **Esto no está limpio.** *esto no esta leempeeo* |
| I'd like to speak to the manager. | **Quisiera hablar con el gerente.** *keeseeyera ablar kon el kherenteh* |

## PAYING

In Mexico, most bills have 10% **IVA (Impuesto de Valor Añadido**) added.

The check, please. **La cuenta, por favor.**
*la kwenta por fabor*

We'd like to pay separately. **Queremos pagar por separado.**
*keremos pagar por separado*

It's all together, please. **Todo junto, por favor.** *todo khoonto
por fabor*

I think there's a mistake
in this bill. **Creo que hay un error en esta cuenta.**
*kreo keh eye oon error en esta kwenta*

What is this amount for? **¿A qué corresponde esta cantidad?**
*a keh korrespondeh esta kanteedath*

I didn't have that. I had … **Yo no comí eso. Yo comí …**
*yo no komee eso. yo komee*

Is service included? **¿Está incluido el servicio?**
*esta eenklooeedo el serbeeseeo*

Can I pay with cash? **¿Puedo pagar en efectivo?**
*pwedo pagar en efekteebo?*

Can I pay with this
credit card? **¿Puedo pagar con esta tarjeta
de crédito?** *pwedo pagar kon esta
tarkheta deh kredeeto*

I've forgotten my wallet. **He olvidado mi billetera.**
*eh olbeedado mee beel-yetera*

I don't have enough money. **No tengo suficiente dinero.**
*no tengo soofeeseeyenteh deenero.*

Could I have a receipt? **¿Me podría dar un recibo?**
*me podreea dar oon reseebo*

That was a very good meal. **La comida estuvo deliciosa.**
*la komeeda estoobo deleeseeyosa*

### IN A RESTAURANT

**La cuenta, por favor.** *la kwenta por fabor*
*(The bill please.)*
**Aquí tiene.** *akee teeyeneh* *(Here you are.)*
**Gracias.** *graseeyas* *(Thanks.)*

## COURSE BY COURSE

### Breakfast

| | |
|---|---|
| I'll have … | **Tomaré …** *tomareh* |
| bread | **pan** *pan* |
| butter | **mantequilla** *mantekeel-ya* |
| eggs | **huevos** *webos* |
| fried eggs | **huevos fritos** *webos freetos* |
| scrambled eggs | **huevos revueltos** *webos rebweltos* |
| jam | **mermelada** *mermelada* |
| honey | **miel** *meeyel* |
| grapefruit juice | **jugo de toronja** *khoogo deh toronkha* |
| orange juice | **jugo de naranja** *khoogo deh narankha* |
| marmalade | **mermelada** *mermelada* |
| milk | **leche** *lecheh* |
| rolls | **bollitos** *bol-yeetos* |
| toast | **pan tostado** *pan tostado* |

### Appetizers/Starters

When in Mexico, try some special appetizers: ask for **antojitos mexicanos**. A few examples:

**guacamole** *gwakamoleh*
Mashed avocado, lime juice, and chilies with **totopos** (small fried pieces of tortilla).

**quesadilla** *kesadeel-ya*
Tortilla (a dry cornmeal pancake) filled with cheese or any other filling you want; it can be fried and it is often served with chili sauce, cream, and cheese.

**tostadas** *tostadas*
Fried tortilla with different fillings on top.

**tacos** *takos*
Tacos are as popular in Mexico as hot dogs in the United States. They are made from tortillas stuffed with all kinds of meat, vegetable, and cheese fillings. They can be fried (**tacos dorados**) in hot oil and spiced with chili-pepper sauce, guacamole, cream, cheese, and lettuce. Tacos can be found in all kinds of restaurants.

## Soups and stews

| | |
|---|---|
| **cazuela de mariscos** | a flavorful seafood stew *(Argentina)* |
| **chipi-chipi** | clam soup *(Venezuela)* |
| **chupe de mariscos** | a superb shellfish dish *(Chile, Peru)* |
| **crema de lima** | lima bean soup |
| **menudo** | tripe in chili-pepper sauce *(Mexico)* |
| **pozole** | pork and ground-corn soup *(Mexico)* |
| **sopa de ajo** | soup with fried bread, paprika, garlic |
| **sopa de arroz** | rice soup |
| **sopa de cebolla** | onion soup |
| **sopa de espárragos** | asparagus soup |
| **sopa de fideos [sopa de pasta]** | vermicelli soup |
| **sopa de frijoles** | bean soup |
| **sopa de mariscos** | seafood soup |
| **sopa de papas** | potato, onion, parsley, and sherry soup |
| **sopa de pescado** | fish soup |
| **sopa de tortuga** | turtle soup |
| **sopa de verduras** | green vegetable soup |

**cazuela de ave** *kaswela deh abeh*
A rich chicken soup with green vegetables cooked in stock *(Chile)*.

**chupe de camarones** *choopeh deh kamarones*
A soup made of potatoes, milk, prawns, hot chilies, peppers, and eggs *(Peru)*.

**cocido [sancocho]** *koseedo [sankocho]*
A stew made with chunks of beef, chicken, or fish, and local vegetables or roots *(Peru)*.

## Fish and seafood

In coastal areas, try the wide variety of fresh fish and seafood.

| | | |
|---|---|---|
| **atún** | *atoon* | tuna |
| **bacalao** | *bakalao* | cod |
| **besugo** | *besoogo* | (sea) bream |

| | | |
|---|---|---|
| **bonito** | _boneeto_ | striped tuna |
| **boquerones** | _bokerones_ | herring |
| **caballa** | _kabal-ya_ | mackerel |
| **calamares** | _kalamares_ | squid |
| **camarones grandes** | _kamarones grandes_ | shrimp [prawns] (large) |
| **gambas** | _gambas_ | shrimp [prawns] (small) |
| **huachinango** | _wacheenango_ | red snapper |
| **langosta** | _langosta_ | lobster |
| **lenguado** | _lengwado_ | sole |
| **merluza** | _merloosa_ | hake |
| **mero** | _mero_ | bass |
| **mújol** | _mookhol_ | mullet |
| **pez espada** | _pes espada_ | swordfish |
| **pulpo** | _poolpo_ | octopus |
| **rape** | _rapeh_ | monkfish |
| **salmón (ahumado)** | _salmon (ahoomado)_ | (smoked) salmon |
| **salmonetes** | _salmonetes_ | red mullet |
| **trucha** | _troocha_ | trout |

**cazuela de mariscos** _kaswela deh mareeskos_
Seafood stew.

**ceviche** _sebeecheh_
Raw fish, marinated in lemon juice, served with onions and hot peppers.

**ceviche de langostinos** _sebeecheh deh langosteenos_
A ceviche (all kinds of shellfish) with sea crayfish [Dublin Bay prawns] as main ingredient.

**ceviche mixto** _sebeecheh meeksto_
A ceviche with a mixture of shrimp, fish, and shellfish.

**pescado a la veracruzana** _peskado a la berakroosana_
Red snapper with tomatoes and pimientos.

**viudo de pescado** _beeoodo deh peskado_
Fish stew, traditionally cooked in holes dug in the ground and covered with hot stones _(Colombia)_.

## Meat

Many Latin-American countries are beef and pork producers. Lamb is common in mountainous countries and chicken is universal.

| | | |
|---|---|---|
| carne de res [carne vacuna] | karneh deh res [karneh bakoona] | beef |
| carnero | karnero | mutton |
| chancho [cerdo, puerco] | chancho [serdo, pwerko] | pork |
| cordero | kordero | lamb |
| filete/lomo/bistec | feeleteh/lomo/beestek | steak |
| hígado | eegado | liver |
| jamón | khamon | ham |
| panceta [tocino] | panseta [toseeno] | bacon |
| pato | pato | duck |
| pavo | pabo | turkey |
| pollo | pol-yo | chicken |
| salchichas | salcheechas | sausages |
| ternera | ternera | veal |

### Meat cuts

| | | |
|---|---|---|
| chuleta | chooleta | chop |
| costilla | kosteel-ya | cutlet/scallop |
| carne molida | karneh moleeda | chopped/minced meat |
| bistec | beestek | steak |
| filete | feeleteh | fillet steak |
| pierna | peeyerna | leg |
| riñones | reeñones | kidneys |

### Meat dishes

**anticucho** anteekoocho

Squares of heart (beef) on skewers, broiled over charcoal, and served with hot sauce *(Peru)*.

**pollo en mole** pol-yo en moleh

Chicken in a sauce of chilies, oil, sugar, sesame seeds, peanuts, cocoa, cinnamon, and other spices, served with small pieces of bread *(Mexico)*.

## Vegetables/Fruit

| | | |
|---|---|---|
| ajo | _akho_ | garlic |
| alcachofas | _alkachofas_ | artichokes |
| berenjena | _berenkhena_ | eggplant [aubergine] |
| calabaza | _kalabasa_ | squash |
| cebollas | _sebol-yas_ | onions |
| champiñones | _champeeñones_ | mushrooms |
| chícharos | _cheecharos_ | peas |
| col | _kol_ | cabbage |
| ejotes | _ekhotes_ | green [French] beans |
| elote/maíx | _eloteh/maeez_ | corn |
| flor de calabaza | _flor deh kalabasa_ | zucchini flowers |
| frijoles | _freekholes_ | beans |
| lechuga | _lechooga_ | lettuce |
| pepino | _pepeeno_ | cucumber |
| rábanos | _rabanos_ | radishes |
| zanahorias | _sanahoreeyas_ | carrots |
| zapallitos | _sapal-yeetos_ | zucchini [courgettes] |
| duraznos | _doorasnos_ | peaches |
| fresas | _fresas_ | strawberries |
| granadas | _granadas_ | pomegranates |
| higos | _eegos_ | figs |
| manzanas | _mansanas_ | apples |
| naranjas | _narankhas_ | oranges |
| piña | _peeña_ | pineapple |
| plátanos | _platanos_ | bananas |

**chile** _cheeleh_

Chili peppers or hot peppers – call them what you like. They come in many varieties; the most popular are: **poblano**, **chipotle**, **jalapeño**, **largo**, **piquín**; but you'll also see **habanero**, **serrano**, and **pimiento**.

**papas [patatas]** _papas [patatas]_

Potatoes; may be ~ **fritas** (~ **a la francesa**) (fries), ~ **hervidas** (boiled), **puré de** ~ (mashed); and varieties of sweet potatoes: **batatas**, **camotes**, **yame**, and **yuca**.

## Cheese

| asadero | a soft, creamy cheese |
|---|---|
| queso añejo | hand-pressed and salted. The flavor is sharp, the texture close-grained and hard with a few small holes; made from ewe's milk |
| queso de Chihuahua | a popular soft cheese named after the province from which it originates |
| queso de Oaxaca | very popular in the south of Mexico, especially used to make **quesadillas** |
| queso enchilado | same as **queso añejo** but a little sharper in taste; the exterior is colored with red chili peppers |
| queso fresco | fresh white cheese; made and sold the same day |

## Dessert

| alborotos | *alborotos* | dessert made of roasted corn |
|---|---|---|
| ante | *anteh* | pastry with coconut and almonds |
| bizcocho | *beeskocho* | sponge cake |
| buñuelos | *booñwelos* | fritters |
| cocada | *kokada* | dessert made of coconut |
| espumilla | *espoomeel-ya* | a kind of meringue |
| flan | *flan* | caramel custard/crème caramel |
| galletas | *gal-yetas* | cookies [biscuits] |
| pastel | *pastel* | layer cake |
| panqué [queque] | *ponkeh [kekeh]* | pound cake |

**capirotada** *kapeerotada*
Bread pudding with cheese, apples, banana, and peanuts *(Mexico)*.

**helado** *elado*
Ice cream; popular flavors include ~ **de chocolate**, ~ **de fresa** (strawberry), and ~ **de vainilla** (vanilla).

**frutas tropicales** *frootas tropeekales*
Tropical fruits. Among the many exotic types you may find are **anona** (scaly custard apple/sweetsop), **carambola** (star fruit), **chirimoya** (custard apple), **fruta de pan** (bread fruit), **guayaba** (guava), **mamey** (sweet fruit), **maracuyá** (passion fruit), and **tamarindo** (sour fruit).

## DRINKS

### Wine

You'll find imported European wines all over Latin America, but try the local ones as well, particularly in Chile, Argentina, and Mexico. Latin America produces almost one tenth of the world's wines.

### South American and Mexican wines

#### Argentina

The fourth largest wine producer in the world. Best wines called **vinos finos**. Major wine areas are **La Rioja**, **Mendoza**, **Rio Negro**, **Salta**, and **San Juan**. The most common grape varieties are **Malbec** (red) and **Criollas** (white). Proprietary names include **Etchart**, **Orfila**, **Suter**, and **Santa Ana**.

#### Chile

The leading quality wine producer in South America. Produces excellent red wines, especially **Merlot** and **Cabernet Sauvignon**; and white wines include **Chardonnay**, **Sauvignon Blanc**, and **Riesling**. The best wines are from **Aconcagua**, **Maule**, **Maipo**, and **Rapel regions**. The geographic diversity of the country allows a wide variety of wines.

#### Mexico

The most popular red wines are **Cepa Urbiñón**, **Calafía**, and **Chatillon**. For a sparkling wine, try **Chambrule**. The best wines are from the **North Baja California** and **Querétaro** regions, such as **Pedro Domecq**.

### Reading the label

| blanco | _blanko_ | white |
|--------|----------|-------|
| dulce | _dool_seh | sweet |
| espumoso | espoo_moso_ | sparkling |
| fuerte | _fwerteh_ | full-bodied |
| ligero | lee_khero_ | light |
| muy seco | mwee _seko_ | very dry |
| rosado | ro_sado_ | blush [rosé] |
| seco | _seko_ | dry |
| tinto | _eento_ | red |

## Beer

Beer is an excellent accompaniment for a hot, spicy, dish; and local beers can be excellent. Popular brands to look for include **Escudo** (Chile), **Cuzqueña** (Peru), **Polar** (Venezuela), **Imperial** (Costa Rica). In Mexico, look for **Bohemia**, **Dos Equis**, **Pacífico**, **Sol**, **Superior**, **Tecate** (served with lime and salt), **Negra Modelo** and **Tres Equis** (both dark beers).

| | | |
|---|---|---|
| Do you have … beer? | **¿Tienen cerveza …?** | _teeyenen serbesa_ |
| light/dark/chilled | **rubia/negra/fría** | _roobeea/negra/freea_ |

## Other alcoholic drinks

Local drinks may provide you with a new experience. They are usually made from tropical fruit. Here are a few national specialties.

**tequila** _tekeela_

The most famous Mexican spirit, distilled from the maguey (**agave**) cactus and reminiscent of gin. Ask your waiter how to drink it Mexican style (with lime and salt on the side). The best is **añejo** or **reposado** (aged). Tequila is the main constituent of margarita cocktails.

**mescal [mexcal]** _meskal_

A less refined version of tequila; the bottle contains a worm (**gusano**) to prove its authenticity.

**pulque** _poolkeh_

Thick, milky beer also made from maguey cactus; the unfermented version is called **aguamiel**.

| | |
|---|---|
| **Mexico** | **chicha**, a strong drink made from fermented sweetened corn and various kinds of fruit **tepache**, a drink made from pulque, pineapple, and cloves |
| **Argentina** | **caña** (cane alcohol), also popular elsewhere in South America; **ginebra bols** are popular local spirits |
| **Chile, Peru, Bolivia** | **pisco**, a local brandy, served with lemon juice, bitters or syrup |
| **Colombia** | **aguardiente**, a fiery spirit; **pisco sour**, brandy with ginger ale (**chilcano**) or vermouth (**capitán**) |
| **Puerto Rico** | **ron** is the word for "rum" here and Puerto Ricans are justly proud of the wide variety available; **ron caldas**, a rum comparable to the Jamaican type **ron medellín**, a lighter rum |
| **Venezuela** | **ponche de crema**, an eggnog punch, spiced with liqueur; **ron,** rum of various varieties |

Here's a list of drinks you'll find in most bars and hotels. Note that Mexican brandy is well worth trying. It's the most popular spirit of that country.

| | |
|---|---|
| aperitif | **un aperitivo** *oon apereeteebo* |
| brandy/rum | **un coñac/ron** *oon koñak/ron* |
| gin | **una ginebra [un gin]** *oona kheenebra [oon "gin"]* |
| gin and tonic | **una tónica con ginebra** *oona toneeka kon kheenebra* |
| liqueur | **un licor** *oon leekor* |
| port/sherry | **un oporto/jerez** *oon oporto/kheres* |
| vermouth | **un vermut** *oon bermoot* |
| vodka/whisky | **un vodka/whisky** *oon bodka/weesky* |
| a glass | **un vaso [una copa]** *oon baso [oona kopa]* |
| a bottle | **una botella** *oona botel-ya* |
| ice cubes | **cubos de hielo** *koobos deh yelo* |
| straight [neat] | **solo** *solo* |
| on the rocks [with ice]/ with water | **con hielo/con agua** *kon yelo/kon agwa* |

### Non-alcoholic drinks

| | |
|---|---|
| I'd like a … | **Quisiera …** *keeseeyera oon(-a)* |
| (hot) chocolate | **un chocolate (caliente)** *chokolateh (kaleeyenteh)* |
| lemonade/cola | **una limonada/coca** *leemonada/koka* |
| milk shake | **un batido de leche** *bateedo deh lecheh* |
| mineral water | **un agua mineral** *oon agwa meeneral* |
| carbonated/non-carbonated | **con gas/sin gas** *kon gas/seen gas* |
| tonic water | **un agua tónica [quina]** *oon agwa toneeka [keena]* |

**atole** *atoleh*
A drink made from the same paste as tortillas and and added flavor.

**café** *kafeh*
Coffee types: **~ chico** (thick, dark in small cup); **~ con crema** (with cream); **~ con leche** (with milk); **~ cortado** (with a little milk); **~ descafeinado** (decaffeinated); **~ de olla** (with cane sugar, cinnamon, and cloves); **~exprés [expreso]** (espresso); **~ solo**, **~ negro** or **~ tinto** (black).

# MENU READER

This is an alphabetical glossary of terms that you may find in a menu. Items that are particularly associated with a region or country are indicated, e.g. *Arg.* – Argentina, *Carib.* – Caribbean, *Col.* – Colombia, *Mex.* – Mexico.

| | | |
|---|---|---|
| baked | **al horno** | al *orno* |
| fried | **frito(-a)** | *freeto* |
| boiled | **cocido(-a)** | *koseedo* |
| grilled | **a la parrilla** | a la *pareel*-ya |
| roasted | **asado(-a)** | a*sado*(-a) |
| poached | **hervido(-a)/** | er*beedo*(-a)/ |
| | **escalfado(-a)** | eskal*fado*(-a) |
| marinated | **en escabeche** | en eska*becheh* |
| sautéed | **salteado(-a)** | salte*ado*(-a) |
| | **[saltado(-a)]** | [sal*tado*(-a)] |
| smoked | **ahumado(-a)** | aoo*mado*(-a) |
| spicy | **condimentado(-a)** | kondeemen*tado*(-a) |
| steamed | **al vapor** | al ba*por* |
| braised | **a la brasa** | a la *brasa* |
| stewed | **guisado(-a)** | gee*sado*(-a) |
| | **[estofado(-a)]** | [esto*fado*] |
| stuffed | **relleno(-a)** | rel-*yeno*(-a) |
| diced | **cortado(-a) en cubos** | kor*tado*(-a) en *koobos* |
| oven-browned | **tostado(-a) al horno** | tos*tado*(-a) al *orno* |
| breaded | **empanado(-a)** | empa*nado*(-a) |
| | **[apanado(-a)]** | [apa*nado*(-a)] |
| deep-fried | **frito(-a)** | *freeto*(-a) |
| very rare | **muy crudo(-a)** | mwee *kroodo*(-a) |
| rare/underdone | **crudo(-a)** | *kroodo*(-a) |
| | **[poco cocinado (-a)]** | [poko kosee*nahdoh*(-a)] |
| medium | **medio hecho(-a)** | me*deeo echo*(-a) |
| | **[a medio cocinar]** | [a *medeeo* kosee*nar*] |
| well-done | **bien hecha** | bee*yen echa* |
| | **[bien cocinada]** | [bee*yen* kosee*nada*] |

**a elegir** of your choice
**a la brasa** braised
**a la parrilla** grilled (broiled)
**a medio cocinar** medium
**aceite** oil
**aceitunas** olives
**acelgas en crema** Swiss chard sautéed with onion, carrot and potato *(Arg.)*
**achicoria** endive
**adobo** sauce made from two types of chili peppers (*chile ancho* and *chile pasilla*), vegetable oil, sesame seeds, peanuts, sugar, salt, and spices
**adobado(-a)** marinated
**agua (caliente)** (hot) water
**agua de jamaica** unfermented drink from flowers
**agua de panela** hot sugar water
**agua mineral** mineral water
**agua tónica/quina** tonic water
**aguacate** avocado
**aguardiente** anise flavored spirit
**ahumado(-a)** smoked
**ají** red pepper
**ají picante** hot pepper
**ajiaco** a pimiento-based sauce; chicken and potato soup *(Col.)*
**ajiaco criollo** creole stew of ribs, steak, corn, sweet potatoes and cassava *(Carib.)*
**ajo** garlic
**al carbón** barbecued
**al horno** baked, roast
**al mojo de ajo** fried in butter and garlic
**al vapor** steamed

**alambre** kebab
**albahaca** basil
**albóndiga** meatball
**alborotos** candy made of roasted corn
**alcachofas** artichokes
**alcaparras** capers
**aliado** ham and cheese
**almejas** clams
**almendras** almonds
**almuerzo** lunch
**ananá[s]** pineapple
**anchoas** anchovies
**anguila (ahumada)** (smoked) eel
**anís** aniseed
**anona** custard apple/sweetsop
**ante** pastry with coconut and almonds
**anticucho** barbequed beef heart with hot sauce *(Peru)*
**antojitos** snacks, starters *(Mex.)*
**apanado(-a)** breaded
**aperitivo** aperitif
**api** sweet corn, lemon, and cinnamon drink
**apio** celery
**aporreado de tasajo** salt-dried beef stew
**arenque** herring
**arenques ahumados** smoked herrings
**arepa** grilled corn dough stuffed with meat, seafood or cheese *(Ven., Col.)*
**aromática** herb tea *(Col.)*
**arreglados** meat sandwiches
**arroz** rice

**arroz a la milanesa** risotto
*(Carib.)*
**arroz con leche** rice pudding
**arvejas** peas
**asadero** a soft, creamy cheese
**asado(-a)** grilled, roasted
**atole** hot drink made from the
same paste as *tortillas*
**atún** tuna
**avellanas** hazelnuts
**aves** poultry
**azafrán** saffron
**azúcar** sugar

## B

**bacalaíto** small cod fritter
**bacalao** cod
**barbacoa** barbequed meat
**batatas** sweet potatoes
**batido de leche** milk shake
**bebida** drink
**bebida sin alcohol** non-alcoholic
drink
**berenjena** eggplant [aubergine]
**besugo** (sea) bream
**betabel** sugar beet
**bien coci[na]do(-a)** well-done
**bien hecho(-a)** well-done
**bife** beef steak
**bife a caballo** "horseback beef";
a steak topped by two fried
eggs *(Arg.)*
**bife de costilla** T-bone steak
**birria** goat or mutton stew
**bistec** steak
**bizcocho** sponge cake
**blanco** white *(wine)*
**blando** soft *(egg)*

**bocaditos** small sandwiches with
various fillings *(Carib.)*
**boliche** stuffed pot roast *(Carib.)*
**bollitos** bread rolls
**boniato** sweet potato
**boniatos asados** caramelized
potatoes
**bonito** striped tuna
**boquerones** herring
**botella** bottle
**budín** pudding
**buñuelos** doughnut fritters with
sugar, anise, and cinnamon
**burrito** filled wheat flour *tortilla*
*(Mex.)*

## C

**caballa** mackerel
**cabeza** head
**cabra** goat
**cabrito** kid
**cacahuetes** peanuts
**cachapa** large corn pancake
**café** coffee; **~ americano** black;
**~ chico** small strong, thick coffee
*(Arg.)*; **~ con leche** with milk;
**~ de olla** coffee with cane sugar,
cinnamon, and cloves; **~ marrón/
con leche** coffee with milk
**cajeta** milk, sugar, and vanilla
dessert
**calabacita** zucchini [courgette]
**calabaza** squash, pumpkin
**calamares** squid
**caldo verde** kale soup *(Mex.)*
**camarones** shrimps; **~ al ajillo**
garlic shrimp; **~ grandes** prawns
**camotes** sweet potatoes
**caña** cane alcohol

54

**canela** cinnamon
**cangrejo** crab
**capirotada** bread pudding with banana, apple, peanuts, and cheese (Mex.)
**capón** capon
**caracoles** snails
**carambola** starfruit
**caramelos** candy, sweets
**carbonada criolla** beef slices sautéed with zucchini [courgette], sweet potatoes, peaches, and sweet corn (Arg.)
**carne** meat
**carne a la tampiqueña** steak strips with guacamole, tacos and fried beans (Mex.)
**carne claveteada** pot-roast studded with almonds and bacon
**carne con papas** fragrant beef stew (Carib.)
**carne de cangrejo** crabmeat
**carne de puerco/cerdo** pork
**carne de res** beef
**carne molida** minced meat
**carne vacuna** beef
**carnero** mutton
**carnes frías** cold cuts of meat
**carnitas** spicy pork
**carta** menu
**castañas** chestnuts
**caza** game
**cazuela de ave** a rich chicken soup with green vegetables cooked in stock (Chile)
**cazuela de mariscos** a flavorful seafood stew (Arg.)

**cazuela de pescado** spicy fish stew
**cebollas** onions; ~ **encurtidas** pickled onion rings (Mex.)
**cebolletas** chives
**centolla** king crab
**cerdo** pork
**cereales** cereal
**cerezas** cherries
**cerveza** beer
**ceviche** raw fish, marinated in lemon juice
**ceviche de corvina** marinated sea bass with yams or potatoes (Peru)
**ceviche de langostinos** shellfish ceviche with sea crayfish [Dublin Bay prawns] as main ingredient
**ceviche mixto** ceviche with a mixture of shrimp, fish, and shellfish
**chabacanos** apricots
**chacarero** beef steak with vegetables
**champiñones** mushrooms
**chancho** pork
**chayote** avocado-like vegetable
**chícharos** peas
**chicharrones** pork rinds
**chicha** a strong drink made from fermented sweet corn
**chicharrón** fried salt pork
**chilaquiles** tortillas filled with beef, spices and egg
**chile** chili peppers, hot peppers or pimientos

**chile con carne** stew of kidney beans and minced beef, well spiced with chili peppers

**chiles en nogada** stuffed green peppers, walnut sauce, and sour cream with red pomegranate *(Mex.)*

**chimichurri** marinade

**chipi-chipi** a soup made with tiny clams *(Ven.)*

**chirimoya** custard apple

**chirivías** parsnips

**chivito** steak, bacon, cheese, lettuce and tomato sandwich *(Urug.)*

**choclo** corn

**chocolate (caliente)** (hot) chocolate

**cholgas** mussels

**chopp** draft beer or lager

**chorizo** a highly spiced type of smoked pork sausage

**chuleta** chop

**chupe de camarones** soup made of potatoes, milk, and eggs *(Peru)*

**chupe de congrio** conger eel stew *(Chile)*

**chupe de marisco** delicious shellfish dish *(Chile, Peru)*

**churrasco** steak

**cilantro** coriander

**ciruelas** plums

**ciruelas secas** prunes

**clavos** cloves

**clericó** white wine and fruit juice

**cocada** coconut cookie [biscuit]

**cochinillo** suckling pig; **~ pibil** slowly baked in a banana-leaf wrapping *(Mex.)*

**cocido** a stew made with chunks of beef, chicken or fish and local vegetables or roots *(Peru)*

**cocido(-a)** boiled, braised

**coco** coconut

**coctel** appetizer in sauce

**codorniz** quail

**col** cabbage; **~ morada** red cabbage

**coles de Bruselas** brussels sprouts

**coliflor** cauliflower

**comino** cumin

**con agua** with water

**con crema** with cream

**con gas** carbonated

**con hielo** on the rocks

**con leche** with milk

**con limón** with lemon

**coñac** brandy

**condimentado(-a)** spicy

**condimentos** spices

**conejo** rabbit

**copa** glass

**cordero** lamb

**cortado** small coffee light

**cortado(-a) en cubos** diced

**corvina** sea bass

**costilla** cutlet

**crema de lima** lima bean soup

**crepa** thin pancake

**criadillas** sweetbreads

**croquetas** croquettes; **~ de jamón** ham croquettes *(Carib.)*

**crudo(-a)** rare/underdone; raw

**cubos de hielo** ice cubes

**cilantro** coriander

**curuba** tropical fruit

## D

**damascos** apricots
**dátiles** dates
**descafeinado** decaffeinated
**desayuno** breakfast
**dulce** sweet
**dulce de camote** puréed yam with nuts and dried fruit *(Mex.)*
**durazno** peach
**duro** hard boiled *(egg)*

## E

**ejotes** green [French] beans
**elote** corn on the cob *(Mex.)*
**empanada** turnover with egg, minced beef, ham, chicken, cheese, vegetables, and other fillings; can be *al horno* (baked) or *frita* (fried); may be highly spiced
**empanado(-a)** breaded
**en barbacoa** barbecued, Mexican style
**en crema** creamed
**en escabeche** marinated
**en salsa** in sauce or gravy
**en su jugo** pot roasted
**enchilada** *tortilla* with filling and sauce, a type of taco *(Mex.);*
**~ de pollo** with a chicken filling in a red or green chili-pepper or *mole* sauce; served with cheese; **~ suiza** with sour cream
**eneldo** dill
**enfrijolada** *tortilla* with cheese, onion, and bean sauce
**ensalada** salad; **~ de aguacate** avocado; **~ de camarones** shrimp; **~ de fruta** fruit; **~ de lechuga** green; **~ de patatas [papas]** potato;

**~ de pepino** cucumber; **~ de tomate [jitomate]** tomato
**entomatada** *tortilla* with cheese, onion, and tomato sauce
**entradas** appetizers, starters
**entremeses** appetizers, starters
**escabeche** pickled or marinated dish
**escalfado(-a)** poached
**escarola** endive/chicory
**espárragos** asparagus
**especialidades de la casa** house specialties
**especialidades locales** local specialties
**especias** spices
**espinacas** spinach; **~ con anchoas** sautéed with anchovies
**espumilla** kind of meringue
**espumoso** sparkling
**estofado(-a)** stewed
**estragón** tarragon
**exprés/expreso** espresso
**exprimado(-a)** fresh *(fruit juice)*

## F

**fainá** baked chickpea dough
**faisán** pheasant
**fiambres** cold meat
**filete** fillet steak
**flan** caramel custard; **~ casero** homemade
**flor de calabaza** zucchini [courgette] flowers
**foie-gras** pâté
**frambuesas** raspberries
**fresas** strawberries
**frijoles** beans; **~ negros** black beans

**fritas** fries [chips]; small fried hamburgers *(Carib.)*
**frito(-a)** fried
**frituras** fritters; ~ **de carita** black-eyed pea fritters *(Carib.)*
**fruta de pan** bread fruit
**frutas** fruit; ~ **tropicales** tropical fruit
**fría** cold
**fuerte** full-bodied
**fugazza** pizza with sweet onions *(Arg.)*

## G

**galletas** cookies [biscuits]
**galletas saladas** crackers
**gallo pinto** "painted rooster", rice with red and white beans *(C. Rica)*
**gambas** shrimp [prawns]
**ganso** goose
**garbanzos** chickpeas
**gaseosas** sodas, carbonated drinks
**gazpacho** chilled vegetable and chili soup
**gelatina** gelatin
**ginebra [gin]** gin
**granadas** pomegranates
**granadilla** passion fruit
**guacamole** mashed avocado with lime juice and chilies
**guanábana** prickly custard apple/soursop
**guaro** spirit *(C. Rica)*
**guayaba** guava *(fruit)*
**guayabada** guava paste
**guisado(-a)** stewed
**guisado** stew
**guisantes** peas

**guiso de maíz** rich corn stew
**guiso de puerco** pork stewed with onions, chilies, cloves, cinnamon, pepper, cumin, garlic, and vinegar *(Mex.)*

## H

**hallaca** chopped meat with vegetables in corn pancake wrapped in banana leaves *(Ven.)*
**helada** ice cream tart
**helado** ice cream
**helado(-a)** iced
**hervidas** boiled, steamed *(potatoes)*
**hervido(-a)** poached
**hígado** liver; ~ **de pollo** chicken liver
**higos** figs
**hoja de laurel** bay leaf
**hongos** mushrooms
**horchata** cooling, unfermented drink made from almonds, cinnamon, and rice
**hormiga culona** large fried ants *(Col.)*
**huachinango** red snapper *(Mex.)*
**huauzontles** vegetable coated and served with a cheese filling *(Mex.)*
**huevos** eggs; ~ **con jamón** ham and eggs; ~ **con tocino** bacon and eggs; ~ **fritos** fried; ~ **mexicanos** scrambled with tomatoes, chilies, garlic, and onions *(Mex.)*; ~ **rancheros** fried with hot chili sauce; ~ **revueltos** scrambled
**humita** corn *tamal*
**húngaro** spicy sausage

## J

**jaiba** crab
**jamón** ham; ~ **ahumado** smoked;
~ **cocido** boiled
**jarra** carafe
**jerez** sherry
**jitomates** tomatoes *(Mex.)*
**jugo de fruta** fruit juice
**jugoso(-a)** rare

## L

**lamprea** eel
**langosta** lobster
**langostino** sea crayfish [Dublin Bay prawns]
**leche** milk
**lechecillas** sweetbreads
**lechón** suckling pig
**lechón asado** roast suckling pig
**lechuga** lettuce
**legumbres** vegetables
**lengua** tongue
**lenguado** sole
**lentejas** lentils
**licor** liqueur
**licuado** milky fruit drink
**liebre** hare
**ligero** light
**lima** lime
**limón** lemon
**limonada** lemonade
**locos** abalone
**locro** corn [maize] stew
**lomito** filet mignon
**lomo** steak
**lomo a lo pobre** beef with eggs and fries [chips] *(Chile)*
**lomo de cerdo** pork fillet

**lomo saltado** chopped steak, potatoes, tomatoes with rice
**lulo** tropical fruit

## M

**maíz** sweet corn
**macarrón de almendras** macaroon
**macarrones** macaroni
**mamey** sweet tropical fruit
**mamoncillo** tropical fruit
**mamones chinos** type of lychee
**mandarina** tangerine
**mango** mango
**maníes** peanuts
**mantequilla** butter
**manzana** apple
**maracuyá** passion fruit
**marañón** tropical fruit with cashew nut seed
**mariquitas** chips; ~ **de plátanos** plantain chips *(Carib.)*
**mariscos** seafood
**masita** pastie
**masitas de puerco fritas** fried pork chunks
**matambre** flank steak;
~ **relleno** stuffed, eaten cold or baked *(Arg.)*
**mate** herb tea; ~ **de coca** coca leaf tea
**mazamorra** corn [maize] mush/porridge
**media botella** half bottle
**medialuna** croissant
**medio hecho(-a)** medium
**medio litro** half a liter
**mejillones** mussels
**melón** melon

**menta** mint
**menú del día** set menu
**menudencias** chicken livers
**menudo** tripe, usually in chili-pepper sauce *(Mex.)*
**merengada** milk shake
**merengue** meringue
**meriendas** snacks
**merluza** hake
**mermelada** jam; **~ de naranja** marmalade
**mero** grouper
**mescal/mezcal** spirit similar to tequila
**miel** honey
**milanés** chocolate fingers
**milanesa** breaded steak
**mojarra** sea bream
**mojo criollo** strong garlic sauce *(Carib.)*
**mole** a composition of chili peppers, oil, sugar, sesame seeds, peanuts, salt, cinnamon, cocoa, and spices, with small pieces of toasted bread; **~ poblano** mole sauce with chili peppers *(Mex.)*
**mondongo** seasoned tripe *(Carib.)*
**mora** blackberry
**morcilla** blood sausage [black pudding]
**mostaza** mustard
**mosto** sugar-cane juice
**mote con huesillo** peach juice with barley kernels *(Chile)*
**muchacho** roast beef in sauce *(Ven.)*
**mújol** mullet
**muslo de pollo** chicken leg
**muy crudo(-a)** very rare

**muy seco(-a)** very dry

## N

**ñame** tropical yam
**naranja** orange
**naranjilla** bitter type of orange
**natilla** sour cream
**negro(-a)** black *(coffee)*; dark *(beer)*
**nieve** flavored ice
**níspero** tropical fruit, medlar
**nopales** cactus/prickly pears
**ñoquis** gnocchi
**nueces** walnuts
**nuez moscada** nutmeg

## O

**olímpico** club sandwich
**olla de carne** meat stew
**omelet** omelette; **~ de cebolla** onion; **~ de hongos** mushroom; **~ de jamón** ham; **~ de queso** cheese
**oporto** port
**orégano** oregano
**ostiones/ostras** oysters

## P

**pabellón** beef, beans, rice, and plantain *(Ven.)*
**paila marina** fish chowder *(Chile)*
**paleta** ice cream
**paleta de cordero** breast of lamb
**palitos de queso** cheese sticks/straws
**palmito** palm heart
**palta a la jardinera** stuffed avocado with vegetables
**pan** bread; **~ tostado** toast
**pan dulce** sweet rolls; **~ chileno** frosted egg-bread *(Chile)*

**panceta** bacon
**pancho** hot dog
**panecillos** rolls
**panqué** pound cake
**papas** potatoes; **~ fritas/a la francesa** (French) fries [chips]; **~ rellenas** mashed potato balls stuffed with meat hash *(Carib.)*
**pargo relleno** stuffed red snapper
**parrillada** mixed grill with everything from steak to sausages grilled over charcoal *(Arg.)*
**parrillada Machu Picchu** beefsteak garnished with avocado, pineapple, and papayas *(Peru)*
**pasas** raisins
**pastas** cookies, [biscuits]; noodles, pasta; pastries
**pastel** cake; **~ de moca** coffee cake; **~ de queso** cheese cake
**pastel de carne** meat pie
**pastel de choclo** corn [maize] casserole with beef, chicken, and vegetables
**pastel de mapueyes** yam pie *(Carib.)*
**pasteles** pastries
**pastelitos** cookies [biscuits]; small puff pastries
**patacones** plantain chips [crisps]
**patas de cerdo** pig's feet [trotters]
**patatas** potatoes
**pato** duck
**pavo** turkey
**pay** fruit pie
**pechuga de pollo** chicken breast
**pepinillos** pickles/gherkins
**pepino** cucumber

**pera** pear
**perca** perch *(fish)*
**perdiz** partridge
**perejil** parsley
**perico** small milk coffee *(Col.)*
**pescadilla** whiting
**pescado** fish
**pescado a la veracruzana** red snapper with tomatoes and pimientos
**pez espada** swordfish
**picadillo** beef hash *(Carib.)*
**pichón** pigeon
**pierna de cordero** leg of lamb
**pierna de puerco asada** roast leg of pork creole *(Carib.)*
**pimienta** pepper
**pimientos** hot peppers
**pimientos morrones** sweet peppers
**piña** pineapple
**pinolillo** corn and milk drink
**pipián** pumpkin seeds, chili peppers, oil, sesame seeds, peanuts, salt, garlic, onions, coriander and caraway seeds, with small pieces of toasted bread
**pisco** brandy served with lemon juice, bitters or syrup *(Chile, Peru, Bol.)*
**pitahayas** tropical fruit
**plátano** plantains *(type of banana)*; **~ fritos** pan-fried; **~ a la tentación** baked sweet
**poco hecho(-a)** rare/underdone
**pollo** chicken; **~ a la brasa/al carbón/al espiedo/rostizado/ asado** roast chicken

**pollo en adobo** chicken in a red-pepper sauce *(Mex.)*

**pollo en mole** chicken in a mole sauce, made of chilies, oil, sugar, sesame seeds, peanuts, salt, cinnamon, cocoa, and spices *(Mex.)*

**pomelo** grapefruit

**ponche** fruit juice and rum punch *(esp. at Christmas)*

**ponche de crema** eggnog punch, spiced with liqueur *(Ven.)*

**porotos** beans

**postre** dessert

**postre vigilante** cheese and preserved fruit

**pozole** pork and ground-corn [maize] soup *(Mex.)*

**puchero** casserole of beef, sausage, bacon, chicken, peppers, tomatoes, sweet potatoes *(Arg.)*

**pudín de bacalao** cod casserole

**puerco** pork; **~ en naranja** pork loin with mustard and orange sauce *(Mex.)*

**puerros** leeks

**pulpo** octopus

**pulque** fermented juice of the agave *(Mex.)*

**pupusa** pancake with cheese or bacon

**puré de papa** mashed potatoes

**quesadilla** tortilla filled with cheese or any other filling you want; it can be fried and it is often served with chili sauce, cream, and cheese

**queque (seco)** pound cake

**queso** cheese

**queso añejo** hand-pressed, salted cheese with a sharp flavor *(Mex.)*

**queso de bola** soft cheese made in the form of a ball *(Mex.)*

**queso de Chihuahua** popular soft cheese named after the province from which it originates *(Mex.)*

**queso de Oaxaca** cheese very popular in the south of Mexico, especially used to make quesadillas *(Mex.)*

**queso enchilado** same as queso añejo but a little sharper in taste *(Mex.)*

**queso fresco** fresh white cheese; made and sold the same day *(Mex.)*

**quinada** tonic water

**rábanos** radishes

**rabo de buey** oxtail

**rabo encendido** oxtail stew

**rape** monkfish

**recomendamos ...** we recommend ...

**refrescos** cold drinks, esp. made with fruit, ice, and milk or water

**relleno(-a)** stuffed

**remolacha** beet

**repollo** cabbage

**res** beef

**riñones** kidneys

**róbalo** sea bass

**rodaballo** turbot

**romero** rosemary

**ron** rum; ~ **caldas** Jamaican-like dark rum *(Col.)*; ~ **medellín** light rum *(Col.)*

**ropa vieja** steak hash in tomato sauce

**rosado** rosé

**rosquilla** doughnut

**rubia** light *(beer)*

**ruibarbo** rhubarb

## S

**saice** spicy meat stew *(Bol.)*

**sajta** chicken in hot pepper sauce

**sal** salt

**salchichas** sausages

**salmón (ahumado)** (smoked) salmon

**salmonetes** red mullet

**salsas** sauces

**salteado(-a), saltado(-a)** sautéed

**salteña** meat and vegetable pasty

**salvia** sage

**sancocho** stew made with chunks of beef, chicken or fish, and local vegetables or roots *(Ven.)*

**sandía** watermelon

**sardinas** sardines

**seco** dry

**silpancho** beef schnitzel

**sin gas** still, non-carbonated

**sincronizada** fried tortilla with ham and cheese filling

**singani** grape spirit *(Bol.)*

**sofrito** onion, tomato, garlic, herb, and spice sauté *(Carib.)*

**solo** black *(coffee)*; straight *(neat)*

**solomillo** pork fillet

**sopa** soup

**sopa a la criolla** spicy noodle soup with beef, egg, and vegetables *(Peru)*

**sopa azteca** dried tortillas with cheese and chilli

**sopa de ajo** soup with fried bread, paprika, and garlic

**sopa de arroz** rice soup

**sopa de cebolla** onion soup

**sopa de elote** corn soup *(Mex.)*

**sopa de espárragos** asparagus soup

**sopa de fideos** vermicelli soup

**sopa de frijoles** bean soup

**sopa de mariscos** seafood soup

**sopa de papas** potato, onion, parsley, and sherry soup

**sopa de pasta** vermicelli soup

**sopa de pescado** fish soup

**sopa de plátanos criolla** creole plantain soup *(Carib.)*

**sopa de tortuga** turtle soup

**sopa de verduras** green vegetable soup

**submarino** milky chocolate drink

**suplemento sobre ...** ... extra

**surubí** type of freshwater fish *(Bol.)*

## T

**tableta de chocolate** chocolate bar

**taco** tortilla with all kinds of meat, chicken or cheese filling

**tamal asado** corn flour cake

**tamales** chopped pork with vegetables and rice in a cornmeal dough, wrapped in banana leaves or corn husks and steamed

**tamarindo** sour tropical fruit;

unfermented drink from it

**tarta** tart; **~ de almendras** almond tart; **~ de manzana** apple tart

**tartaletas** small tarts

**tasajo** salt-dried beef;
**~ a la cubana** stir-fried

**té** tea; **~ con leche** with milk;
**~ de manzanilla** camomile

**tenedor libre** all you can eat

**tepache** a drink made of pulque, pineapple, and cloves *(Mex.)*

**tequila** alcoholic drink reminiscent of gin, distilled from agave

**término medio** medium

**ternera** veal

**tiburón** shark

**tinto** small black coffee *(Col.)*; red *(wine)*

**tocino** bacon

**tomate** tomato; green tomato *(Mex.)*

**tónica con ginebra** gin and tonic

**toronja** grapefruit

**torrejas** French toast

**torta** cake; white bread sandwich

**torta del cielo** almond sponge cake *(Mex.)*

**tortilla** cornmeal pancake; **~ al ron** rum; **~ de cebolla** onion; **~ de hongos** mushroom; **~ de jamón** ham; **~ de papas** potato; **~ de plátanos maduros** plantain *(Carib.)*; **~ de queso** cheese

**tortilla de huevo** omelette

**tostada** fried tortilla with fillings such as sausage, beans, avocado

**tostado** cheese and ham toasted sandwich

**tostado(-a) al horno** oven-browned

**tostones** crispy fried plantains *(Carib.)*

**tres leches** cake soaked in syrup and milk

**tripas** tripe

**trucha** trout

**tucumana** meat and vegetable pastry

**tumbo** type of tropical fruit

**tuna** prickly pear

## U

**uvas** grapes

## VWXYZ

**vaca** beef; **~ frita** stir-fried *(Carib.)*

**vainilla** vanilla

**vaso** glass

**venado** venison

**verduras** vegetables

**vermut** vermouth

**vinagre** vinegar

**vino** wine

**viudo de pescado** fish stew, traditionally cooked in holes dug in the ground and covered with hot stones *(Col.)*

**whisky con soda** whisky and soda

**yame** yam *(sweet potato)*

**yogur** yogurt

**yuca** cassava *(type of potato)*

**zanahorias** carrots

**zapallitos** zucchini [courgettes]

**zapallo** pumpkin

**zapote** tropical fruit

**zarzuela de mariscos** spicy shellfish stew *(Carib.)*

**zuppa inglesa** egg custard and lady fingers *(sponge fingers)*

# TRAVEL

| ESSENTIAL | |
|---|---|
| 1/2/3 for … | **un/dos/tres para …** |
| | *oon/dos/tres para* |
| To …, please. | **A …, por favor.** *a por fabor* |
| one-way [single] | **de ida** *deh eeda* |
| round-trip [return] | **de ida y vuelta** *deh eeda ee bwelta* |
| How much? | **¿Cuánto?** *kwanto* |

Because of the often difficult terrain encountered in South America, rail services are generally less developed than bus and air services. However, Mexico, Argentina and Chile do have extensive rail networks. Air travel is often the best option (and quickest, by far) for covering the vast distances involved. Alternatively, long-distance buses are comfortable and economical. Don't be confused in Mexico when talking with the natives, who call their capital **México** or **el DF** (**Distrito Federal**), while their nation is generally referred to as **la República**.

## SAFETY

It is wise to take precautions against crime, particularly in major cities. Don't wear expensive jewelry when traveling on public transportation; do not take unofficial taxis on your own, especially at night; avoid carrying large amounts of money; and don't walk alone along empty streets.Germany, Austria and Switzerland have well-developed public transport systems. You should be able to enjoy trouble-free traveling.

## ARRIVAL

To enter Mexico, travelers from most Western countries (excluding South Africa) require only a valid visa and a tourist card (**FMT** or **folleto de migración turística**, available from consulates, airports, and border crossings). U.S. and Canadian citizens only require proof of citizenship.

For Argentina, most foreigners require only a passport, though Australians and New Zealanders need a visa.

For Uruguay, West European and U.S. citizens need tourist cards; all other foreigners need visas.

Customs clearance systems vary. Some airports have adopted an honor system: follow the green arrow if you have nothing to declare, the red arrow for items to declare. Elsewhere, including Mexico, travelers are required to press a button: a green light means pass through, a red light means the baggage must be checked.

## Passport control

| | |
|---|---|
| We have a joint passport. | **Tenemos pasaporte conjunto.** *tenemos pasaporteh konkhoonto* |
| The children are on this passport. | **Los niños están en este pasaporte.** *los neeños estan en esteh pasaporteh* |
| I'm here on vacation/ holiday/business. | **Vengo de vacaciones/en viaje de negocios.** *bengo deh bakaseeyones/en beeyakheh deh negoseeos* |
| I'm just passing through. | **Estoy de paso.** *estoy deh paso* |
| I'm going to ... | **Voy hacia ...** *boy aseea* |
| I'm coming from... | **Vengo de ...** *bengo deh* |
| I'm ... | **Vengo ...** *bengo* |
| on my own | **solo(-a)** *solo(-a)* |
| with my family | **con mi familia** *kon mee fameeleeya* |
| with a group | **con un grupo** *kon oon groopo* |

## Customs

| | |
|---|---|
| I have nothing to declare. | **No tengo nada que declarar.** *no tengo nada keh deklarar* |
| It's a gift. | **Es un regalo.** *es oon regalo* |
| It's for my personal use. | **Es de uso personal.** *es deh ooso personal* |
| I would like to declare ... | **Quisiera declarar ...** *keeseeyera deklarar* |
| I don't understand. | **No entiendo.** *no enteeyendo* |
| Does anyone here speak English? | **¿Hay alguien aquí que hable inglés?** *eye algeeyen akee keh ableh eengles* |

## Duty-free shopping

| | |
|---|---|
| What currency is this in? | **¿En qué moneda hay que pagar?** |
| | *en keh moneda eye keh pagar* |
| Can I pay in … | **¿Puedo pagar en …** *pwedo pagar en* |
| dollars | **dólares** *dolares* |
| Mexican pesos | **pesos mexicanos** *pesos mekheekanos* |
| pounds | **libras esterlinas** *leebras esterleenas* |

### YOU MAY SEE

| | |
|---|---|
| **CONTROL DE PASAPORTES** | passport control |
| **CRUCE DE FRONTERA** | border crossing |
| **ADUANA** | customs |
| **NADA QUE DECLARAR** | nothing to declare |
| **ARTÍCULOS PARA DECLARAR** | goods to declare |
| **ARTÍCULOS LIBRES DE IMPUESTOS** | duty-free goods |

### YOU MAY HEAR

| | |
|---|---|
| **¿Tiene algo que declarar?** | Do you have anything to declare? |
| **Tiene que pagar impuesto por esto.** | You must pay duty on this. |
| **¿Dónde compró usted esto?** | Where did you buy this? |
| **Abra esta bolsa, por favor.** | Please open this bag. |
| **¿Tiene más equipaje?** | Do you have any more luggage? |

## PLANE

The main hubs for international flights into Mexico from the United States are Miami, Houston, Dallas and Los Angeles. There are more than 50 airports in Mexico with regular internal passenger flights. Popular flights within Mexico are cheap; *Mexicana*, *Aero-méxico* and *Inter* offer multi-flight air passes, only available outside Mexico.

Air passes can greatly reduce the cost of air travel within South America, though check their conditions and restrictions first. Some national airlines (e.g. *Aerolíneas Argentinas*, *AeroPerú*, *LanChile* and *Líneas Aéreas Paraguayas*) offer multi-country air passes.

## Tickets and reservations

| | |
|---|---|
| When is the … flight to Lima? | **¿A qué hora sale el … vuelo a Lima?** *a keh ora saleh el … bwelo a leema* |
| first/next/last | **primero/próximo/último** *preemero/prokseemo/oolteemo* |
| I'd like 2 tickets. | **Quiero dos boletos [tiquetes].** *keeyero dos boletos [teeketes]* |
| one-way [single] | **de ida** *deh eeda* |
| round-trip [return] | **de ida y vuelta** *deh eeda ee bwelta* |
| first class | **primera clase** *preemera klaseh* |
| business class | **clase ejecutiva** *klaseh ekhekooteeba* |
| economy class | **clase económica [clase de turista]** *klaseh ekonomeeka [klaseh deh tooreesta]* |
| How much is a flight to …? | **¿Cuánto cuesta el pasaje a …?** *kwanto kwesta el pasakheh a* |
| Are there any supplements/ reductions? | **¿Hay algún sobrecargo [recargo]/ descuento?** *eye algoon sobrekargo [rekargo]/deskwento* |
| I'd like to … my reservation for flight number … | **Quisiera … mi reservación para el vuelo número …** *keeseeyera … mee reserbaseeyon para el bwelo noomero* |
| cancel/change/confirm | **cancelar/cambiar/confirmar** *kanselar/kambeeyar/konfeermar* |
| What time does the plane leave? | **¿A qué hora sale el avión?** *a keh ora saleh el abeeyon* |
| What time will we arrive? | **¿A qué hora llegamos?** *a keh ora lyegamos* |
| What time do I have to check in? | **¿A qué hora tengo que presentarme?** *a keh ora tengo keh presentarmeh* |

## Checking in

| | |
|---|---|
| Where is the check-in desk for flight …? | **¿Dónde queda la ventanilla para el vuelo número …?** _dondeh keda la bentaneel-ya para el bwelo noomero_ |
| I have … | **Tengo …** _tengo_ |
| three suitcases to check in | **tres maletas para registrar** _tres maletas para rekheestrar_ |
| two carry-ons [pieces of hand luggage] | **dos maletas de mano** _dos maletas deh mano_ |

### YOU MAY HEAR

| | |
|---|---|
| **Me permite su boleto [tiquete]/ pasaporte, por favor.** | Your ticket/passport, please. |
| **¿Desea un asiento cerca de la ventanilla o del pasillo?** | Would you like a window or an aisle seat? |
| **¿Fumadores o no fumadores?** | Smoking or non-smoking? |
| **Diríjase/pase, por favor a la sala de embarque.** | Please go through to the departure lounge. |
| **¿Cuántas maletas tiene?** | How many pieces of baggage do you have? |
| **Tiene exceso de equipaje.** | You have excess baggage. |
| **Tiene que pagar un sobrecargo [sobrecupo] de … pesos mexicanos.** | You'll have to pay a supplement of … Mexican pesos. |
| **Esto está demasiado pesado/ grande para llevar en la mano.** | That's too heavy/large for hand baggage. |
| **¿Empacó usted mismo su equipaje?** | Did you pack these bags yourself? |
| **¿Contienen artículos cortantes o aparatos eléctricos?** | Do they contain any sharp or electronic items? |

### YOU MAY SEE

| | |
|---|---|
| LLEGADAS | arrivals |
| SALIDAS | departures |
| NO DESCUIDE SU EQUIPAJE | do not leave bags unattended |
| SEGURIDAD | security check |

## Information

| Is flight … delayed? | ¿Está retrasado el vuelo …? *esta retrasado el bwelo* |
| How late will it be? | ¿Cuánto se demora en llegar? *kwanto seh demora en l-yegar* |
| Has the flight from … landed? | ¿Ha llegado ya el vuelo de …? *a l-yegado ya el bwelo deh* |
| Which gate does flight … leave from? | ¿De qué puerta sale el vuelo …? *de keh pwerta sale el bwelo* |

## In-flight

| Could I have something to drink/eat, please? | ¿Podría traerme algo para tomar/comer, por favor? *podreea trayermeh algo para tomar/komer por fabor* |
| Please wake me for the meal. | Despiérteme a la hora de la comida, por favor. *despeeyertemeh a la ora deh la komeeda por fabor* |
| What time will we arrive? | ¿A qué hora llegamos? *a keh ora l-yegamos* |
| An airsickness bag, please. | Una bolsa para el mareo, por favor. *oona bolsa para el mareo por fabor* |

## Arrival

| Where is/are the …? | ¿Dónde puedo encontrar …? *dondeh pwedo enkontrar* |
| buses | las paradas de autobuses *las paradas deh aootobooses* |
| car rental | un local de alquiler de carros *oon lokal deh alkeeler deh karros* |
| currency exchange | una oficina de cambio [una casa de cambio] *oona ofeeseena deh kambeeo [oona kasa deh kambeeo]* |
| exit | la salida *la saleeda* |
| taxi | un taxi *oon taksi* |
| Is there a bus into town? | ¿Hay algún bus que entre a la ciudad? *eye algoon boos keh entreh a la seeoodath* |

## Baggage

| | |
|---|---|
| Porter! Excuse me! | **¡Disculpe, señor!** *deeskoolpeh señor* |
| Could you take my luggage to …? | **¿Podría llevar mi equipaje a …?** *podreea l-yebar mee ekeepakheh a* |
| a taxi/bus | **un taxi/bus** *oon taksi/boos* |
| Where is/are (the) …? | **¿Dónde está(n) …?** *dondeh esta(n)* |
| luggage carts [trolleys] | **los carritos de equipaje** *los karreetos deh ekeepakheh* |
| luggage lockers | **los casilleros [los lóckers]** *los kaseel-yeros [los lokers]* |
| baggage check [left-luggage office] | **el depósito de equipaje** *el deposeeto deh ekeepakheh* |
| Where is the luggage from flight …? | **¿Dónde está el equipaje del vuelo …?** *dondeh esta el ekeepakheh del bwelo* |

## Loss, damage, and theft

| | |
|---|---|
| I've lost my baggage. | **Perdí mi equipaje.** *perdee mee ekeepakheh* |
| My baggage has been stolen. | **Me han robado mi equipaje.** *meh an robado mee ekeepakheh* |
| My suitcase was damaged. | **Mi maleta se dañó.** *mee maleta seh daño* |
| Our baggage has not arrived. | **Nuestro equipaje no ha llegado.** *nwestro ekeepakheh no a l-yegado* |

---

### YOU MAY HEAR

| | |
|---|---|
| **¿Cómo es su equipaje?** | What does your baggage look like? |
| **¿Tiene la etiqueta de reclamo?** | Do you have the claim check [reclaim tag]? |
| **Su equipaje …** | Your luggage … |
| **pudo haberse llevado a …** | may have been sent to … |
| **puede llegar más tarde** | may arrive later today |
| **Vuelva mañana, por favor.** | Please come back tomorrow. |
| **Llame a este número para averiguar si su equipaje ya llegó.** | Call this number to check if your baggage has arrived. |

## TRAIN

### Autovía  *aootoveeya*

Fast intercity train. In Mexico, they resemble track-bound buses rather than trains, and space is limited (3 cars).

### Tren de lujo  *tren deh lookho*

Long-distance express train; can also be called **tren de larga distancia**. The trains are generally very comfortable and well-equipped, with bars, sleeping cars, and lounges. Compartments, with reclining seats, are air conditioned.

### Tren directo  *tren deerekto*

Fast train stopping at main stations.

### Ómnibus  *omneeboos*

Train stopping at all stations; also called **tren local**. Not very comfortable; all second class.

### Coche cama  *kocheh kama*

Sleeping car with individual compartments (single or double) and washing facilities.

### Coche comedor  *kocheh komedor*

Dining car. Not all trains have a dining car, even night trains. However, if not, a trolley service is common, and there may be a small bar.

Mexico, Argentina, and Chile have extensive rail networks. If you have time to travel around, the train can be a convenient means of transportation and it certainly gives you a better feel for the country and the people.

Children aged 5–12 travel half-fare, those under 5 travel free.

In Mexico, there are special overnight trains such as **El Tapatío** (Mexico City to Guadalajara) with waitress service.

For a spectacular train journey, take the Lima to Huancayo train on the highest normal gauge railway in the world. However, most train services in Peru tend to be unreliable.

Reservations are essential during vacation times.

## To the station

| | |
|---|---|
| How do I get to the train station? | **¿Cómo se llega a la estación de tren?** *komo seh l-yega a la estaseeyon deh tren* |
| Do trains to … leave from … station? | **¿Los trenes para … salen de la estación de …?** *los trenes para … salen deh la estaseeyon deh* |

| | |
|---|---|
| How far is it? | **¿A qué distancia está?** |
| | *a keh deestantheeya esta* |
| Can I leave my car there? | **¿Puedo dejar mi carro allí?** |
| | *pwedo dekhar mee karro al-yee* |

## At the station

| | |
|---|---|
| Where is/are the …? | **¿Dónde está(n) …?** |
| | *dondeh esta(n)* |
| currency-exchange office | **la oficina [casa] de cambio** |
| | *la ofeeseena [kasa] deh kambeeo* |
| baggage check | **el depósito de equipaje** |
| [left-luggage office] | *el deposeeto deh ekeepakhe* |
| information desk | **la oficina [ventanilla] de información** |
| | *la ofeeseena [betaneel-ya] deh eenformaseeyon* |
| lost and found | **la oficina de objetos perdidos** |
| [lost-property office] | *la ofeeseena deh obkhetos perdeedos* |
| luggage lockers | **los casilleros [los lóckers]** |
| | *los kaseel-yeros [los lokers]* |
| platforms | **los andenes** |
| | *los andenes* |
| snack bar | **la cafetería** |
| | *la kafetereeya* |
| ticket office | **la venta de boletos [tiquetes]** |
| | *la benta deh boletos [teeketes]* |
| waiting room | **la sala de espera** |
| | *la sala deh espera* |

## YOU MAY SEE

| | |
|---|---|
| **SALIDA** | exit |
| **A LOS ANDENES** | to the platforms |
| **INFORMACIÓN** | information |
| **RESERVACIONES** | reservations |
| **LLEGADAS** | arrivals |
| **SALIDAS** | departures |

## Tickets

| | |
|---|---|
| Where can I buy a ticket? | **¿Dónde puedo comprar un boleto [tiquete]?** _dondeh pwedo komprar oon boleto [teeketeh]_ |
| I'd like a ... ticket to ... | **Quisiera un boleto [tiquete] ... para ...** _keeseeyera oon boleto [teekete] ... para_ |
| one-way [single] | **de ida** _de eeda_ |
| round-trip [return] | **de ida y vuelta** _de eeda ee bwelta_ |
| first/second class | **de primera/segunda clase** _de preemera/segoonda klaseh_ |
| concessionary | **concesionario** _konseseeyonareeo_ |
| I'd like to reserve a(n) ... seat. | **Quisiera reservar un asiento ...** _keeseeyera reserbar oon aseeyento_ |
| aisle seat | **cerca del pasillo** _serka del pasil-yo_ |
| window seat | **en la ventanilla** _en la bentaneel-ya_ |
| Is there a sleeping car [sleeper]? | **¿Hay algún coche cama en el tren?** _eye algoon kocheh kama en el tren_ |
| I'd like a ... berth. | **Quisiera una litera ...** _keeseeyera oona leetera_ |
| upper/lower | **superior/inferior** _soopereeyor/eenfereeyor_ |

## Price

| | |
|---|---|
| How much is that? | **¿Cuánto es?** _kwanto es_ |
| Is there a reduction for ...? | **¿Hay descuentos para ...?** _eye deskwentos para_ |
| children/families | **niños/familias** _neeños/fameeleeas_ |
| senior citizens | **ancianos** _anseeyanos_ |
| students | **estudiantes** _estoodeeyantes_ |
| Do you offer a cheap same-day round-trip [return]? | **¿Hay una tarifa especial para viajes de ida y vuelta en el mismo día?** _eye oona tareefa espeseeyal para beeyakhes deh eeda ee bwelta en el meesmo deeya_ |
| Is it cheaper to travel after a certain time? | **¿Sale más barato viajar después de determinada hora?** _saleh mas barato beeakhar despwes deh determeenada ora_ |

## Train times

| | |
|---|---|
| Could I have a timetable? | **¿Podría darme un horario de trenes?** _podreeya darmeh oon orareeo deh trenes_ |
| When is the … train to …? | **¿A qué hora sale el … tren para …?** _a keh ora saleh el … tren para_ |
| first/next/last | **primer/próximo/último** _preemer/prokseemo/oolteemo_ |
| How frequent are trains to …? | **¿Con qué frecuencia salen los trenes para …?** _kon keh frekwenseea salen los trenes para_ |
| once/twice a day | **una vez/dos veces al día** _oona bes/dos beses al deeya_ |
| five times a day | **cinco veces al día** _seenko beses al deeya_ |
| every hour | **cada hora** _kada ora_ |
| What time do they leave? | **¿A qué hora salen?** _a keh ora salen_ |
| on the hour | **a la hora en punto** _a la ora en poonto_ |
| 20 minutes past the hour | **a la hora y veinte [a las y veinte]** _a la ora ee beynteh [a las ee beynteh]_ |
| What time does the train stop at …? | **¿A qué hora para el tren en …?** _a keh ora para el tren en_ |
| What time does the train arrive in …? | **¿A qué hora llega el tren a …?** _a keh ora l-yega el tren a_ |
| How long is the trip [journey]? | **¿Cuánto dura el viaje?** _Kwanto doora el beeyakheh_ |
| Is the train on time? | **¿Viene a tiempo el tren ?** _beeyeneh a teeyempo el tren_ |

### IN A TRAIN STATION

**Dos boletos a Veracruz, por favor.** _dos beelyetehs a veracruz por fabor (Two tickets to Veracruz, please.)_
**¿De ida o de ida y vuelta?** _deh eehda o deh eehda ee bwelta (One way or round trip?)_
**De ida y vuelta, por favor.** _deh eehda ee bwelta por fabor (Round trip, please.)_

## Departures

Which platform does the
train to … leave from?
**¿De qué plataforma sale el tren para …?**
*de keh plataforma sale el tren para*

Where is platform 4?
**¿Dónde está la plataforma 4?**
*dondeh esta la plataforma kwatro*

on the right/left
**a la derecha/izquierda**
*a la derecha/eeskeeyerda*

Where do I change for …?
**¿Dónde puedo cambiar de tren para
ir a …?** *dondeh pwedo kambeeyar deh
tren para eer a*

How long will I have to
wait for a connection?
**¿Cuánto tiempo tengo que esperar
para hacer el trasbordo?** *kwanto
teeyempo tengo keh esperar para
aser el trasbordo*

## Boarding

Is this the right platform
for the train to …?
**¿Es éste la plataforma para el tren a …?** *es
esteh la plataforma para el tren a*

Is this the train to …?
**¿Es éste el tren a …?** *es esteh el tren a*

Is this seat taken?
**¿Está ocupado este asiento?**
*esta okoopado esteh aseeyento*

I think that's my seat.
**Creo que ése es mi asiento.**
*kreyo keh eseh es mee aseeyento*

Here's my reservation.
**Aquí está mi reservación.**
*akee esta mee reserbaseeyon*

Are there any seats/berths
available?
**¿Queda algún asiento/alguna litera
disponible?** *keda algoon aseeyento/
algoona leetera deesponeebleh*

Do you mind if …?
**¿Le molesta si …?** *le molesta see*

I sit here
**me siento aquí** *me seeyento akee*

I open the window
**abro la ventana** *abro la bentana*

## During the trip

How long are we
stopping here?
**¿Cuánto tiempo vamos a parar aquí?**
*kwanto teeyempo bamos a parar akee*

| | |
|---|---|
| When do we get to …? | **¿A qué hora llegamos a …?** _a keh ora l-yegamos a_ |
| Have we passed …? | **¿Hemos pasado …?** _emos pasado_ |
| Where is the dining/ sleeping car? | **¿Dónde está el coche comedor/el coche cama?** _dondeh esta el kocheh komedor/ el kocheh kama_ |
| Where is my berth? | **¿Dónde está mi litera?** _dondeh esta mee leetera_ |
| I've lost my ticket. | **Se me perdió mi boleto [tiquete].** _seh meh perdeeyo mee boleto [teeketeh]_ |

## Queries

| | |
|---|---|
| Do I have to change trains? | **¿Tengo que cambiar de tren?** _tengo keh kambeeyar deh tren_ |
| It's a direct train. | **Es un tren directo.** _es oon tren deerekto_ |
| You have to change at … | **Tiene que cambiar en …** _teeyeneh keh kambeeyar en_ |
| Can I return on the same ticket? | **¿Puedo regresar con el mismo boleto [tiquete]?** _pwedo regresar kon el meesmo boleto [teeketeh]_ |
| How long is this ticket valid? | **¿Por cuánto tiempo es válido este boleto [tiquete]?** _por kwanto teeyempo es baleedo esteh boleto [teeketeh]_ |
| Can I take my bicycle on the train? | **¿Puedo llevar mi bicicleta en el tren?** _pwedo jayyahr mee beeseekleta en el tren_ |
| In which car [coach] is my seat? | **¿En qué coche [vagón] está mi asiento?** _en keh kocheh esta mee eseeyento_ |
| Is there a dining car on the train? | **¿Hay un coche comedor en el tren?** _eye oon kocheh komedor en el tren_ |

## YOU MAY SEE

| | |
|---|---|
| **ALARMA** | alarm |
| **FRENO DE EMERGENCIA** | emergency brake |
| **PUERTAS AUTOMÁTICAS** | automatic doors |

## LONG-DISTANCE BUS [COACH]

Mexico, Chile, and Argentina provide good regional long-distance coach services. Most cities have a **terminal de autobuses**. Service is categorized as first, second, and third class; and **sin escalas** (nonstop), **directo** (few stops), and **ordinario** (stops on demand).

| | |
|---|---|
| Where is the bus [coach] station? | **¿Dónde queda la estación de autobuses?** _dondeh keda la estaseeyon deh aootobooses_ |
| When's the next bus to …? | **¿A qué hora sale el próximo autobús para …?** _a keh ora saleh el prokseemo aootoboos para_ |
| Which stop [bay] does it leave from? | **¿De qué parada [paradero] sale el bus?** _deh keh parada [paradero] saleh el aootoboos_ |
| Does the bus stop at …? | **¿Se detiene el autobús en …?** _seh deteeyeneh el aootoboos en_ |
| How long does the trip [journey] take? | **¿Cuánto dura el viaje?** _kwanto doora el beeyakheh_ |

## YOU MAY SEE

| | |
|---|---|
| **CONVALIDE SU TIQUETE** | validate your ticket |

## BUS/STREETCAR [TRAM]

Most towns have a bus station (**Central de Autobuses** or **Central Camionera**), but city buses vary in name: **el bus/autobús** (the general term), **el camión** (Mexico), **el ómnibus** (Peru), **el micro** (Chile) and **la guagua** (Caribbean).

| | |
|---|---|
| Could you tell me when to get off? | **¿Podría avisarme cuándo tengo que bajarme?** _podreeya abeesarmeh kwando tengo keh bakharmeh_ |
| Do I have to change buses? | **¿Tengo que cambiar de autobús?** _tengo keh kambeeyar deh aootoboos_ |
| How many stops are there to …? | **¿Cuántas paradas [paraderos] hay hasta …?** _kwantas paradas [paraderos] eye asta_ |
| Next stop, please! | **¡El proximo paradero, por favor!** _la prokseema parada por fabor_ |

78

| Where can I get a bus/ streetcar [tram] to …? | ¿Dónde puedo tomar un autobús/ tranvía para…? _dondeh pwedo tomar oon aootoboos/tranbeeya para_ |
| What time is the … bus to …? | ¿A qué hora sale el … autobús para …? _a keh ora sale el … aootoboos para_ |
| first/next/last | primer/próximo/último _preemer/prokseemo/oolteemo_ |

### Buying tickets

| Where can I buy tickets? | ¿Dónde se compran los boletos [tiquetes]? _dondeh seh kompran los boletos [teeketes]_ |
| A … ticket to …, please. | Un boleto [tiquete] … para …, por favor. _oon boleto [teeketeh] … para … por fabor_ |
| one-way [single] | de ida _deh eeda_ |
| round-trip [return] | de ida y vuelta _deh eeda ee bwelta_ |
| How much is the fare to …? | ¿Cuál es la tarifa para …? _kwal es la tareefa para_ |

### Traveling

| Is this the right bus/ streetcar [tram] to …? | ¿Es éste el autobús/tranvía para …? _es este el aootoboos/tranbeeya para_ |

---

### YOU MAY SEE

| PARADA DE AUTOBUSES | bus stop |
| PROHIBIDO FUMAR | no smoking |
| SALIDA (DE EMERGENCIA) | (emergency) exit |
| SOLICITE LA PARADA | request stop |

---

### AT A BUS STOP

¿Es éste el autobús al centro? _es este el awtoboos al thentro (Is this the bus to downtown?)_
Sí, es el número ocho. _see es el noomero ocho (Yes, bus number 8.)_
Muchas gracias. _moochas gratseeyas (Thank you very much.)_
De nada. _de nada (You're welcome.)_

## SUBWAY/METRO

There are metro systems in Mexico City, Buenos Aires, Santiago, and Caracas. Buy a single flat-rate ticket or a book of tickets (**un abono**) at ticket offices or automatic machines, found in every station.

The Mexico City metro runs from 5 a.m. till midnight (7 a.m. on Sundays); but try to avoid it during rush hour; passengers are allowed to carry only one package (no bigger than a briefcase) each.

## General Inquiries

Where's the nearest subway [metro] station?
**¿Dónde queda la estación de metro más cercana?** _dondeh keda la estaseeyon deh metro mas serkana_

Where do I buy a ticket?
**¿Dónde se compran los boletos [tiquetes]?** _dondeh seh kompran los boletos [teeketes]_

Could I have a subway [metro] map?
**¿Me podría dar un mapa del metro, por favor?** _meh podreeya dar oon mapa del metro por fabor_

## Traveling

Which line should I take for …?
**¿Qué línea debo tomar para ir a…?** _keh leenea debo tomar para eer a_

Is this the right train for …?
**¿Es éste el metro para …?** _es esteh el metro para_

Which stop is this?
**¿Qué parada [paradero] es ésta?** _keh parada [paradero] es esta [esteh]_

How many stops is it to …?
**¿Cuántos paraderos faltan para llegar a …?** _kwantos paraderos faltan para l-yegar a_

Is the next stop …?
**¿Es … la próxima parada?** _es…la prokseema parada_

Where are we?
**¿Dónde estamos?** _dondeh estamos_

Where do I change for …?
**¿Dónde debo cambiar para …?** _dondeh debo kambeeyar para_

What time is the last train to …?
**¿A qué hora sale el último metro para …?** _a keh ora saleh el oolteemo metro para_

## YOU MAY SEE

| CONEXIÓN CON OTRAS LÍNEAS | to other lines/transfer |
| --- | --- |

## FERRY

Ferries run between mainland Mexico and Baja California, and Cozumel and Isla Mujeres and the Yucatán peninsula.

| | |
|---|---|
| When is the … car ferry to …? | **¿A qué hora sale el … transbordador de carros para …?** *a keh ora saleh el … transbordador deh karros para* |
| first/next/last | **primer/próximo/último** *preemer/prokseemo/oolteemo* |
| hovercraft/ship | **el hidrodeslizador/el barco** *el eedrodesleesador/el barko* |
| A round-trip [return] ticket for … | **Un boleto [tiquete] de ida y vuelta para …** *oon boleto [teeketeh] deh eeda ee bwelta para* |
| one car and one trailer [caravan] | **un carro y una casa móvil** *oon karro ee oona kasa mobeel* |
| two adults and three children | **dos adultos y tres niños** *dos adooltos ee tres neeños* |
| I want to reserve a … cabin. | **Quiero reservar una cabina …** *keeyero reserbar oona kabeena* |
| single/double | **sencilla/doble** *senseel-ya/dobleh* |

## BOAT TRIPS

| | |
|---|---|
| Is there a …? | **¿Hay …?** *eye* |
| boat trip/river cruise | **un viaje en barco/crucero por el río** *oon beeyakheh en barko/kroosero por el reeyo* |
| What time does it leave/return? | **¿A qué hora sale/regresa?** *a keh ora saleh/regresa* |
| Where can we buy tickets? | **¿Dónde se pueden comprar los boletos [tiquetes]?** *dondeh seh pweden komssprar los boletos [teeketes]* |

### YOU MAY SEE

| | |
|---|---|
| **BOTE SALVAVIDAS** | life boat |
| **CINTURÓN SALVAVIDAS** | life preserver [belt] |
| **SITIO DE CONCENTRACIÓN DE PASAJEROS** | muster station |
| **PROHIBIDO EL ACCESO A LOS ESTACIONAMIENTOS** | no access to car decks |

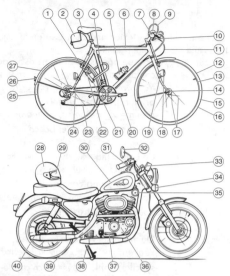

| | | |
|---|---|---|
| 1 | brake pad **la pastilla de frenos** | 20 | pedal **el pedal** |
| 2 | bicycle bag **la mochila** | 21 | lock **la cerradura contra robos** |
| 3 | saddle **el asiento** | 22 | generator [dynamo] **el dínamo** |
| 4 | pump **la bomba** | 23 | chain **la cadena** |
| 5 | water bottle **la cantimplora** | 24 | rear light **el faro trasero/luz** |
| 6 | frame **el cuadro [la armadura]** | 25 | rim **la llanta** |
| 7 | handlebars **los manubrios** | 26 | reflectors **los reflectores** |
| 8 | bell **la campana** | 27 | fender [mudguard] **el guardafango** |
| 9 | brake cable **el cable de los frenos** | 28 | helmet **el casco** |
| 10 | gear shift **la barra de cambios** | 29 | visor **la visera** |
| 11 | gear control cable **el cable de los cambios** | 30 | fuel tank **el tanque de la gasolina** |
| 12 | inner tube **cámara de aire/llanta** | 31 | clutch lever **el pedal de embrague** |
| 13 | front/back wheel **la rueda delantera/trasera** | 32 | mirror **el espejo** |
| 14 | axle **el eje** | 33 | ignition switch **la llave de encendido** |
| 15 | tire [tyre] **la llanta** | 34 | turn signal **la direccional** |
| 16 | wheel **la rueda** | 35 | horn **la bocina [el pito]** |
| 17 | spoke **el radio/rayo** | 36 | engine **el motor** |
| 18 | bulb **la bombilla/el foco** | 37 | gear shift **la barra de cambios** |
| 19 | headlamp **faro** | 38 | kick stand **la varilla de la bicicleta** |
| | | 39 | exhaust pipe **el tubo de escape** |
| | | 40 | chain guard **la barra** |

## BICYCLE/MOTORBIKE

| | |
|---|---|
| I'd like to rent a … | **Quisiera alquilar …**<br>*keeseeyera alkeelar* |
| 3-/10-speed bicycle | **una bicicleta de cambio tres/diez** *oona*<br>*beeseekleta deh kambeeo tres/deeyes* |
| moped | **un velomotor**<br>*oon belomotor* |
| motorbike | **una motocicleta**<br>*oona motoseekleta* |
| How much does it cost per day/week? | **¿Cuál es el precio por día/semana?**<br>*kwal es el preseeyo por deeya/semana* |
| Do you require a deposit? | **¿Hay que pagar un depósito?**<br>*eye keh pagar oon deposeeto* |
| The brakes don't work. | **Los frenos no funcionan.**<br>*los frenos no foonseeyonan* |
| There are no lights. | **No tiene luces.**<br>*no teeyene looses* |
| The front/rear tire [tyre] has a flat [puncture]. | **La llanta delantera/trasera está pinchada.**<br>*la lyanta trasera/delantera esta peenchada* |

## HITCHHIKING

Hitchhiking is not safe in Mexico; you are advised not to hitch alone.

| | |
|---|---|
| Where are you heading? | **¿Adónde va usted?**<br>*adondeh ba oosteth* |
| I'm heading for … | **Voy hacia …** *boy aseeya* |
| Is that on the way to …? | **¿Está eso en la vía a …?**<br>*esta eso en la beeya a* |
| Could you drop me off …? | **¿Podría dejarme …?**<br>*podreeya dekharmeh* |
| here/at … | **aquí/en …** *akee/en* |
| at the … exit | **en la salida …**<br>*en la saleeda* |
| in the center | **en el centro** *en el sentro* |
| Thanks for the lift. | **Gracias por el aventón [el viaje].**<br>*graseeyas por el abenton [el beeyakheh]* |

## Taxi/Cab

Most taxis have meters, but it is generally wise to ask the fare beforehand. Extra charges are added for night trips and often for baggage. In most major cities there are official taxis (at airports, bus stations, etc.) which should be used for your security. No tip is generally required for taxi drivers in most Central and South American countries; it is considered optional in Argentina.

| | |
|---|---|
| Where can I get a taxi? | **¿Dónde puedo tomar un taxi?** _dondeh pwedo tomar oon taksi_ |
| Do you have the number for a taxi? | **¿Tiene el número de alguna empresa de taxis?** _teeyeneh el noomero deh algoona empresa deh taksis_ |
| I'd like a taxi … | **Quisiera un taxi …** _keeseeyera oon taksi_ |
| now | **para ahora mismo** _para aora meesmo_ |
| in an hour | **para dentro de una hora** _para dentro deh oona ora_ |
| for tomorrow at 9:00 | **para mañana a las nueve** _para mañana a las nwebeh_ |
| The pick-up address is … | **La dirección es …** _la deerekseeyon es_ |
| Please take me to the … | **Por favor, lléveme a/a la…** _por fabor lyebemeh a/a la_ |
| airport | **el aeropuerto** _el aeropwerto_ |
| train station | **la estación de tren** _la estaseeyon deh tren_ |
| this address | **esta dirección** _esta deerekseeyon_ |
| How much will it cost? | **¿Cuánto va a costar el viaje [la carrera]?** _kwanto ba a kostar el beeyakheh [la karrera]_ |
| How much is that? | **¿Cuánto es?** _kwanto es_ |
| On the meter it's … | **Según el taxímetro son …** _segoon el takseemetro son_ |
| Keep the change. | **Guarde el cambio.** _gwardeh el kambeeo_ |

## AT A TAXI STAND

**¿Cuánto va a costar al aeropuerto?** _kwanto ba a kostar al ayropwerto_ *(How much is it to the airport?)*

**Doscientos pesos.** _dosseeyentos pesos_ *(200 pesos.)*

**Gracias.** _gratseeyas_ *(Thank you.)*

## CAR/AUTOMOBILE

Most foreign drivers' licenses are valid in Mexico.

If driving into Mexico, take out insurance on your own car, available from agencies at the border.

You are not allowed to sell your car in Mexico; you will be required to fill out a vehicle import form at the border.

Carry a spare tire [tyre], a jack, and water for your radiator; and spare parts, if possible. In Mexico, it is best to avoid driving at night in case of banditry and road hazards.

In Mexico, illegal parking may result in your license plate being removed. Pay an on-the-spot fine to the nearby policeman to retrieve it.

In Mexico City, vehicles are banned from driving one day per week, which is set according to the final digit of each vehicle's license plate.

### Speed limits

| *Speed limits* | **Built-up area** | **Outside built-up area** | **Highway** |
|---|---|---|---|
| | *kmph (mph)* | *kmph (mph)* | *kmph (mph)* |
| *Mexico* | 25 (40) | 43 (70) | 68 (110) |

Watch out for speed bumps (**topes**) on entering most towns in Mexico.

### Fuel

| **Gas [Petrol]** | **Leaded** | **Lead-free** | **Diesel** |
|---|---|---|---|
| Mexico | Nova (80) | Magna Sin (87) | Gas-oil |
| | Blue pump | Green pump | Red/Purple pump |

Check that gas [petrol] pumps are set at zero before pumping. Have enough cash for your fuel, credit cards are not accepted at gas [petrol] stations.

### Conversion Chart

| km | 1 | 10 | 20 | 30 | 40 | 50 | 60 | 70 | 80 | 90 | 100 | 110 | 120 | 130 |
|---|---|---|---|---|---|---|---|---|---|---|---|---|---|---|
| **miles** | 0.62 | 6 | 12 | 19 | 25 | 31 | 37 | 44 | 50 | 56 | 62 | 68 | 74 | 81 |

## Car rental

Car rental firms will require to see a valid driver's license and identification. The minimum age varies between countries.

Local firms tend to be cheaper than major chains, but check the cost of insurance, tax, and mileage when comparing prices.

| | |
|---|---|
| Where can I rent a car? | **¿Dónde puedo alquilar un carro?** *dondeh pwedo alkeelar oon karro* |
| I'd like to rent/hire a(n) … | **Quisiera alquilar …** *keeseeyera alkeelar* |
| 2-/4-door car | **un carro de dos/cuatro puertas** *oon karro deh dos/kwatro pwertas* |
| automatic | **un carro automático** *oon karro aootomateeko* |
| car with air conditioning | **un carro con aire acondicionado** *oon karro kon ayreh akondeeseeonado* |
| I'd like it for a day/week. | **Lo quiero para un día/una semana.** *lo keeyero para oon deeya/oona semana* |
| How much does it cost per day/week? | **¿Cuál es el precio por día/semana?** *kwal es el preseeo por deeya/semana* |
| Is mileage/insurance included? | **¿Está incluido el kilometraje/el seguro?** *esta eenklooeedo el kilometrakheh/el segooro* |
| Are there special weekend rates? | **¿Hay precios especiales para los fines de semana?** *eye preseeos espeseeyales para los feenes deh semana* |
| Can I leave the car at your office in …? | **¿Puedo dejar el carro en la sucursal de …?** *pwedo dekhar el karro en la sookoorsal deh* |
| What kind of fuel does it take? | **¿Qué clase de gasolina consume?** *keh klaseh deh gasoleena konsoomeh* |
| Where's the high [full]/ low [dipped] beam? | **¿Dónde están las luces altas/las luces bajas?** *dondeh estan las looses altas/las looses bakhas* |
| Could I have full insurance, please? | **Quiero seguro completo, por favor.** *keeyero segooro kompleto por fabor* |

## Gas [Petrol] station

Where's the next gas [petrol] station?
**¿Dónde está la próxima gasolinera [estación] de gasolina?** _dondeh esta la prokseema gasoleenera [estaseeyon deh gasoleena]_

Is it self-service?
**¿Es autoservicio?** _es aootoserbeeseeo_

Fill it up, please.
**Llene el tanque, por favor.** _l-yeneh el tankeh por fabor_

… liters of gas [petrol], please.
**… litros de gasolina, por favor.** _leetros deh gasoleena por fabor_

premium [super]/regular
**súper/normal** _sooper/normal_

lead-free/diesel
**sin plomo/diesel** _seen plomo/deesel_

I'm at pump number …
**Bomba número …** _bomba noomero_

Where is the air pump?
**¿Dónde está la bomba de aire?** _dondeh esta la bomba deh ayreh_

Where is the water?
**¿Dónde está el agua?** _dondeh esta el agwa_

## YOU MAY SEE

| | |
|---|---|
| **PRECIO POR LITRO** | price per liter/litre |

## Parking

Is there a parking lot [car park] nearby?
**¿Hay un estacionamiento [parqueadero] de carros por aquí?** _eye oon estaseeonameeyento [parkeadero] deh karros por akee_

What's the charge per hour/day?
**¿Cuál es la tarifa por hora/día?** _kwal es la tareefa por ora/deeya_

Do you have some change for the parking meter?
**¿Tiene cambio para el parquímetro [contador de estacionamiento]?** _teeyeneh kambeeo para el parkeemetro/kontador deh estaseeonameeyento_

My car has been booted [clamped]. Who do I call?
**Han inmobilizado [bloqueado] mi carro. ¿Con quién tengo que hablar?** _an eenmobeeleesado [blokeado] mee karro. kon keeyen tengo keh ablar_

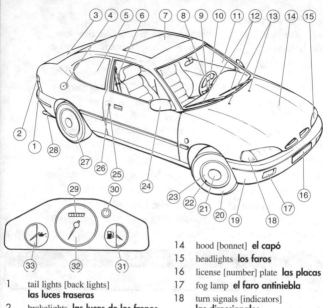

1. tail lights [back lights] **las luces traseras**
2. brakelights **las luces de los frenos**
3. trunk [boot] **la cajuela [el maletero]**
4. gas tank door [petrol cap] **la tapa del depósito de gasolina**
5. window **la ventana**
6. seat belt **el cinturón de seguridad**
7. sunroof **el techo solar**
8. steering wheel **el volante**
9. starter/ignition **el encendido**
10. ignition key **la llave (de encendido)**
11. windshield [windscreen] **el parabrisas**
12. windshield [windscreen] wipers **las escobillas**
13. windshield [windscreen] washer **el limpiaparabrisas**
14. hood [bonnet] **el capó**
15. headlights **los faros**
16. license [number] plate **las placas**
17. fog lamp **el faro antiniebla**
18. turn signals [indicators] **las direccionales**
19. bumper **el parachoques**
20. tires [tyres] **las llantas**
21. wheel cover [hubcap] **el tapacubos**
22. valve **la válvula**
23. wheels **las ruedas**
24. outside/wing mirror **el espejo retrovisor**
25. automatic locks [central locking] **el cierre centralizado**
26. lock **el seguro [la cerradura]**
27. wheel rim **el rin de la rueda**
28. exhaust pipe **el tubo de escape**
29. odometer [milometer] **el medidor de kilometraje**

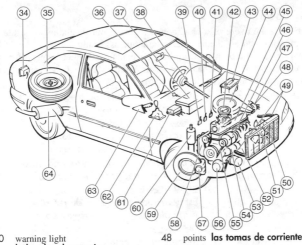

| | | | |
|---|---|---|---|
| 30 | warning light **la luz de advertencia** | 48 | points **las tomas de corriente** |
| 31 | fuel gauge **el indicador** | 49 | radiator hose (top/bottom) **la manguera del radiador (arriba/abajo)** |
| 32 | speedometer **el velocímetro** | 50 | radiator **el radiador** |
| 33 | oil gauge **el indicador del nivel de aceite** | 51 | fan **el ventilador** |
| 34 | backup [reversing] lights **las luces de reversa** | 52 | engine **el motor** |
| 35 | spare wheel **la llanta de repuesto** | 53 | oil filter **el filtro de aceite** |
| 36 | choke **el estárter [ahogador]** | 54 | starter motor **el motor de arranque** |
| 37 | heater **la calefacción** | 55 | fan belt **la correa del ventilador** |
| 38 | steering column **la columna de dirección** | 56 | horn **la bocina [el pito]** |
| 39 | accelerator **el acelerador** | 57 | brake pads **las pastillas de los frenos** |
| 40 | pedal **el pedal** | 58 | transmission [gear box] **la caja de cambio** |
| 41 | clutch **el embrague [el cloche]** | 59 | brakes **los frenos** |
| 42 | carburetor **el carburador** | 60 | shock absorbers **los amortiguadores** |
| 43 | battery **la batería** | 61 | fuses **los fusibles** |
| 44 | air filter **el filtro de aire** | 62 | gear shift [lever] **la barra de cambios** |
| 45 | camshaft **el árbol de levas** | 63 | handbrake **el freno de mano** |
| 46 | alternator **el alternador** | 64 | muffler [silencer] **el silenciador** |
| 47 | distributor **el distribuidor** | | |

## Breakdown

For help in the event of a breakdown: refer to your breakdown assistance documents or contact the national automobile association.

In the event of a breakdown in Mexico, contact the Green Angels (**Ángeles Verdes**), a free mechanic service. Within Mexico City, contact the Mexican Automobile Association (**AAM**).

| | |
|---|---|
| Where is the nearest garage? | **¿Dónde está el taller de mecánica más cercano?** _dondeh esta el tal-yer deh mekaneeka mas serkano_ |
| My car broke down. | **Mi carro se ha descompuesto.** _mee karro seh a deskompwesto_ |
| Can you send a mechanic/ tow [breakdown] truck? | **¿Puede enviar un mecánico/una grúa?** _pwedeh enbeear oon mekaneeko/ oona grooa_ |
| I belong to … rescue [recovery] service. | **Estoy afiliado al servicio de rescate …** _estoy afeeleeyado al serbeeseeo deh reskateh_ |
| My license plate [registration] number is … | **Mi número de matrícula es …** _mee noomero deh matreekoola es_ |
| The car is … | **El carro está …** _el karro esta_ |
| on the highway [motorway] | **en la autopista** _en la aootopeesta_ |
| 2 km from … | **a dos kilómetros de …** _a dos kilometros deh_ |
| How long will you be? | **¿Cuánto se demorará?** _kwanto seh demorara_ |

## What is wrong?

| | |
|---|---|
| My car won't start. | **Mi carro no quiere arrancar.** _mee karro no keeyereh arrankar_ |
| The battery is dead. | **La batería está descargada.** _la batereeya esta deskargada_ |
| I've run out of gas [petrol]. | **Se me acabó la gasolina.** _seh meh akabo la gasoleena_ |
| I have a flat [puncture]. | **Tengo una llanta pinchada.** _tengo oona l-yanta peenchada_ |
| There is something wrong with … | **Algo anda mal con …** _algo anda mal kon_ |
| I've locked the keys in the car. | **Dejé las llaves dentro del carro.** _dekheh las l-yabes dentro del karro_ |

## Repairs

| | |
|---|---|
| Do you do repairs? | **¿Hace usted reparaciones?** *aseh oosteth reparaseeyones* |
| Can you repair it? | **¿Podría repararlo?** *podreeya repararlo* |
| Please make only essential repairs. | **Por favor haga sólo las reparaciones indispensables.** *por fabor aga solo las reparaseeyones eendeespensables* |
| Can I wait for it? | **¿Puedo esperar a que lo repare?** *pwedo esperar a keh lo repareh* |
| Can you repair it today? | **¿Puede repararlo hoy mismo?** *pwedeh repararlo oy meesmo* |
| When will it be ready? | **¿Cuándo estará listo?** *kwando estara leesto* |
| How much will it cost? | **¿Cuánto me va a costar la reparación?** *kwanto meh ba a kostar la reparaseeyon* |
| That's outrageous! | **¡Es un precio escandaloso!** *es oon preseeyo eskandaloso* |
| Can I have a receipt for my insurance? | **¿Podría darme un recibo para el trámite de seguro?** *podreeya darmeh oon reseebo para el trameeteh deh segooro* |

### YOU MAY HEAR

| | |
|---|---|
| **... no está funcionando.** | The ... isn't working. |
| **No tengo los repuestos necesarios.** | I don't have the necessary parts. |
| **Tendría que encargar los repuestos.** | I will have to order the parts. |
| **Sólo puedo repararlo temporalmente.** | I can only repair it temporarily. |
| **Su carro no sirve para nada.** | Your car is beyond repair. |
| **No se puede reparar.** | It can't be repaired. |
| **Estará listo ...** | It will be ready ... |
| **dentro de un rato/más tarde** | later today |
| **mañana** | tomorrow |
| **dentro de ... días** | in ... days |

## Accidents

In the event of a minor accident in Mexico, you may find it simpler to sort things out with the other driver without involving the police. For a serious incident, contact your consulate and Mexican insurance company.

| | | |
|---|---|---|
| There has been an accident. | **Ha habido un accidente.** | |
| | *a abeedo oon akseedenteh* | |
| It's … | **Ocurrió…** *okooreeyo* | |
| on the highway [motorway] | **en la autopista** *en la aootopeesta* | |
| near … | **cerca de …** *serka deh* | |
| Where's the nearest telephone? | **¿Dónde está el teléfono más cercano?** *dondeh esta el telefono mas serkano* | |
| Call … | **Llame …** *l-yameh* | |
| an ambulance | **a una ambulancia** | |
| | *a oona amboolanseea* | |
| a doctor | **a un doctor** *a oon doktor* | |
| the fire department [brigade] | **a los bomberos** *a los bomberos* | |
| the police | **a la policía** *a la poleeseeya* | |
| Can you help me, please? | **¿Puede ayudarme, por favor?** *pwedeh ayoodarmeh por fabor* | |

## Injuries

| | |
|---|---|
| There are people injured. | **Hay personas heridas.** *eye personas ereedas* |
| No one is hurt. | **Nadie resultó herido.** *nadeeyeh resoolto ereedo* |
| He is seriously injured. | **Él está gravemente herido.** *el esta grabementeh ereedo* |
| She's unconscious. | **Ella está inconsciente.** *el-ya esta eenkonseeyenteh* |
| He can't breathe/move. | **Él no puede respirar/moverse.** *el no pwedeh respeerar/moberseh* |
| Don't move him. | **No lo mueva.** *no lo mweba* |

## Legal matters

| | |
|---|---|
| What's your insurance company? | **¿Cuál es su compañía de seguros?** *kwal es soo kompañeeya deh segooros* |

| What's your name and address? | **¿Cuál es su nombre y dirección?** |
|---|---|
| | *kwal es soo nombreh ee deereekseeyon* |
| He ran into me. | **Él me chocó.** *el meh choko* |
| She was driving too fast/too close. | **Ella estaba conduciendo [manejando] demasiado rápido/demasiado cerca.** |
| | *el-ya estaba kondooseeyendo [manekhando] demaseeyado rapeedo/demaseeyado serka* |
| I had the right of way. | **Yo tenía el derecho a la vía.** |
| | *yo teneeya el derecho a la beeya* |
| I was (only) driving at … kmph. | **Yo (sólo) estaba conduciendo [manejando] a … kilómetros por hora.** *yo solo estaba kondooseeyendo [manekhando] a … kilometros por ora* |
| I'd like an interpreter. | **Quisiera un intérprete.** |
| | *keeseeyera oon eenterpreteh* |
| I didn't see the sign. | **Yo no vi la señal.** *yo no bee la señal* |
| He/She saw it happen. | **Él/ella vio lo que sucedió.** |
| | *el/el-ya beeo lo keh soosedeeyo* |

## YOU MAY HEAR

| | |
|---|---|
| **¿Me permite su …?** | Can I see your …? |
| **licencia de conducir** | driver's license |
| **certificado del seguro** | insurance card [certificate] |
| **documento del registro del carro** | vehicle registration |
| **¿A qué hora sucedió?** | What time did it happen? |
| **¿Dónde sucedió?** | Where did it happen? |
| **¿Hubo alguien más involucrado en el accidente?** | Was anyone else involved? |
| **¿Hay testigos?** | Are there any witnesses? |
| **Usted estaba conduciendo [manejando] a gran velocidad.** | You were speeding. |
| **Sus luces no están funcionando.** | Your lights aren't working. |
| **Usted tendrá que pagar una multa ahora mismo.** | You'll have to pay a fine (on the spot). |
| **Necesitamos que haga una declaración en la estación.** | We need you to make a statement at the station. |

## Asking directions

| | |
|---|---|
| Excuse me, please. | **Disculpe, por favor.** _deeskoolpeh por fabor_ |
| How do I get to …? | **¿Cómo se llega a …?** _komo se l-yega a_ |
| Where is …? | **¿Dónde queda …?** _dondeh keda_ |
| Can you show me on the map where I am? | **¿Puede mostrarme en el mapa dónde estoy ahora?** _pwedeh mostrarmeh en el mapa dondeh estoy aora_ |
| I've lost my way. | **Estoy perdido(-a).** _estoy perdeedo(-a)_ |
| Can you repeat that, please? | **¿Puede repetírmelo, por favor?** _pwedeh repeteermelo por fabor_ |
| More slowly, please. | **Más despacio, por favor.** _mas despaseeo por fabor_ |
| Thanks for your help. | **Gracias por su ayuda.** _graseeas por soo ayooda_ |

## Traveling by car

| | |
|---|---|
| Is this the right road for …? | **¿Es ésta la carretera que va a…?** _es esta la karretera keh ba a_ |
| How far is it to … from here? | **¿A qué distancia queda … de aquí?** _a keh distancia keda deh akee_ |
| Where does this road lead? | **¿Adónde va esta carretera?** _adondeh ba esta karretera_ |
| How do I get onto the highway [motorway]? | **¿Cómo puedo llegar a la autopista?** _komo pwedo l-yegar a la aootopeesta_ |
| What's the next town called? | **¿Cómo se llama el próximo pueblo?** _komo seh l-yama el prokseemo pweblo_ |
| How long does it take by car? | **¿Cuánto dura el viaje en carro?** _kwanto doora el beeyakheh en karro_ |

---

### ON THE STREET

**¿A qué distancia queda la estación de tren?**
_a keh deestantheeya keda la estatheeyon deh tren_
*(How far is it to the train station?)*

**Diez minutos en carro.** _deeyeth meenootos en karro_
*(10 minutes by car.)*

**Gracias.** _gratseeyas_ *(Thank you.)*

## Location

| Está... | It's ... |
|---|---|
| derecho | straight ahead |
| a la izquierda | on the left |
| a la derecha | on the right |
| al otro lado de la calle | on the other side of the street |
| en la esquina | on the corner |
| a la vuelta de la esquina | around the corner |
| en dirección a... | in the direction of ... |
| enfrente de.../detrás de... | opposite .../behind ... |
| al lado de.../después de... | next to .../after ... |
| Baje ... | Go down ... |
| la calle lateral/la calle principal | side street/main street |
| Cruce ... | Cross the ... |
| la plaza/el puente | square/bridge |
| Tome el tercer giro a la derecha. | Take the third turn on the right. |
| Gire a la izquierda... | Turn left ... |
| después del primer semáforo | after the first traffic light |

## By car

| Está al ... de aquí. | It's ... of here. |
|---|---|
| norte/sur | north/south |
| este/oeste | east/west |
| Tome la carretera hacia ... | Take the road for ... |
| Usted está en la carretera equivocada. | You're on the wrong road. |
| Tiene que regresar a... | You'll have to go back to ... |
| Siga las señales para ... | Follow the signs for ... |

## How far?

| Está ... | It's ... |
|---|---|
| cerca/muy lejos | close/a long way |
| a cinco minutos a pie/en carro | 5 minutes on foot/by car |
| a diez kilómetros de aquí | about 10 km away |

## Road signs

### YOU MAY SEE

| | |
|---|---|
| **CAMINO CERRADO** | road closed |
| **DE [CEDA] LA VÍA** | yield [give way] |
| **DESVÍO** | detour [diversion] |
| **ESCUELA/COLEGIO** | school |
| **MÉTASE AL CARRIL** | stay in lane [get in lane] |
| **PUENTE BAJO** | low bridge |
| **RUTA ALTERNATIVA** | alternative route |
| **UNA SOLA VÍA** | one-way street |
| **ENCIENDA LOS FAROS** | use headlights |
| **VÍA DE ACCESO SOLAMENTE** | access only |

## Town plans

### YOU MAY SEE

| | |
|---|---|
| **aeropuerto (m)** | airport |
| **calle (f) principal** | main [high] street |
| **campos (mpl) deportivos** | playing field[sports ground] |
| **cine (m)** | movie theater [cinema] |
| **ciudad (f) vieja** | old town |
| **cruce (m) peatonal** | pedestrian crossing |
| **edificio (m) público** | public building |
| **estación (f)** | station |
| **estación (f) del metro** | subway [metro] station |
| **estación (f) de policía** | police station |
| **estacionamiento [parqueadero] (m)** | parking lot [car park] |
| **estadio (m)** | stadium |
| **iglesia (f)** | church |
| **oficina (f) de correo** | post office |
| **oficina (f) de información** | information office |
| **parada (f) de autobús** | bus stop |
| **parada (f) de taxi** | taxi stand [rank] |
| **parque (m)** | park |
| **pasadizo (m) subterráneo** | underpass [subway] |
| **ruta (f) de buses** | bus route |
| **teatro (m)** | theater |
| **Usted está aquí.** | You are here. |
| **zona (f) peatonal** | pedestrian zone [precinct] |

# SIGHTSEEING

## TOURIST INFORMATION OFFICE

Tourist offices (**turismos**) are very helpful with plenty of free brochures about services and attractions.

| | |
|---|---|
| Where's the tourist office? | **¿Dónde queda la oficina de turismo?** _dondeh keda la ofeeseena deh tooreesmo_ |
| What are the main points of interest? | **¿Cuáles son los principales sitios de interés?** _kwales son los preenseepales seeteeos deh eenteres_ |
| We're here for … | **Vamos a estar aquí …** _bamos a estar akee_ |
| only a few hours | **sólo un par de horas** _solo oon par deh oras_ |
| a day | **un día** _oon deeya_ |
| a week | **una semana** _oona semana_ |
| Can you recommend …? | **¿Puede recomendarme … por favor?** _pwedeh rekomendarmeh … por fabor_ |
| a sightseeing tour | **un recorrido por los lugares turísticos** _oon rekorreedo por los loogares tooreesteekos_ |
| an excursion | **una excursión** _oona eskoorseeyon_ |
| a boat trip | **un viaje en barco** _oon beeyakheh en barko_ |
| Do you have any information on …? | **¿Tiene alguna información sobre …?** _teeyeneh algoona eenformaseeyon sobreh_ |
| Are there any trips to …? | **Hay algún viaje a …?** _eye algoon beeyakheh a_ |

## ESSENTIAL

| | |
|---|---|
| How much is it? | **¿Cuánto cuesta?** _kwanto kwesta_ |
| When do we leave? | **¿A qué hora salimos?** _a keh ora saleemos_ |
| Where do we leave from? | **¿De dónde salimos?** _de dondeh saleemos_ |
| Can we take pictures? | **¿Podemos tomar fotografías?** _podemos tomar fotografeeyas_ |

## EXCURSIONS

| How much does the tour cost? | **¿Cuánto cuesta el tour?** _kwanto kwesta el toor_ |
| Is lunch included? | **¿Está incluida la comida [el almuerzo]?** _esta eenklooeeda la komeeda [el almwerso]_ |
| Where do we leave from? | **¿De dónde salimos?** _deh dondeh saleemos_ |
| What time does the tour start? | **¿A qué hora empieza el recorrido?** _a keh ora empeeyesa el rekoreedo_ |
| What time do we get back? | **¿A qué hora regresamos?** _a keh ora regresamos_ |
| Do we have free time in …? | **¿Tenemos tiempo libre en …?** _tenemos teeyempo leebreh en_ |
| Is there an English-speaking guide? | **¿Hay algún guía que hable inglés?** _eye algoon geeya keh able eengles_ |

## ON TOUR

| Are we going to see …? | **¿Vamos a ver …?** _bamos a ber_ |
| We'd like to have a look at … | **Quisiéramos echar un ojo [vistazo] al/a la …** _keeseeyeramos echar oon okho [beestaso] al/a la_ |
| Can we stop here …? | **¿Podemos parar aquí?** _podemos parar akee_ |
| to take photographs | **para tomar fotografías** _para tomar fotografeeyas_ |
| to buy souvenirs | **para comprar recuerdos** _para komprar rekwerdos_ |
| for the bathrooms [toilets] | **para ir al baño** _para eer al baño_ |
| Would you take a photo of us, please? | **¿Podría tomarnos una fotografía, por favor?** _podreeya tomarnos oona fotografeeya por fabor_ |
| How long do we have here …? | **¿Cuánto tiempo vamos a estar aquí?** _kwanto teeyempo bamos a estar akee_ |
| Wait! … isn't back. | **¡Un momento! … no ha regresado.** _oon momento. … no a regresado_ |

## SIGHTS

| | |
|---|---|
| Where is the …? | **¿Dónde está …** _dondeh esta_ |
| abbey | **la abadía** _la aba<u>dee</u>ya_ |
| art gallery | **la galería de arte** _la gale<u>ree</u>ya deh <u>ar</u>teh_ |
| battle site | **el campo de batalla** _el <u>kam</u>po deh ba<u>tal</u>-ya_ |
| botanical garden | **el jardín botánico** _el khar<u>deen</u> bo<u>ta</u>neeko_ |
| castle | **el castillo** _el kas<u>teel</u>-yo_ |
| cathedral | **la catedral** _la kate<u>dral</u>_ |
| cemetery | **el cementerio** _el semen<u>te</u>reeo_ |
| church | **la iglesia** _la ee<u>gle</u>seea_ |
| downtown area | **el centro (de la ciudad)** _el <u>sen</u>tro (deh la seeoo<u>dath</u>)_ |
| fountain | **la fuente** _la <u>fwen</u>te_ |
| market | **el mercado** _el mer<u>ka</u>do_ |
| (war) memorial | **el monumento (conmemorativo)** _el monoo<u>men</u>to konmemora<u>tee</u>bo_ |
| monastery | **el monasterio** _el monas<u>te</u>reeo_ |
| museum | **el museo** _el moo<u>se</u>yo_ |
| old town | **la ciudad vieja** _la seeoo<u>dath</u> bee<u>ye</u>kha_ |
| opera house | **el teatro de la ópera** _el te<u>a</u>tro deh la <u>o</u>pera_ |
| palace | **el palacio** _el pa<u>la</u>seeo_ |
| park | **el parque** _el <u>par</u>keh_ |
| parliament building | **la Cámara de Senadores [la Cámara de Representantes/Asamblea Nacional]** _la <u>ka</u>mara deh sena<u>do</u>res [la <u>ka</u>mara deh represen<u>tan</u>tes/asam<u>ble</u>a naseeo<u>nal</u>]_ |
| ruins | **las ruinas** _las roo<u>ee</u>nas_ |
| shopping area | **la zona comercial** _la <u>so</u>na komersee<u>yal</u>_ |
| statue | **la estatua** _la esta<u>too</u>a_ |
| theater | **el teatro** _el te<u>a</u>tro_ |
| tower | **la torre** _la <u>to</u>rreh_ |
| town hall | **la alcaldía [el consejo municipal]** _la alkal<u>dee</u>a [el kon<u>se</u>kho mooneesee<u>pal</u>]_ |
| viewpoint | **el mirador** _el meera<u>dor</u>_ |

## ADMISSION

| | |
|---|---|
| Is the … open to the public? | **¿Está … abierto(-a) al público?** *esta … abee<u>yer</u>to(-a) al <u>poo</u>bleeko* |
| Can we look around? | **¿Podemos dar una vuelta?** *po<u>de</u>mos dar <u>oo</u>na <u>bwel</u>ta* |
| What are the hours? | **¿Cuáles son los horarios?** *<u>kwa</u>les son los o<u>ra</u>reeos* |
| When does it close? | **¿A qué hora cierran?** *a keh <u>o</u>ra see<u>ey</u>eran* |
| Is … open on Sundays? | **¿Está abierto(-a) … los domingos?** *esta abee<u>yer</u>to(-a) … los do<u>meen</u>gos* |
| When's the next guided tour? | **¿Cuándo es el próximo tour con guía?** *<u>kwan</u>do es el <u>prok</u>seemo toor kon <u>gee</u>ya* |
| Do you have a guide book (in English)? | **¿Tiene usted una guía turística en inglés?** *tee<u>ey</u>eneh oos<u>teth</u> <u>oo</u>na <u>gee</u>ya too<u>rees</u>teeka en een<u>gles</u>* |
| Can I take photos? | **¿Puedo tomar fotografías?** *<u>pwe</u>do to<u>mar</u> fotogra<u>fee</u>yas* |
| Is there access for the disabled? | **¿Hay una entrada especial para personas incapacitadas?** *eye <u>oo</u>na en<u>tra</u>da espe<u>see</u>yal <u>pa</u>ra per<u>so</u>nas eenkapasee<u>ta</u>das* |
| Is there an audioguide in English? | **¿Hay alguna guía grabada en inglés?** *eye al<u>goo</u>na <u>gee</u>ya gra<u>ba</u>da en een<u>gles</u>* |

## PAYING/TICKETS

| | |
|---|---|
| How much is the entrance fee? | **¿Cuánto cuesta la entrada?** *<u>kwan</u>to <u>kwes</u>ta la en<u>tra</u>da* |
| Are there any discounts for …? | **¿Hay descuentos/concesiones para …?** *eye des<u>kwen</u>tos/konsesee<u>ey</u>ones <u>pa</u>ra* |
| children/students | **niños/estudiantes** *<u>nee</u>ños/estoodee<u>yan</u>tes* |
| the disabled | **personas incapacitadas** *per<u>so</u>nas eenkapasee<u>ta</u>das* |
| groups/senior citizens | **grupos/pensionados** *<u>groo</u>pos/pensee<u>yo</u>nados* |
| One adult and two children, please. | **un boleto [tiquete] para adulto y dos para niño, por favor.** *oon bo<u>le</u>to [tee<u>ke</u>te] <u>pa</u>ra a<u>dool</u>to ee dos <u>pa</u>ra <u>nee</u>ño por fa<u>bor</u>* |

## AT THE TICKET COUNTER

**Dos adultos, por favor.** *dos adooltos por fabor*
*(Two adults, please.)*
**Tres mil colones.** *tres meel colones (3000 colones.)*
**Aquí tiene.** *akee teeyeneh (Here you are. )*

## YOU MAY SEE

| | |
|---|---|
| **ABIERTO** | open |
| **CERRADO** | closed |
| **ENTRADA LIBRE [GRATUITA]** | admission free |
| **HORAS DE VISITA** | visiting hours |
| **PROHIBIDA LA ENTRADA** | no entry |
| **PROHIBIDO TOMAR FOTOGRAFÍAS CON FLASH** | no flash photography |
| **PRÓXIMO TOUR A LAS ...** | next tour at ... |
| **TIENDA DE REGALOS** | gift shop |
| **ÚLTIMA ENTRADA A LAS 5 P.M.** | last entry at 5 p.m. |

## IMPRESSIONS

| | |
|---|---|
| It's ... | **Es ...** *es* |
| amazing | **asombroso(-a)** *asombroso(-a)* |
| beautiful/ugly | **hermoso(-a)/feo(-a)** *ermoso(-a)/feo(-a)* |
| boring | **aburrido(-a)** *aboorreedo(-a)* |
| brilliant | **brillante** *breel-yanteh* |
| great fun | **divertido(-a)** *deeberteedo(-a)* |
| interesting | **interesante** *interesanteh* |
| magnificent | **suntuoso(-a) [majestuoso(-a)]** *soontoooso(-a) [makhestoooso(-a)]* |
| romantic | **romántico(-a)** *romanteeko(-a)* |
| stunning | **sensacional** *sensaseeonal* |
| terrible | **terrible** *terreebleh* |
| It's good value. | **Es dinero bien gastado.** *es deenero beeyen gastado* |
| It's a rip-off. | **Es una estafa.** *es oona estafa* |
| I like it./I don't like it. | **Me gusta./No me gusta.** *meh goosta/no meh goosta* |

101

## TOURIST GLOSSARY

**AC** B.C.
**acuarela** watercolor
**alfiz** frame around arch
**al estilo de ...** in the style of ...
**ala** wing (of building)
**alfarería** pottery
**almenas** battlements
**antigüedades** antiquities
**aposentos reales** apartments (royal)
**arco** arch
**arma** weapon
**arquitecto** architect
**arsenal** armory [armoury]
**arte moderno** modern art
**artesanías** crafts
**artista** artist
**atlas** sculpted figure support
**auditorio** auditorium
**azulejo** glazed tile
**balcón** balcony
**baluarte** defensive wall
**baño** baths
**biblioteca** library
**boleadoras** bolas/weighted thongs
**bosquejo** sketch
**bóveda** vault
**cacique** Indian chief
**camarín** side chapel
**camarote** stateroom
**capilla abierta** open-air chapel
**casona** large colonial mansion
**cementerio** churchyard
**cenotafio** cenotaph
**cerámica** ceramic/pottery
**Chac** Mayan rain god
**chac-mool** recumbent stone sculpture
**chapitel** spire
**chinampas** Aztec floating gardens
**colección** collection

**completado(-a) en ...** completed in ...
**conferencia** lecture
**construido-(a) en ...** built in ...
**contrafuerte** buttress
**corona** crown
**cripta** crypt
**cuadro** picture
**cúpula** dome
**DC** A.D.
**de oro** gold(en)
**decoración** decoration
**decorado(-a) por ...** decorated by ...
**demostración** demonstration
**descubierto(-a) en ...** discovered in ...
**destruido(-a) por ...** destroyed by ...
**detalle** detail
**dibujo** drawing
**diseñado(-a) por ...** designed by ...
**diseño** design
**disfraz** costume
**documento** document
**donado(-a) por ...** donated by ...
**dorado(-a)** gilded
**edificio** building
**emperador** emperor
**emperatriz** empress
**empezó en ...** started in ...
**encargado(-a) por ...** commissioned by ...
**escala de 1 a 100** scale 1:100
**escalera** staircase
**escenario** stage
**escuela de ...** school of ...
**escultor** sculptor
**escultura** sculpture/carving
**estela** standing stone monument
**estípite** pedestal
**exhibición** display

**exponer** exhibit
**exposición** exhibition
**exposición temporal** temporary exhibit
**fachada** facade
**figura de cera** waxwork
**fósil** fossil
**foso** moat
**fotografía** photograph
**friso** frieze
**fundado(-a) en ...** founded in ...
**gárgola** gargoyle
**grabado** engraving/etching
**guaca** burial ground/tomb
**joyas** jewelry [jewellery]
**juego de pelota** ball court
**laberinto** formal garden
**lápida** headstone
**lienzo** canvas
**manuscrito** manuscript
**mármol** marble
**miniatura** miniature
**modelo** model
**moneda** coin
**muebles** furniture
**muerto(-a) en ...** died in ...
**mural** mural
**muro** wall
**na** Mayan hut
**nacido(-a) en ...** born in ...
**obra maestra** masterpiece
**óleos** oils
**órgano** organ
**pabellón** pavilion
**paisaje** landscape *(painting)*
**palacio** palace
**parroquia** parish church
**pastel** pastel
**patio** courtyard
**piedra** stone
**piedra preciosa** gemstone
**pila bautismal** font

**pilar** pillar
**pintado(-a) por ...** painted by ...
**pintor(-a)** painter
**pintura** painting
**pirámide** pyramid
**placa** plaque
**plata** silver
**por** by *(person)*
**porcelana** porcelain
**portal** doorway
**presidio** fort/garrison
**prestado(-a) a ...** on loan to ...
**primer nivel** level 1
**puerta** gate
**púlpito** pulpit
**quero** Mayan vase
**quipu** Inca knotted cord
**reconstruido(-a) en ...** rebuilt in ...
**reina** queen
**reinado** reign
**reloj** clock
**representa ...** represents ...
**restaurado(-a) en ...** restored in ...
**retablo** altarpiece
**retrato** portrait
**rey** king
**sacbe** Mayan sacred causeway
**siglo** century
**silla de coro** choir *(stall)*
**tapiz** tapestry
**telamon** sculpted figure support
**templo** church, temple
**toqui** Indian chieftain
**torre** tower
**tumba** grave, tomb
**vajilla de plata** silverware
**vestíbulo** foyer
**vitral** stained-glass window
**vivió** lived
**yácata** ceremonial structure

## WHAT?/WHEN?

| | |
|---|---|
| What's that building? | **¿Qué es ese edificio?** keh es _eseh_ edee_fee_syo |
| When was it built? | **¿En qué época fue construido(-a)?** en keh _epoka_ fweh konstroo_ee_do(-a) |
| What style/period is that? | **¿Qué estilo/periodo es ése?** keh es_tee_lo/peree_yo_do es _eseh_ |

### la cultura maya   2000 b.c.–1500 a.d.

The great Mayan culture flowered in the Classic period (250–900 a.d.). Excavated ruins reveal grand monuments, pyramids, ceremonial buildings, stone causeways, stelae, and altars. Surviving artifacts include stone carvings and mosaics, multicolored pottery, and murals.

### la cultura azteca   ca. 15–early 16

The Aztecs, or Mexica, centered their empire on the vast, regulated ancient city of Tenochtitlan (in the Mexico City valley). Among the few remains of their culture are mural art and frescoes, huge pyramids adorned with stylized carved heads of the god Quetzalcoatl (plumed serpent), and records of extensive human sacrifice.

### la civilización inca   ca. 15–early 16

The Incas extended their Andean empire from Ecuador to Chile. Major sites at Machu Picchu and Cuzco feature temples, courtyards, trapezoidal stonework, terraces, and zigzag walls. Surviving cultural artifacts include ceramics, textiles, and vases.

### gótico-renacimiento   ca. 16–17

Very elaborate Gothic and Renaissance styles (especially Plateresque intricate lacelike carving) predominated in the colonial cities of Mexico and South America, particularly in the religious architecture.

### barroco   ca. 17–18

An exuberant architectural style, evident in the great cathedrals of Mexico City and Puebla, and also in Zacatecas. This developed in Latin America into the more extravagant Churriqueresque style.

### neoclásico   ca. 19

The influence of neoclassical art can be seen in the grandiose public buildings in Mexico City, e.g. the Palacio de Bellas Artes and the Post Office.

### modernismo   ca. late 19–20

The originality of modern architecture in Mexico is seen in the buildings of the National Archeology Museum and University City in Mexico City.

# History

### prehispánico 2000 b.c.–1519 a.d.

Settlements by ancient Mexican cultures in the preclassic period (2000 b.c.–300 a.d.): Olmecs (at San Lorenzo, La Venta, Tres Zapotes, Monte Alban), Mayans (across southern Mexico and Guatemala), and Zapotecs (southern Mexico, especially Oaxaca). The classic period (300–900) saw the flowering of Mayan culture in the Yucatan. The postclassic (900–1500) period: Toltecs (in Tula), Mixtecs (Monte Alban, Mitla), and Aztecs (at Tenochtitlan). Incas built up the most extensive empire, ruling about 12 million people from Ecuador to Chile. The Picunche and Mapuche Indians predominated in Argentina and Chile.

### colonial ca.15–18

Cristóbal Colón (Christopher Columbus) "discovered" the Americas in 1492. Treaty of Tordesillas (1494) split the continent into Spanish and Portuguese zones of influence. Prominent among the Conquistadors was Cortés, who captured and destroyed the vast city of Teonochtitlan in central Mexico (1519–21). Meanwhile, Pizarro plundered the Inca Empire. Conquest was followed by centuries of economic exploitation of land and native Indian labor. Cruelty and European diseases led to a catastrophic collapse in the native Indian population.

### independencia ca.19

Independence from Spanish control was prompted by Napoleon's military occupation of Spain. Mexico fought a 10-year war for independence (1810–21), while in South America the heroic campaigns of Simón Bolívar brought independence to Colombia, Venezuela, Eduador, Peru, and Bolivia (1817–24). Other years of statehood: Paraguay (1811), Argentina (1816); Chile (1818), Uruguay (1828).

### dictadura ca.19–20

The history of Latin America since independence has rarely been peaceful. Mexico suffered huge loss of territory to the U.S., French invasions (1838, 1863–66), and the Mexican Revolution (1910–21). Elsewhere, miliary coups and dicatorship, guerrilla warfare, and economic crises have been the norm. Only recently has democracy taken root in many countries.

## Religion

Central and South America are predominantly Roman Catholic.

| | |
|---|---|
| Catholic/Protestant church | **la iglesia católica/protestante** _la eegleseea katoleeka/protestanteh_ |
| mass/the service | **la misa/el oficio** _la meesa/el ofeeseeyo_ |

## IN THE COUNTRYSIDE

| | |
|---|---|
| I'd like a map of … | **Quisiera un mapa de …** *keeseeyera oon mapa deh* |
| this region | **esta región** *esta rekheeyon* |
| walking routes | **las rutas peatonales** *las rootas peatonales* |
| bicycle routes | **las rutas para tránsito de bicicletas** *las rootas para transeeto deh beeseekletas* |
| How far is it to …? | **¿A qué distancia está …?** *a keh distancia esta* |
| Is there a trail/scenic route to …? | **¿Hay alguna ruta pintoresca hacia …?** *eye algoona roota peentoreska aseea* |
| Can you show me on the map? | **¿Puede mostrarme en el mapa?** *pwedeh mostrarmeh en el mapa* |
| I'm lost. | **Estoy perdido(-a).** *estoy perdeedo(-a)* |

## ORGANIZED WALKS

| | |
|---|---|
| When does the guided walk start? | **¿A qué hora empieza la caminata?** *a keh ora empeeyesa la kameenata* |
| When will we return? | **¿A qué hora regresamos?** *a keh ora regresamos* |
| What is the walk like? | **¿Cómo es la caminata?** *komo es la kameenata* |
| gentle/medium/tough | **suave/media/dura** *swabeh/medeea/doora* |
| I'm exhausted. | **Estoy muy cansado(-a).** *estoy mwee kansado(-a)* |
| What kind of … is that? | **¿Qué clase de … es ése(-a)?** *keh klase deh … es ese(-a)* |
| animal/bird | **animal/pájaro** *aneemal/pakharo* |
| flower/tree | **flor/árbol** *flor/arbol* |

## GEOGRAPHICAL FEATURES

| | |
|---|---|
| bridge | **el puente** *el pwente* |
| cave | **la cueva** *la kweba* |
| cliff | **el acantilado [el precipicio]** *el akanteelado [el preseepeeseeo]* |
| farm | **la finca** *la feenka* |
| field | **el campo** *el kampo* |
| footpath | **el sendero** *el sendero* |
| forest | **la selva** *la selba* |
| hill | **la colina** *la koleena* |
| lake | **el lago** *el lago* |
| mountain | **la montaña** *la montaña* |
| mountain pass | **el cruce de montaña** *el kroose deh montaña* |
| mountain range | **la cordillera** *la kordeel-yera* |
| nature reserve | **la reserva natural** *la reserba natooral* |
| panorama | **el panorama** *el panorama* |
| park | **el parque** *el parkeh* |
| peak | **el pico** *el peeko* |
| picnic area | **la zona de picnic** *la sona deh peekneek* |
| pond | **la laguna** *la lagoona* |
| rapids | **los rápidos** *los rapeedos* |
| river | **el río** *el reeo* |
| sea | **el mar** *el mar* |
| stream | **el arroyo** *el arroyo* |
| tropical rainforest | **la selva tropical** *la selba tropicahl* |
| valley | **el valle** *el bal-yeh* |
| viewpoint | **el mirador** *el meerador* |
| village | **la aldea** *la aldeya* |
| vineyard/winery | **la viña** *la beeña* |
| waterfall | **la cascada [la catarata]** *la kaskada [la katarata]* |
| wood | **el bosque** *el boskeh* |

# LEISURE

## EVENTS

Local papers and weekly entertainment guides will tell you what's on.

| | |
|---|---|
| Do you have a program of events? | **¿Tiene usted el programa de eventos?** teeyeneh oosteth el programa deh ebentos |
| Can you recommend a …? | **¿Puede recomendarme un …?** pwedeh rekomendarmeh oon |
| ballet/concert | **algún ballet/algún concierto** algoon baleh/algoon konseeyerto |
| movie [film] | **alguna película** algoona peleekoola |
| opera | **alguna ópera** algoona opera |

## AVAILABILITY

| | |
|---|---|
| Are there any seats for tonight? | **¿Hay entradas para esta noche?** eye entradas para esta nocheh |
| Where can I get tickets? | **¿Dónde puedo conseguir boletos [tiquetes]?** dondeh pwedo konsegeer boletos [teeketes] |
| There are … of us. | **Somos …** somos |
| When does it start? | **¿A qué hora empieza?** a keh ora empeeyesa |
| When does it end? | **¿A qué hora termina?** a keh ora termeena |

---

### YOU MAY HEAR

| | |
|---|---|
| **¿Cuál es su … de tarjeta de crédito?** | What's your credit card …? |
| **número/tipo** | number/type |
| **fecha de vencimiento** | expiration [expiry] date |
| **Por favor, reclame sus boletos [tiquetes] …** | Please pick up the tickets … |
| **a la(s) … de la tarde** | by … p.m. |
| **en la taquilla [ventanilla]** | at the reservation desk |

## TICKETS

| | |
|---|---|
| Do you have tickets for…? | **¿Tiene entradas para …?** _tiene entradas para …_ |
| How much are the seats? | **¿Cuánto cuestan las entradas?** _kwanto kwestan las entradas_ |
| Do you have anything cheaper? | **¿Hay entradas más baratas?** _eye entradas mas baratas_ |
| I'd like to reserve … | **Quisiera reservar …** _keeseeyera reserbar_ |
| three for Sunday evening | **tres entradas para la función del domingo por la noche** _tres entradas para la foonseeyon del domeengo por la nocheh_ |
| one for Friday matinée | **una entrada para la función de matiné del viernes** _oona entrada para la foonseeyon deh mateeneh del beeyernes_ |
| May I have a program? | **¿Podría darme un programa?** _podreeya darmeh oon programa_ |
| Where's the coatcheck [cloakroom]? | **¿Dónde queda el guardarropa?** _dondeh keda el gwardarropa_ |

### YOU MAY SEE

| | |
|---|---|
| **AGOTADOS(-AS) /VENDIDOS(-AS)** | sold out |
| **BOLETOS [TIQUETES] PARA LA FUNCIÓN DE HOY** | tickets for today |
| **RESERVACIONES POR ADELANTADO** | advance reservations |

### AT THE BOX OFFICE

**¿Tiene un programa de eventos?** _teeyeneh oon programa de ebentos_ (Do you have a program of events?)

**Por supuesto.** _por soopwesto_ (Of course.)

**Gracias.** _gratseeyas_ (Thank you.)

## MOVIES [CINEMA]

| | |
|---|---|
| Is there a movie theater [multiplex cinema] near here? | **¿Hay un cine múltiple cerca de aquí?** *eye oon seeneh moolteepleh serka deh akee* |
| What's playing at the movies [at the cinema]? | **¿Qué películas están en el cine?** *keh peleekoolas estan en el seeneh* |
| Is the film dubbed/subtitled? | **¿Está doblada/subtitulada la película?** *esta doblada/soobteetoolada la peleekoola* |
| Is the film in the original English? | **¿Presentan el original en inglés?** *presentan el oreekheenal en eengles* |
| A ..., please. | **Un(a) ..., por favor.** *oon(a) ... por fabor* |
| box [carton] of popcorn | **unas palomitas de maíz [maíz pira]** *oonas palomeetas deh maees [maees peera]* |
| chocolate ice cream [choc-ice] | **un helado de chocolate** *oon elado deh chokolateh* |
| hot dog | **un hot dog [un perro caliente]** *oon hot dog [oon perro kaleeyenteh]* |
| soft drink | **un refresco [una gaseosa]** *oon refresko [oona gaseyosa]* |
| small | **pequeño(-a)** *pekeño(-a)* |
| regular | **mediano(-a)** *medeeyano(-a)* |
| large | **grande** *grandeh* |

## THEATER

| | |
|---|---|
| What's playing at the ... theater? | **¿Qué están presentando en el teatro ...?** *keh estan presentahndo en el teatro* |
| Who's the playwright? | **¿Quién es el autor?** *keeyen es el aootor* |
| Do you think I'd enjoy it? | **¿Cree que la/lo voy a disfrutar?** *kreye keh la/lo boy a deesfrootar* |
| I don't know much Spanish. | **No sé mucho español.** *no se moocho español* |

## OPERA/BALLET/DANCE

Where's the opera house? **¿Dónde queda el teatro de la ópera?**
_dondeh keda el teatro deh la opera_

Who's the soloist/ **¿Quién es el/la solista/el compositor?**
composer? _keeyen es el/la soleesta/el komposeetor_

Is evening dress required? **¿Se exige traje formal?**
_seh ekseekheh trakheh formal_

Who's dancing? **¿Quién baila?** _keeyen baeela_

I'm interested in **Me interesa la danza contemporánea**
contemporary dance. _meh eenteresa la dansa kontemporanea_

## MUSIC/CONCERTS

Popular music styles include **mariachi** (brass, violin, and guitar ensemble),
**marimba** (played on xylophone), **música ranchera** (country music), **música tropical** (rhythmic dance music), and Andean pan-pipe music, played at
Latin American folk evenings (**peñas**).

Where's the concert hall? **¿Dónde queda la sala de conciertos?**
_dondeh keda la sala deh konseeyertos_

Which orchestra/band **¿Qué orquesta/banda toca esta noche?**
is playing? _keh orkesta/banda toka esta nocheh_

What are they playing? **¿Qué están tocando?** _keh estan tokando_

Who is the **¿Quién es el director/el (la) solista?**
conductor/soloist? _keeyen es el deerektor/el (la) soleesta_

I really like … **Soy aficionado(-a) a …**
_soy afeeseeyonado(-a) a_

country music **la música country** _la mooseeka kontree_

folk music/jazz **la música folklórica/el jazz**
_la mooseeka folkloreeka/el yas_

music of the 60s **la música de los años sesenta**
_la mooseeka deh los años sesenta_

pop/rock/soul music **la música pop/rock/soul**
_la mooseeka pop/rok/soool_

Have you heard **¿Lo/La has oído nombrar/mencionar?**
of her/him? _lo/la as oeedo nombrar/menseeonar_

Are they popular? **¿Son muy famosos?** _son mwee famosos_

## NIGHTLIFE

| | |
|---|---|
| What's there to do in the evenings? | **¿Qué se puede hacer por las noches?** *keh seh pwedeh aser por las noches* |
| Can you recommend a …? | **¿Puede usted recomendarme un(a) …** *pwedeh oosteth rekomendarme oon(a)* |
| Is there a … in town? | **¿Hay … en el pueblo?** *eye … en el pweblo* |
| bar | **un bar** *oon bar* |
| casino | **un casino** *oon kaseeno* |
| discotheque | **una discoteca** *oona diskoteka* |
| gay club | **un club de gays** *oon kloo deh geys* |
| nightclub | **un club nocturno** *oon kloo noktoorno* |
| restaurant | **un restaurante** *oon restoranteh* |
| What type of music do they play? | **¿Qué clase de música tocan?** *keh klaseh deh mooseeka tokan* |
| How do I get there? | **¿Cómo se llega allí?** *komo seh l-yega al-yee* |

## ADMISSION

| | |
|---|---|
| What time does the show start? | **¿A qué hora empieza la función?** *a keh ora empeeyesa la foonseeyon* |
| Is evening dress required? | **¿Se exige traje formal?** *seh ekseekheh trakheh formal* |
| Is there a cover charge? | **¿Hay consumo minimo [cover]?** *eye konsoomo meeneemo [kober]* |
| Is a reservation necessary? | **¿Hay que reservar?** *eye keh reserbar* |
| Do we need to be members? | **¿Hay que ser miembros?** *eye keh ser meeyembros* |
| How long will we have to stand in line [queue]? | **¿Por cuánto tiempo tendremos que hacer cola [fila]?** *por kwanto teeyempo tendremos keh aser kola [feela]* |
| I'd like a good table. | **Quisiera una buena mesa.** *keeseeyera oona bwena mesa* |

### YOU MAY SEE

| | |
|---|---|
| **INCLUYE UNA BEBIDA DE CORTESÍA** | includes one complimentary drink |

## CHILDREN

Can you recommend
something for the children?
**¿Me puede recomendar algo para los niños?** *meh pwedeh rekomendar algo para los neeños*

Are there changing
facilities here for babies?
**¿Hay algún lugar especial para cambiar a los bebés?** *eye algoon loogar espeseeyal para kambeeyar a los bebes*

Where are the bathrooms
[toilets]?
**¿Dónde están los baños?** *dondeh estan los baños*

amusement arcade
**el local de maquinitas [de juegos electrónicos]** *el lokal deh makeeneetas [deh khwegos elektroneekos]*

kiddie [paddling] pool
**la piscina para niños** *la peeseena para neeños*

playground
**el patio de recreo [el patio de juego]** *el pateeo deh rekreo [el pateeo deh khwego]*

play group
**la guardería** *la gwardereeya*

zoo
**el zoológico** *el soo-olokheeko*

## BABYSITTING

Can you recommend
a reliable babysitter?
**¿Me puede recomendar una niñera confiable?** *meh pwedeh rekomendar oona neeñera konfeeyableh*

Is there constant
supervision?
**¿Hay vigilancia continua?** *eye beekheelanseea konteenooa*

Is the staff properly trained?
**¿Hay personal debidamente cualificado?** *eye personal debeedamenteh kaleefeekado*

When can I bring them?
**¿A qué hora puedo traer a los niños?** *a keh ora pwedo trahair a los neeños*

I'll pick them up at …
**Paso a recogerlos a las …** *paso a rekokherlos a las*

We'll be back by …
**Regresamos a las …** *regresamos a las*

She's 3, and he's
18 months.
**Ella tiene tres años y él tiene dieciocho meses.** *el-ya teeyeneh tres años y el teeyeneh deeyes-ee-ocho meses*

113

## SPORTS

Central and South Americans are avid soccer fans. Successful club teams include Boca Juniors (Buenos Aires) and River Plate in Argentina; matches between América (Mexico City) and Guadalajara (nicknamed Las Chivas) raise tremendous passions. There are some huge stadiums, particularly Estadio Azteca in Mexico City.

Other spectator sports include baseball (**el béisbol**) in Central America; boxing (**el boxeo**) and show-biz wrestling (**la lucha libre**) are also enjoyed in Mexico. In Argentina, popular participation sports include polo, rugby, and field hockey. For the adventurous, there is trekking in the Andes foothills, as well as hang-gliding and white-water rafting.

### Spectator sports

| | |
|---|---|
| Is there a soccer [football] game [match] this Saturday? | **¿Hay algún partido de fútbol este sábado?** _eye algoon parteedo deh footbol esteh sabado_ |
| Which teams are playing? | **¿Qué equipos juegan?** _keh ekeepos khwegan_ |
| Can you get me a ticket? | **¿Puede conseguirme un tiquete?** _pwedeh consegeermeh oon teeketeh_ |
| What's the admission charge? | **¿Cuánto cuesta la entrada?** _kwanto kwesta la entrada_ |
| Where's the racetrack? [racecourse]? | **¿Dónde queda la pista de carreras?** _dondeh keda la peesta deh karreras_ |
| Where can I place a bet? | **¿Dónde puedo hacer una apuesta?** _dondeh pwedo aser oona apwesta_ |
| What are the odds on ...? | **¿Cuáles son las probabilidades para ...?** _kwales son las probabeeleedades para_ |
| athletics | **el atletismo** _el atleteesmo_ |
| basketball | **el baloncesto** _el balonsesto_ |
| cycling | **el ciclismo** _el seekleesmo_ |
| golf | **el golf** _el golf_ |
| horse racing | **las carreras de caballos** _las karreras deh kabal-yos_ |
| soccer [football] | **el fútbol** _el footbol_ |
| swimming | **la natación** _la nataseeyon_ |
| tennis | **el tenis** _el tenees_ |
| volleyball | **el voleibol** _el boleybol_ |

**charreada** *charreada*

The Mexican equivalent of an American rodeo. It can be seen mostly on Sunday mornings in Mexico City at the Rancho del Charro.

**corrida** *korreeda*

Bullfight; **la corrida** (literally "running of the bulls") will either fascinate or appall you. In some ways the spectacle resembles a ballet. There are colorful moments when the procession (**paseo**) arrives. The entry of the bull into the arena is a moment of high tension. The movement of cape and bullfighter are graceful and precise.

The **matador** and his teams of assistants goad the bull so as to assess its reactions to the cape. The **picador** weakens the bull by piercing its neck muscles with a lance. A **banderillo** then confronts the animal and thrusts three sets of barbed sticks between its shoulder blades. The crowd will be watching critically, weighing the fearlessness of bull and man, the matador's skill as he executes a series of dangerous passes, leading to the final climax of the kill.

You'll be asked whether you want a seat in the sun or shade (**sol o sombra**). Be sure to specify **sombra**, for the sun is hot. Rent a cushion (**almohadilla**) for the hard concrete stands.

**jai-alai** *kheye leye*

Also known as **pelota vasca** or **frontón**, this game is a popular cross between handball and racketball or squash. Players carry a kind of curved wicker basket or scoop (**cesta**), using it to catch and fling a hard, goatskin-covered ball (**pelota**) against the end wall of a court.

| | |
|---|---|
| I'd like to see a bullfight. | **Quisiera ver una corrida.** |
| | *keeseeyera ber oona koreeda* |

## Participation sports

| | |
|---|---|
| Where's the nearest …? | **¿Dónde queda … más cercano(-a)?** |
| | *dondeh keda … mas serkano(-a)* |
| golf course | **el campo de golf** *el kampo deh golf* |
| sports club | **el club deportivo** *el kloo deporteebo* |
| Where are the tennis courts? | **¿Dónde quedan las canchas de tenis?** |
| | *dondeh kedan las kanchas deh tenees* |
| What's the charge per …? | **¿Cuál es el precio [la tarifa] por …?** |
| | *kwal es el preseeo [la tareefa] por* |
| day/round/hour | **día/ronda/hora** *deeya/ronda/ora* |

| Do I need to be a member? | **¿Hay que ser miembro?** |
| | *eye keh ser meeyembro* |
| Where can I rent …? | **¿Dónde puedo alquilar …?** |
| | *dondeh pwedo alkeelar* |
| boots | **unas botas** *oonas botas* |
| clubs | **unos palos de golf** *oonos palos deh golf* |
| equipment | **el equipo** *el ekeepo* |
| racket | **una raqueta** *oona raketa* |
| Can I get lessons? | **¿Puedo tomar clases?** |
| | *pwedo tomar klasses* |
| Do you have a fitness room? | **¿Tienen gimnasio?** *teeyenen kheemnaseeo* |
| Can I join in? | **¿Puedo jugar con ustedes?** |
| | *pwedo khoogar kon oostedes* |

## AT THE BEACH

The Mexican resorts of Acapulco on the Pacific coast, and Cancun and Cozumel in the Caribbean are famed for their beaches.

| Is the beach …? | **¿La playa es …?** *la playa es* |
| pebbly/sandy | **de graba/de arena** *deh graba/deh arena* |
| Is there a … here? | **¿Hay … por aquí?** *eye … por akee* |
| children's pool | **un chapoteadero [una piscina para niños]** |
| | *oon chapoteadero [oona peeseena* |
| | *para neeños]* |

<table>
<tr><th colspan="2">YOU MAY HEAR</th></tr>
<tr><td>Lo siento, todo está reservado / no tenemos nada libre.</td><td>I'm sorry, we're booked.</td></tr>
<tr><td>Hay que pagar un depósito de …</td><td>There is a deposit of …</td></tr>
<tr><td>¿Qué talla es usted?</td><td>What size are you?</td></tr>
<tr><td>Usted necesita una fotografía tamaño pasaporte.</td><td>You need a passport-size photo.</td></tr>
</table>

<table>
<tr><th colspan="2">YOU MAY SEE</th></tr>
<tr><td>PERMISO CON LICENCIA</td><td>permit holders only</td></tr>
<tr><td>PROHIBIDA LA PESCA</td><td>no fishing</td></tr>
<tr><td>VESTIDORES</td><td>changing rooms</td></tr>
</table>

| | |
|---|---|
| swimming pool | **una piscina …** _oona peeseena_ |
| indoor/outdoor | **cubierta/al aire libre** _koobeeyerta/al ayreh leebreh_ |
| Is it safe to swim/ dive here? | **¿Se puede nadar/bucear aquí sin peligro?** _seh pwedeh nadar/boosear akee seen peleegro_ |
| Is it safe for children? | **¿Es seguro(-a) para niños?** _es segooro(-a) para neeños_ |
| Is there a lifeguard? | **¿Hay algún salvavidas?** _eye algoon salbabeedas_ |
| I want to rent a/some … | **Quisiera alquilar …** _keeseeyera alkeelar_ |
| deck chair | **una silla de lona** _oona seel-ya deh lona_ |
| diving equipment | **un equipo de buceo** _oon ekeepo deh booseo_ |
| jet-ski | **un jet-ski [una moto acuática]** _oon yet-skee [oona moto akwateeka]_ |
| motorboat | **una lancha de motor** _oona lancha deh motor_ |
| umbrella [sunshade] | **una sombrilla** _oona sombreel-ya_ |
| surfboard | **una tabla de surf** _oona tabla deh soorf_ |
| water skis | **unos esquíes acuáticos** _oonos eskeeyes akwateekos_ |
| For … hours. | **Por … horas.** _por … oras_ |

## Skiing

There are winter-sport resorts in Chile and Argentina, notably San Carlos de Bariloche.

| | |
|---|---|
| I'd like to ski. | **Quisiera esquiar.** _keeseeyera eskeeyar_ |
| Are there any ski lifts? | **¿Hay telesquí?** _eye teleskee_ |
| I'd like to rent/hire … | **Quisiera alquilar …** _keeseeyera alkeelar_ |

117

# MAKING FRIENDS

## INTRODUCTIONS

Central and South Americans are generally open, friendly, and helpful. It is considered good manners to exchange pleasantries when meeting, before getting down to conversation.

In Spanish, when referring to someone by their title, the definite article (the) is required. For example, **"Este(a) es el señor/la señora/la señorita …"** is literally "This is the Mr./Mrs./Miss …". Spanish names generally consist of 3 parts; the second is the most important for formal purposes.

In Spanish, there are three forms for "you" (each taking a different form of the verb): **tú** (singular) and **vosotros** (plural) are used when talking to relatives, close friends and children (and between young people); **usted** (singular) and **ustedes** (plural) – often abbreviated to **Vd./Vds.** – are used in all other cases. If in doubt, use **usted/ustedes**.

| | |
|---|---|
| Hello, we haven't met. | **Hola, no nos conocemos.**<br>_ola no nos konosemos_ |
| My name is … | **Me llamo …**<br>_meh l-yamo_ |
| May I introduce …? | **Quiero presentarle a …**<br>_keeyero presentarleh a_ |
| Pleased to meet you. | **Mucho gusto.**<br>_moocho goosto_ |
| What's your name? | **¿Cómo se llama?**<br>_komo seh l-yama_ |
| How are you? | **¿Cómo está?**<br>_komo esta_ |
| Fine, thanks. And you? | **Bien, gracias. ¿Y usted?**<br>_beeyen graseeas. y oosteth_ |

### AT A RECEPTION

**Me llamo Sheryl.** _meh l-yamo sheryl_ (*My name is Sheryl.*)

**Mucho gusto. Me llamo José.** _moocho goostoh meh l-yamo hoseh_ (*My pleasure. My name is José.*)

**El gusto es mío.** _el goostoh es meeoh_ (*The pleasure is mine.*)

## Where are you from?

| | | |
|---|---|---|
| Where do you come from? | ¿De dónde es Ud.? | de _dondeh_ es oos_teth_ |
| Where were you born? | ¿Dónde nació usted? | _dondeh_ naseeyo oos_teth_ |
| I'm from … | Soy de … | soy deh |
| Australia | Australia | aoos_tra_leea |
| Britain | Gran Bretaña | gran bre_ta_ña |
| Canada | Canadá | _kana_da |
| England | Inglaterra | eengla_te_rra |
| Ireland | Irlanda | eer_lan_da |
| Scotland | Escocia | es_ko_seea |
| the United States | Los Estados Unidos | los es_ta_dos oo_nee_dos |
| Wales | (País de) Gales | (pa_ees_ deh) _ga_les |
| Where do you live? | ¿Dónde vive usted? | _dondeh_ _bee_beh oos_teth_ |
| What part of … are you from? | ¿De qué parte de … es usted? | de keh _parteh_ deh … es oos_teth_ |
| Argentina | Argentina | arkhen_tee_na |
| Chile | Chile | _chee_leh |
| Mexico | México | _mekhee_ko |
| Venezuela | Venezuela | benes_we_la |
| We come here every year. | Venimos todos los años. | ve_nee_mos _todos_ los _a_ños |
| It's my/our first visit. | Ésta es la primera vez que vengo/venimos. | _esta_ es la pree_me_ra ves ke _vengo_/ve_nee_mos |
| Have you ever been to Britain/the U.S.? | ¿Ha(n) ido alguna vez a la Gran Bretaña/los Estados Unidos? | a(n) _eedo_ al_goo_na ves a gran bre_ta_ña/los es_ta_ dos oo_nee_dos |
| Do you like it here? | ¿Le gusta este lugar? | le _goos_ta _este_ loo_gar_ |
| What do you think of the …? | ¿Qué opina de …? | ke o_pee_na deh |
| I love the … here. | Me encanta el/la … de aquí. | me en_kan_ta el/la … deh a_kee_. |
| I don't really like the … here. | A mí no me gusta mucho (el/la) … de aquí. | a mee no me _goos_ta _moo_cho (el/la) … deh a_kee_. |
| food/people | la comida/la gente | la ko_mee_da/la _khen_teh |

## Who are you with?

| | |
|---|---|
| Who are you with? | **¿Con quién viene usted?** *kon keeyen beeyeneh oosteth* |
| I'm on my own. | **Vengo solo(-a).** *bengo solo(-a)* |
| I'm with a friend. | **Vengo con un(a) amigo(-a).** *bengo kon oon ameego(-a)* |
| I'm with … | **Vengo con …** *bengo kon (mee/mees)* |
| my wife | **mi esposa** *mee esposa* |
| my husband | **mi esposo** *mee esposo* |
| my family | **mi familia** *mee fameelya* |
| my children | **mis niños/hijos** *mees neeños/eekhos* |
| my parents | **mis padres** *mees padres* |
| my boyfriend/girlfriend | **mi novio/novia** *mee nobeeyo/nobeeya* |
| my father/mother | **mi padre/madre** *mee padreh/madreh* |
| my son/daughter | **mi hijo/hija** *mee eekho/eekha* |
| my brother/sister | **mi hermano/hermana** *mee hermano/hermana* |
| my uncle/aunt | **mi tío/tía** *mee teeo/teea* |
| What's your son's/ wife's name? | **¿Cómo se llama su hijo/esposa?** *komo se lyama soo eekho/esposa* |
| Are you married? | **¿Es usted casado(-a)?** *e oosteth kasado(-a)* |
| I'm … | **Soy …** *soy* |
| married/single | **casado(-a)/soltero(-a)** *kasado(-a)/soltero(-a)* |
| divorced/separated | **divorciado(-a)/separado(-a)** *deeborseeyado(-a)/separado(-a)* |
| engaged | **(Estoy) comprometido(-a)** *(estoy) komprometeedo(-a)* |
| We live together. | **Vivimos juntos.** *beebeemos khoontos* |
| Do you have any children? | **¿Tienen hijos?** *teeyenen eekhos* |
| We have two sons and a daughter. | **Tenemos dos hijos y una hija.** *tenemos dos eekhos ee oona eekha* |
| How old are they? | **¿Qué edad tienen?** *keh edad teeyenen* |

## What do you do?

| | | |
|---|---|---|
| What do you do? | **¿Qué hace usted?** | *keh aseh oosteth* |
| What are you studying? | **¿Qué está estudiando?** | *keh esta estoodeeyando* |
| I'm studying … | **Estoy estudiando …** | *estoy estoodeeyando* |
| science | **ciencia** | *seeyenseeyas* |
| the arts | **bellas artes** | *bel-yas artes* |
| I'm in … | **Trabajo en …** | *trabakho en* |
| business | **administración de empresas** | *admeeneestraseeyon deh empresas* |
| engineering | **ingeniería** | *eenkheneeyereea* |
| retail | **ventas al menudeo** | *bentas al menoodeo* |
| sales | **ventas** | *bentas* |
| Who do you work for …? | **¿Para quién trabaja?** | *para keeyen trabakha* |
| I work for … | **Trabajo para …** | *trabakho para* |
| I'm a(n) … | **Soy (un/una) …** | *soy (oon/oona)* |
| accountant | **un(a) contador(a)** | *oon(a) kontador(a)* |
| housewife | **una ama de casa** | *oona ama deh kasa* |
| student | **un(a) estudiante** | *oon(a) estoodeeyanteh* |
| I'm retired. | **Estoy retirado(-a).** | *reteerado(-a)* |
| I'm self-employed. | **Soy independiente.** | *soy eendependeeyenteh* |
| I'm between jobs. | **No tengo trabajo en este momento.** | *no tengo trabakho en este momento* |
| What are your interests/ hobbies? | **¿Cuáles son sus pasatiempos?** | *kwales son soos passateeyempos* |
| I like … | **Me gusta …** | *me goosta* |
| music | **la música** | *la moosyka* |
| reading | **la lectura** | *la lektoora* |
| sports | **el deporte** | *el deporteh* |
| Would you like to play …? | **¿Le gustaría jugar …?** | *le goostareea khoogar* |
| cards | **cartas** | *kartas* |
| chess | **ajedrez** | *akhedres* |

## What weather!

| | |
|---|---|
| What a lovely day! | **¡Qué día tan hermoso!** <br> *keh deeya tan ermoso* |
| What awful weather! | **¡Qué tiempo tan malo!** <br> *keh teeyempo tan malo* |
| Isn't it cold/hot today! | **¡Qué frío/calor hace hoy! ¿Verdad?** <br> *keh freeyo/kalor aseh oy. berdath* |
| Is it usually as warm as this? | **¿Hace normalmente este calor?** <br> *aseh normalmente este kalor* |
| Do you think it's going to … tomorrow? | **¿Cree que va a … mañana?** <br> *kreyeh keh ba a … mañana* |
| be a nice day | **hacer buen tiempo** *aser bwen teeyempo* |
| rain | **llover** *l-yober* |
| snow | **nevar** *nebar* |
| What is the weather forecast? | **¿Qué dice "El tiempo meteorológico"?** <br> **[la predicción del tiempo]?** <br> *keh deeseh "El teeyempo metereolokhiko"* <br> *[la predeekseeyon del teeyempo]* |
| It's … | **Está …** *esta* |
| cloudy | **nublado** *nooblado* |
| rainy | **lloviendo** *l-yobeeyendo* |
| snowy | **nevando** *nebando* |
| thundering | **tronando** *tronando* |
| It's foggy. | **Hay niebla.** *eye neeyebla* |
| It was frosty last night. | **Anoche heló [hubo heladas].** <br> *anocheh elo [oobo eladas]* |
| It's ice cold. | **Hace un frío helado.** *aseh oon freeyo elado* |
| It's windy. | **Hace viento.** *aseh beeyento* |
| Has the weather been like this for long? | **¿Ha estado así el tiempo últimamente?** <br> *a estado asee el teeyempo oolteemamenteh* |
| What's the pollen count? | **¿Cuál es el recuento polínico?** <br> *kwal es el rekwento poleeneeko* |
| high/medium/low | **alto/medio/bajo** <br> *alto/medeeo/bakho* |

### Enjoying your trip?

| | |
|---|---|
| I'm here on … | **Estoy aquí …** _estoy akee_ |
| a business trip | **en viaje de negocios**<br>_en beeyakheh deh negoseeos_ |
| vacation [holiday] | **de vacaciones** _de bakaseeyones_ |
| We came by … | **Vinimos en…** _beeneemos en_ |
| train/bus/plane | **tren/bus/avión** _tren/boos/abeeyon_ |
| car/ferry | **carro/transbordador [ferry]**<br>_karro/transbordador [ferree]_ |
| I have a rental car. | **He alquilado un carro.** _eh alkeelado_<br>_oon karro_ |
| We're staying in … | **Nos hospedamos en …** _nos ospedamos en_ |
| an apartment | **un departamento** _oon departamento_ |
| a hotel/campsite | **un hotel /una zona de campamento**<br>_oon otel/oona sona deh kampamento_ |
| with friends | **la casa de unos amigos**<br>_la kasa deh oonos ameegos_ |
| Can you suggest …? | **¿Puede sugerirme …?** _pwedeh sookhereerme_ |
| places to eat | **sitios para ir a comer**<br>_seeteeyos para eer a komer_ |
| places to visit | **lugares para visitar** _loogares para beeseetar_ |
| We're having a great time. | **Nos estamos divirtiendo mucho.**<br>_nos estamos deebeerteeyendo moocho_ |
| We're having an awful time. | **No nos ha ido nada bien.**<br>_no nos a eedo nada beeyen_ |

---

#### YOU MAY HEAR

| | |
|---|---|
| **¿Está de vacaciones?** | Are you on vacation? |
| **¿En qué vino?** | How did you get here? |
| **¿Qué tal el viaje?** | How was the trip? |
| **¿Dónde se hospeda?** | Where are you staying? |
| **¿Qué tal el alojamiento?** | How are the accommodations? |
| **¿Cuánto tiempo lleva aquí?** | How long have you been here? |
| **¿Cuánto tiempo piensa quedarse aquí?** | How long are you staying? |

## INVITATIONS

Would you like to have dinner with us on …?
**¿Le gustaría cenar con nosotros el …?**
*leh goostareea senar kon nosotros el*

Are you free for lunch?
**¿Puedo invitarlo(-a) a comer [almorzar]?**
*pwedo eenbeetarlo(-a) a komer [almorsar]*

Can you come for a drink this evening?
**¿Puede venir a tomar una copa esta noche?**
*pwedeh beneer a tomar oona kopa esta nocheh*

We are having a party. Can you come?
**Tenemos una fiesta. ¿Puede venir?**
*tenemos oona feeyesta. pwedeh beneer*

May we join you?
**¿Podemos ir con usted/ustedes?**
*podemos eer kon oosteth/oostedes*

Would you like to join us?
**¿Le gustaría ir con nosotros?**
*leh goostareeya eer kon nosotros*

## Going out

What are your plans for …?
**¿Qué planes tiene para …?**
*keh planes teeyeneh para*

today/tonight
**hoy/esta noche** *oy/esta nocheh*

tomorrow
**mañana** *mañana*

Are you free this evening?
**¿Está libre esta noche?**
*esta leebreh esta nocheh*

Would you like to …?
**¿Le gustaría …?** *leh goostareeya*

go dancing
**ir a bailar** *eer a baeelar*

go for a drink/meal
**ir de copas [salir a tomar algo]/ir a cenar**
*eer deh kopas [saleer a tomar algo]/ eer a senar*

go for a walk
**dar un paseo** *dar oon paseyo*

go shopping
**ir de compras** *eer deh kompras*

Where would you like to go?
**¿Adónde le gustaría ir?**
*adondeh leh goostareea eer*

I'd like to go to …
**Quisiera ir a …** *keeseeyera eer a*

I'd like to see…
**Quisiera ver …** *keeseeyera behr*

Do you enjoy …?
**¿Le gusta …?** *leh goosta*

Shall we go to the movies?
**¿Vamos al cine?** *bamos al seeneh*

## Accepting/Declining

| | | |
|---|---|---|
| That's very kind of you. | **Es usted muy amable.** | |
| | *es oosteth mwee amableh* | |
| Great. I'd love to. | **Estupendo. Me encantaría.** | |
| | *estoopendo. meh enkantareeya* | |
| Thank you, but I'm busy. | **Gracias, pero estoy muy ocupado(-a).** | |
| | *graseeas pero estoy mwee okoopado(-a)* | |
| May I bring a friend? | **¿Puedo llevar a un(a) amigo(-a)?** | |
| | *pwedo l-yebar a oon ameego(-a)* | |
| Where shall we meet? | **¿Dónde nos encontramos?** | |
| | *dondeh nos enkontramos* | |
| I'll meet you … | **Nos encontramos …** *nos enkontramos* | |
| in the bar | **en el bar** *en el bar* | |
| in front of your hotel | **enfrente del hotel** *enfrenteh del otel* | |
| I'll call for you at 8. | **Iré a recogerlo(-a) [Paso por usted] a las 8.** | |
| | *eereh a rekokherlo(-a) [paso por oosteth] a las ocho* | |
| What time shall I come? | **¿A qué hora vengo?** *a keh ora bengo* | |
| How about …? | **¿Qué le parece a las …?** | |
| | *keh leh pareseh a las* | |
| Could we make it a bit later? | **¿Puede ser un poquito más tarde?** | |
| | *pwedeh ser oon pokeeto mas tardeh* | |
| How about another day? | **¿Qué le parece otro día?** | |
| | *keh leh parehseh otro deeya* | |
| That will be fine. | **Me parece bien.** *meh pareseh beeyen* | |

## Dining out/in

| | | |
|---|---|---|
| Where would you like to sit? | **¿Dónde quiere sentarse?** | |
| | *dondeh keeyereh sentarseh* | |
| Let me bring you a drink. | **Voy a traerle una copa [algo de tomar].** | |
| | *boy a trayerleh oona kopa [algo deh tomar].* | |
| What would you like? | **¿Qué desea?** *keh deseea* | |
| Do you like …? | **¿Le gusta …?** *leh goosta* | |
| That was a lovely meal. | **Fue una cena deliciosa.** | |
| | *fweh oona sena deleeseeyosa* | |

## ENCOUNTERS

| | |
|---|---|
| Do you mind if …? | **¿Le molesta si …?** *leh molesta see* |
| I sit here/smoke | **me siento aquí/fumo** *meh seeyento akee/foomo* |
| Can I get you a drink? | **¿Puedo ofrecerle una copa [algo de tomar]?** *pwedo ofreserleh oona kopa [algo deh tomar]* |
| I'd love to have some company. | **Me encantaría tener un poco de compañía.** *meh enkantareeya tener oon poko deh kompañeeya* |
| Why are you laughing? | **¿Por qué se ríe?** *por keh seh reeyeh* |
| Is my Spanish that bad? | **¿Es tan malo mi español?** *es tan malo mee español* |
| Shall we go somewhere quieter? | **¿Vamos a un sitio más tranquilo?** *bamos a oon seeteeo mas trankeelo* |
| Leave me alone, please! | **¡Déjeme tranquilo(-a), por favor!** *dekhemeh trankeelo(-a) por fabor* |
| You look great! | **¡Qué bien luces! [¡Te ves muy bien!]** *keh beeyen looses [teh bes mwee beeyen]* |
| Thanks for the evening. | **Gracias por la velada.** *graseeas por la belada* |
| I'm afraid I have to leave. | **Lo siento, tengo que irme ahora.** *lo seeyento tengo keh eermeh aora* |
| Can I see you … ? | **¿Puedo verlo(-a) … ?** *pwedo berlo(-a)* |
| tomorrow | **mañana** *mañana* |
| next week | **la próxima semana** *la prokseema semanah* |
| See you soon. | **Hasta luego.** *asta lwego* |
| Can I have your address? | **¿Puedo anotar su dirección?** *pwedo anotar soo deerekseeyon* |

## TELEPHONING

In Mexico, international calls can be made from modern phone booths (blue, marked **Lada** or **Larga Distancia** for international; orange, for local). Most have instructions in English. Some take phone cards (available from stores nearby, telephone offices, and bus and train stations). In **casetas de teléfono** an operator will connect you and bill you afterward according to a meter reading.

To phone abroad from Mexico, dial 95 + area code (for U.S. and Canada); 98 + country code (for outside Americas). In Argentina, tokens (**cospeles** or **fichas**) and cards (**tarjetas**) are used in public phones.

| | |
|---|---|
| Can I have your telephone number? | **¿Puedo anotar su número de teléfono?** _pwedo anotar soo noomero deh telefono_ |
| Here's my number. | **Éste es mi número.** _esteh es mee noomero_ |
| Please call me. | **Llámeme, por favor.** _l-yamemeh por fabor_ |
| I'll give you a call. | **Yo lo (la) llamaré.** _yo lo (la) l-yamareh_ |
| Where's the nearest telephone booth? | **¿Dónde está el teléfono público más cercano [la cabina de teléfono]?** _dondeh esta el telefono poobleeko mas serkano [la kabeena deh telefono]_ |
| May I use your phone? | **¿Puedo usar su teléfono?** _pwedo oosar soo telefono_ |
| It's an emergency. | **Es una emergencia.** _es oona emerkhenseea_ |
| I'd like to call someone in… | **Quisiera llamar a alguien en …** _keeseeyera l-yamar a algeeyen en_ |
| What's the area [dialling] code for …? | **¿Cuál es el código para …?** _kwal es el kodeego para_ |
| I'd like a phone card. | **Quisiera una tarjeta de teléfono.** _keeseeyera oona tarkheta deh telefono_ |
| What's the number for Information [Directory Enquiries]? | **¿Cuál es el número de Información?** _kwal es el noomero deh eenformaseeyon_ |
| I'd like the number for … | **Quisiera el número de teléfono de …** _keeseeyera el noomero deh telefono deh_ |
| I'd like to call collect [reverse the charges]. | **Quisiera llamar por cobrar [por cobro revertido].** _keeseeyera l-yamar por kobrar [por kobro reberteedo]_ |

## Speaking on the phone

| | |
|---|---|
| Hello. This is … | **Aló, habla …** *alo abla* |
| I'd like to speak to … | **Quisiera hablar con …** *keeseeyera ablar kon* |
| Extension … | **Extensión …** *extenseeyon* |
| Speak louder, please. | **¿Podría hablar más fuerte?** *podreeya ablar mas fwairteh* |
| Speak more slowly, please. | **¿Podría hablar más despacio?** *podreeya ablar mas despaseeo* |
| Could you repeat that, please? | **¿Me lo repite, por favor?** *meh lo repeeteh por fabor* |
| I'm afraid he's/she's not in. | **Lo siento. Él/ella no se encuentra en este momento.** *lo seeyento. el/el-ya no se enkwentra en esteh momento* |
| You've got the wrong number. | **Lo siento. Tiene el número equivocado.** *lo seeyento. teeyeneh el noomero ekeebokado* |
| Just a moment, please. | **Un momento, por favor.** *oon momento por fabor* |
| Hold on, please. | **Espere un momento, por favor.** *espereh oon momento por fabor* |
| When will he/she be back? | **¿A qué hora regresará?** *a keh ora regresara* |
| Will you tell him/her that I called? | **¿Podría decirle que le llamé?** *podreeya deseerleh keh leh l-yameh* |
| My name is … | **Mi nombre es …** *mee nombreh es* |
| Would you ask him/her to call me? | **¿Podría pedirle que me llame?** *podreeya pedeerleh keh meh l-yameh* |
| I must go now. | **Tengo que irme.** *tengo keh eermeh* |
| Nice to speak to you. | **Fue un placer hablar con usted.** *fweh oon plaser ablar kon oosteth* |
| I'll be in touch. | **Me mantendré en contacto.** *meh mantendreh en kontakto* |
| Bye. | **Adiós.** *adeeyos* |

# STORES & SERVICES

Stores are generally small and individual; however, large chain stores have appeared. In Mexico, for example, you will see department stores (**Palacio de Hierro**, **Sears**, **Sanborn's**, and **Liverpool**) and supermarket chains (**Aurrera**, **Comercial Mexicana**, **Superama**, and **Gigante**).

For souvenir shopping in Mexico City, go to **Mercado Artesanal Buenavista** for a huge range of goods.

Most cities and towns have at least one market; some permanent, others open just one morning a week. There is generally an opportunity to bargain over prices. Flea markets (**tianguis**) and street peddlers are also common.

| | |
|---|---|
| I'd like … | **Quisiera …** _keeseeyera_ |
| Do you have …? | **¿Tiene …?** _teeyeneh_ |
| How much is that? | **¿Cuánto cuesta eso?** _kwanto kwesta eso_ |
| Thank you. | **Gracias.** _graseeas_ |

## STORES AND SERVICES
### Where is …?

| | |
|---|---|
| Where's the nearest …? | **¿Dónde está … más cercano(-a)?** _dondeh esta … mas serkano(-a)_ |
| Where's there a good …? | **¿Dónde hay un(a) buen(a) …?** _dondeh eye oon(a) bwen(a)_ |
| Where's the main shopping mall [centre]? | **¿Dónde está la principal zona de tiendas?** _dondeh esta la preenseepal sona deh teeyendas_ |

| YOU MAY SEE | |
|---|---|
| **ABIERTO** | open |
| **CERRADO** | closed |

### IN A STORE

**¿Le puedo ayudar en algo?** le _pwedo ayudar en algo?_
(Can I help you with anything?)
**Gracias. Sólo estoy mirando.** _gratseeyas solo estoy meerando_ (Thanks. I'm just browsing.)

| Is it far from here? | ¿Está lejos de aquí? _esta lekhos deh akee_ |
| How do I get there? | ¿Cómo se llega allá? _komo seh l-yega al-ya_ |

## Stores

| antiques store | el almacén de antigüedades |
| | _el almasen deh antigwedades_ |
| bakery | la panadería _la panadereeya_ |
| bookstore | la librería _la leebrereeya_ |
| butcher | la carnicería _la karneesereeya_ |
| camera store | la tienda de fotografía |
| | _la teeyenda deh fotografeeya_ |
| clothing store | la tienda de ropa _la teeyenda deh ropa_ |
| delicatessen | el delicatessen _el deleekatesen_ |
| department store | el almacén _el almasen_ |
| drugstore | la farmacia [la droguería] |
| | _la farmaseea [la drogereeya]_ |
| fish store [fishmonger] | la pescadería _la peskadereeya_ |
| florist | la floristería _la floreestereeya_ |
| gift shop | la tienda de regalos |
| | _la teeyenda deh regalos_ |
| greengrocer | la verdulería _la berdoolereeya_ |
| health food store | la tienda de alimentos naturales |
| | _la teeyenda deh aleementos natoorales_ |
| liquor store [off-licence] | la vinetería [la licorería] |
| | _la beenetereeya [la leekorereeya]_ |
| market | el mercado _el merkado_ |
| newsstand [newsagent] | el quiosco de periódicos y revistas |
| | _el keeyosko deh pereeyodeekos ee rebeestas_ |
| pastry shop | la pastelería _la pastelereeya_ |
| pharmacy [chemist] | la farmacia _la farmaseea_ |
| produce [grocery] store | la tienda de abarrotes |
| | _la teeyenda deh abarrotes_ |
| record [music] store | la tienda de discos _la teeyenda deh deeskos_ |
| souvenir store | la tienda de recuerdos [souvenirs] |
| | _la teeyenda deh rekwerdos [soobeneers]_ |

| | |
|---|---|
| sporting goods store | **la tienda de artículos deportivos** |
| | *la teeyenda deh arteekoolos deporteebos* |
| supermarket | **el supermercado** *el soopermerkado* |
| toy store | **la juguetería** *la khoogetereeya* |

## Services

| | |
|---|---|
| clinic | **la policlínica** *la poleekleeneeka* |
| dentist | **el dentista** *el denteesta* |
| doctor | **el doctor** *el doktor* |
| dry cleaner | **la tintorería** *la teentorereeya* |
| hairdresser | **la peluquería** *la pelookereeya* |
| hospital | **el hospital** *el ospeetal* |
| laundromat | **la lavandería** *la labandereeya* |
| library | **la biblioteca** *la beebleeoteka* |
| optician | **el oculista** *el ocooleesta* |
| police station | **la estación de policía** |
| | *la estaseeyon deh poleeseeya* |
| post office | **la oficina de correo** |
| | *la ofeeseena de korreo* |
| travel agency | **la agencia de viajes** |
| | *la akhenseea deh beeyakhes* |

## Opening hours

| | |
|---|---|
| When does the … open/close? | **¿A qué hora abre/cierra …?** *a keh ora abre/seeyera* |
| Are you open in the evening? | **¿Está abierto(-a) por las noches?** *esta abeeyerto(-a) por las noches* |
| Do you close for lunch? | **¿Cierran al mediodía?** *seeyeran al medeeodeeya* |
| Where is the … | **¿Dónde está …?** *dondeh esta* |
| cashier [cash desk] | **la caja** *la kakha* |
| elevator [lift] | **el ascensor** *el asensor* |
| escalator | **la escalera eléctrica** *la eskalera elektreeka* |
| store directory [guide] | **la guía del almacén** *la geeya del almasen* |

| Where's the … department? | ¿Dónde está el departamento [la sección] de …? _dondeh esta el departamento [la sekseeyon] deh_ |
| first [ground (U.K.)] floor | **la planta baja** _la planta bakha_ |
| second [first (U.K.)] floor | **el primer piso** _el preemer peeso_ |

| General times for: | Opening | Closing | Lunch break | Closed |
|---|---|---|---|---|
| **shops** | 10 | 8 | none | some on Sunday |
| **pharmacy** | 9 | 8 | none | Sunday |
| **post office** | 8 | 7 | none | most on Sunday |
| **banks** | 9 | 5 | none | weekend |

## Service

| Can you help me? | ¿Puede ayudarme? _pwedeh ayoodarmeh_ |
| I'm looking for … | Estoy buscando …_estoy booskando_ |
| I'm just browsing. | Sólo estoy mirando. _solo estoy meerando_ |
| It's my turn. | Es mi turno. _es mee toorno_ |
| Do you have …? | ¿Tiene usted …? _teeyeneh oosteth_ |
| I'd like to buy … | Quisiera comprar … _keeseeyera komprar_ |
| Could you show me …? | ¿Podría mostrarme …? _podreeya mostrarmeh_ |
| How much is this/that? | ¿Cuánto cuesta esto/eso? _kwanto kwesta esto/eso_ |

### YOU MAY SEE

| HORAS DE ATENCIÓN | business hours |
| CERRADO AL MEDIODÍA | closed for lunch |
| ABIERTO TODO EL DÍA | open all day |
| SALIDA | exit |
| SALIDA DE EMERGENCIA/ INCENDIOS | emergency/fire exit |
| ENTRADA | entrance |
| ESCALERA ELÉCTRICA | escalator |
| ASCENSOR | elevator [lift] |
| ESCALERAS | stairs |

## ESSENTIAL

| | |
|---|---|
| **Buenos días/Buenas tardes señora/señor.** | Good morning/afternoon, madam/sir. |
| **¿Ya lo/la atendieron?** | Are you being served? |
| **¿Qué desea?** | What would you like? |
| **Voy a revisar [averiguar].** | I'll just check that for you. |
| **¿Eso es todo?** | Is that everything? |
| **¿Algo más?** | Anything else? |

### Preferences

| | |
|---|---|
| I want something … | **Quiero algo …** keeyero algo |
| It must be … | **Tiene que ser …** teeyeneh keh sehr |
| big/small | **grande/pequeño(-a)** grandeh/pekeño(-a) |
| cheap/expensive | **barato(-a)/caro(-a)** barato(-a)/karo(-a) |
| dark/light | **oscuro(-a)/claro(-a)** oskooro(-a)/klaro(-a) |
| light/heavy | **liviano(-a)/pesado(-a)** leebeeyano(-a)/pesado(-a) |
| oval/round/square | **ovalado(-a)/redondo(-a)/cuadrado(-a)** obalado(-a)/redondo(-a)/kwadrado(-a) |
| genuine/imitation | **original [un ejemplar auténtico]/imitación** oreekheenal [oon ekhemplar aootenteeko]/eemeetaseeyon |
| I don't want anything too expensive. | **No quiero nada demasiado caro.** no keeyero nada demaseeyado karo |
| Around … pesos. | **Alrededor … pesos.** alrededor … pesos |
| Do you have anything …? | **¿Tiene algo …?** teeyeneh algo |
| larger | **más grande** mas grandeh |
| better quality | **de mejor calidad** deh mekhor kaleedath |
| cheaper | **más barato** mas barato |

### YOU MAY SEE

| | |
|---|---|
| **INFORMACIÓN AL CLIENTE** | customer service |
| **REBAJA** | clearance [sale] |

| smaller | **más pequeño** *mas pekeño* |
| Can you show me …? | **¿Podría mostrarme …?** |
| | *podreeya mostrarmeh* |
| this/that | **éste(-a)/ése(-a)** *este(-a)/ese(-a)* |
| these/those | **éstos(-as)/ésos(-as)** *estos(-as)/esos(-as)* |

## Conditions of purchase

| Is there a guarantee? | **¿Tiene garantía?** *teeyeneh garanteeya* |
| Are there any instructions with it? | **¿Trae las instrucciones?** *trayeh las eenstrookseeyones* |

## Out of stock

| Can you order it for me? | **¿Podría encargármelo?** |
| | *podreeya encargarmelo* |
| How long will it take? | **¿Cuánto tiempo demorará?** |
| | *kwanto teeyempo demorara* |

### YOU MAY HEAR

| **Disculpe, no nos quedan más.** | I'm sorry, we don't have any. |
| **Se nos han agotado.** | We're out of stock. |
| **¿Desea que le muestre algo diferente?** | Can I show you something else? |
| **¿Desea que se lo encarguemos?** | Shall we order it for you? |

## Decisions

| That's not quite what I want. | **Eso no es exactamente lo que quiero.** |
| | *eso no es eksaktamenteh lo keh keeyero* |
| No, I don't like it. | **No, no me gusta.** *no no meh goosta* |
| That's too expensive. | **Es demasiado caro(-a).** |
| | *es demaseeyado karo(-a)* |
| I'll take it. | **Me lo/la llevo.** *meh lo/la l-yebo* |

### IN A STORE

**¿Quiere comprarlo?** *keeyere komprarloh (Would you like to buy this?)*

**Quiero pensarlo. Gracias.** *keeyero pensarlmeoh gratseeyas (I'd like to think about it. Thanks.)*

134

## PAYING

Small businesses may not accept credit cards; however, large stores, restaurants and hotels accept major credit cards and traveler's checks – look for the signs on the door.

| | |
|---|---|
| Where do I pay? | **¿Dónde se paga?** _dondeh seh_ _paga_ |
| How much is that? | **¿Cuánto cuesta eso?** _kwanto_ _kwesta_ eso |
| Could you write it down, please? | **¿Podría escribírmelo, por favor?** podreeya eskreebeermelo por fabor |
| Do you accept traveler's checks [cheques]? | **¿Aceptan cheques de viajero?** aseptan chekes deh beeyakhero |
| I'll pay … | **Voy a pagar …** boy a pagar |
| by cash | **en efectivo** en efekteebo |
| by credit card | **con tarjeta de crédito** kon tarkheta deh kredeeto |
| I don't have any smaller change. | **No tengo cambio [suelto].** no tengo kambeeyo [swelto] |
| Sorry, I don't have enough money. | **Disculpe, no tengo suficiente dinero.** deeskoolpeh no tengo soofeeseeyenteh deenero |
| Could I have a receipt, please? | **¿Me podría dar un recibo, por favor?** meh podreeya dar oon reseebo por fabor |

### YOU MAY SEE

| | |
|---|---|
| **PAGUE AQUÍ, POR FAVOR.** | Please pay here. |
| **SE DETENDRÁ A QUIEN SE SORPRENDA ROBANDO.** | Shoplifters will be prosecuted. |

### YOU MAY HEAR

| | |
|---|---|
| **¿Cómo desea pagar?** | How are you paying? |
| **Esta transacción no ha sido autorizada.** | This transaction has not been approved/accepted. |
| **Esta tarjeta no es válida [no tiene validez].** | This card is not valid. |
| **¿Tiene otro documento de identificación?** | May I have additional identification? |
| **¿Tiene cambio [suelto]?** | Have you got any smaller change? |

## Complaints

| | |
|---|---|
| This doesn't work. | **Esto está defectuoso.** _esto esta defektoooso_ |
| Can you exchange this, please? | **¿Puede cambiarme esto, por favor?** _pwedeh kambeeyarmeh esto por fabor_ |
| I'd like a refund. | **Quisiera que me devolvieran el dinero.** _keeseeyera keh meh debolbeeyeran el deenero_ |
| Here's the receipt. | **Aquí está el recibo.** _akee esta el reseebo_ |
| I don't have the receipt. | **No tengo el recibo.** _no tengo el reseebo_ |
| I'd like to see the manager. | **Quisiera hablar con el gerente.** _keeseeyera ablar kon el kherenteh_ |

## Repairs/Cleaning

| | |
|---|---|
| This is broken. Can you repair it? | **Esto está roto. ¿Puede arreglarlo?** _esto esta roto. pwedeh arreglarlo_ |
| Do you have … for this? | **¿Tiene … para esto?** _teeyeneh … para esto_ |
| a battery | **una pila** _oona peela_ |
| replacement parts | **repuestos** _repwestos_ |
| There's something wrong with … | **Algo anda mal con …** _algo anda mal kon_ |
| Can you … this? | **¿Puede … esto?** _pwedeh … esto_ |
| clean | **lavar** _labar_ |
| press | **planchar** _planchar_ |
| mend | **remendar** _remendar_ |
| alter | **arreglar** _arreglar_ |
| When will it/they be ready? | **¿Cuándo estará(n) listo(s)/-a(s)?** _kwando estara(n) leesto(s)/-a(s)_ |
| There's … missing. | **Falta …** _falta_ |

## YOU MAY SEE

| | |
|---|---|
| **EMPUJE/HALE/OPRIMA** | push/pull/press |
| **CAJEROS** | cashiers |
| **TODO TIPO DE TRANSACCIONES** | all transactions |
| **CAJERO AUTOMÁTICO** | (ATM) [cash machine] |

## BANK/CURRENCY EXCHANGE

Currency exchange offices (**oficina/casa de cambio**) can be found in most tourist centers; they generally offer better exchange rates than hotels and banks.

Remember your passport when you want to change money. Money can be obtained from **Bancomer** and **Banamex** ATMs [cash machines] in most Mexican towns with major credit cards and cash cards.

| | |
|---|---|
| Where's the nearest …? | **¿Dónde está … más cercano(-a)?** *dondeh esta … mas serkano(-a)* |
| bank | **el banco** *el banko* |
| currency exchange office [bureau de change] | **la oficina de cambio** *la ofeeseena de kambeeo* |

### Changing money

| | |
|---|---|
| Can I exchange foreign currency here? | **¿Puedo cambiar moneda extranjera aquí?** *pwedo kambeeyar moneda ekstrankhera akee* |
| I'd like to change some dollars/pounds into pesos. | **Quisiera cambiar unos dólares/libras esterlinas por pesos.** *keeseeyera kambeeyar oonos dolares/leebras esterleenas por pesos* |
| I want to cash some traveler's checks [cheques]. | **Quisiera cambiar unos cheques de viajero.** *keeseeyera kambeeyar oonos chekes deh beeakhero* |
| What's the exchange rate? | **¿Cuál es la tasa de cambio?** *kwal es la tasa de kambeeo* |
| How much commission do you charge? | **¿Cuál es la comisión?** *kwal es la komeeseeyon* |
| I've lost my traveler's checks. These are the numbers. | **Se me perdieron mis cheques de viajero. Éstos son los números.** *seh meh perdeeyeron mees chekes de beeakhero. estos son los noomeros* |
| Could I have some smaller change? | **¿Podría darme cambio [suelto]?** *podreeya darmeh kambeeo [swelto]* |
| Could I have large bills? | **¿Podría darme billetes de alta denominación?** *podreeya darmeh beel-yetes de alta denomeenasion* |

## SECURITY
### Cash machines/ATMs

| YOU MAY HEAR | |
|---|---|
| **¿Me permite …?** | Could I see …? |
| **su pasaporte** | your passport |
| **un documento de identificación** | some identification |
| **su tarjeta del banco** | your bank card |
| **¿Cuál es su dirección?** | What's your address? |
| **¿Dónde se hospeda?** | Where are you staying? |
| **Llene este formulario, por favor.** | Fill out this form, please. |
| **Firme aquí, por favor.** | Please sign here. |

Can I withdraw money on my credit card here? **¿Puedo retirar dinero con mi tarjeta de crédito aquí?** *pwedo reteerar deenero kon mee tarkheta deh kredeeto akee*

Where are the ATMs [cash machines]? **¿Dónde están los cajeros automáticos?** *dondeh estan los kakheros aootomateekos*

Can I use my … card in the ATM? **¿Puedo utilizar mi tarjeta… en este cajero automático?** *pwedo ooteeleesar mee tarkheta … en esteh kakhero aootomateeko*

The ATM [cash machine] has eaten my card. **El cajero automático se ha quedado con mi tarjeta.** *el kakhero aootomateeko seh a kedado kon mee tarkheta*

| Various Currencies | |
|---|---|
| **Argentina** | *Coins:* 1, 5, 10, 25, 50 ct. |
| | *Notes:* 1, 2, 5, 10, 50, 100 pesos |
| **Chile** | *Coins:* 1, 5, 10, 50, 100 pesos (Ch$) |
| | *Notes:* 500, 1000, 5000, 10,000 pesos (Ch$) |
| **Colombia** | *Coins:* 10, 20, 50, 100, 200, 500 pesos |
| | *Notes:* 500, 1000, 5000, 10,000 pesos |
| **Mexico** | *Coins:* 5, 10, 20, 50 ct.; 1, 2, 5, 10, 50 pesos |
| | *Notes:* 10, 20, 50, 100, 200, 500 pesos |
| **Venezuela** | *Coins:* 1, 2, 5 bolívares |
| | *Notes:* 5, 10, 20, 50, 100, 500, 1000 |

## PHARMACY

Some pharmacies in major cities are open 24 hours; others offer a home delivery service. For their address and phone number, consult your hotel reception or call the information line (e.g. 04 in Mexico City). Most pharmacies are easily recognized by their green cross and **farmacia** sign.

| | |
|---|---|
| Where's the nearest (all-night) pharmacy? | **¿Dónde está la farmacia [droguería] de veinticuatro horas más cercana?** *dondeh esta la farmaseea [drogereeya] deh beynteekwatro oras mas serkana* |
| What time does the pharmacy open/close? | **¿A qué hora abren/cierran la farmacia [droguería]?** *a keh ora abren/seeyeran la farmaseea [drogereeya]* |
| Can you make up this prescription for me? | **¿Podría prepararme esta receta [fórmula]?** *podreeya prepararmeh esta reseta [formoola]* |
| Shall I wait? | **¿Debo esperar?** *debo esperar* |
| I'll come back for it. | **Pasaré más tarde a recogerla.** *pasareh mas tardeh a rekokherla* |

### Dosage instructions

| | |
|---|---|
| How much should I take? | **¿Cuánto debo tomar?** *kwanto debo tomar* |
| How often should I take it? | **¿Cuántas veces al día debo tomarlo(-a)?** *kwantas beses al deeya debo tomarlo(-a)* |
| Is it suitable for children? | **¿Es apropiado(-a) [recomendable] para niños?** *es apropeeyado(-a) [rekomendableh] para neeños* |

---

### YOU MAY SEE

| | |
|---|---|
| **Tome ...** | Take ... |
| **... pastillas/cucharaditas** | ... tablets/... teaspoons |
| **antes/después de cada comida** | before/after meals |
| **con agua** | with water |
| **enteras** | whole |
| **por la mañana/por la noche** | in the morning/at night |
| **durante ... días** | for ... days |

## Asking advice

| | |
|---|---|
| What would you recommend for a(n) …? | **¿Qué me recomienda para …?** *keh meh rekomeeyenda para* |
| cold | **el resfriado** *el resfreeyado* |
| cough | **la tos** *la tos* |
| diarrhea | **la diarrea** *la deearreya* |
| hangover | **la cruda [la resaca/el guayabo]** *la krooda [la resaka/el gwayabo]* |
| hayfever | **la fiebre del heno** *la feeyebreh del eno* |
| insect bites | **las mordeduras de insectos** *las mordedooras deh insektos* |
| sore throat | **el dolor de garganta** *el dolor deh garganta* |
| sunstroke | **la insolación** *la eensolaseeyon* |
| motion [travel] sickness | **el mareo** *el mareo* |
| upset stomach | **el trastorno [malestar] estomacal** *el trastorno [malestar] estomakal* |
| Can I get it without a prescription? | **¿Puedo conseguirlo sin receta [fórmula] médica?** *pwedo konsegeerlo seen reseta [formoola] medeeka* |
| Can I have a(n)/some …? | **¿Puede darme …?** *pwedeh darmeh* |
| antiseptic cream | **una crema antiséptica** *oona krema anteesepteeka* |
| aspirin | **unas aspirinas** *oonas aspeereenas* |
| gauze [bandages] | **una venda** *oona benda* |
| condoms | **unos condones** *oonos kondones* |
| cotton [cotton wool] | **un paquete de algodón** *oon paketeh deh algodon* |
| insect repellent | **un repelente contra insectos** *oon repelenteh kontra eensektos* |
| painkillers | **unos analgésicos** *oonos analkheseekos* |
| vitamins | **unas vitaminas** *oonas beetameenas* |

## YOU MAY SEE

| | |
|---|---|
| **SÓLO PARA USO EXTERNO** | for external use only |
| **NO INGERIR** | not to be taken internally |

## Toiletries

| | |
|---|---|
| I'd like some … | **Quisiera …** *keeseeyera* |
| aftershave | **una loción para después de afeitar** *oona loseeyon para despwes deh afeytar* |
| deodorant | **un desodorante** *oon desodoranteh* |
| moisturizing cream | **crema humectante** *krema oomektanteh* |
| razor blades | **unas hojas de afeitar** *oonas okhas deh afeytar* |
| sanitary napkins [towels] | **unas toallas higiénicas** *oonas toal-yas eekheeyeneekas* |
| soap | **un jabón** *oon khabon* |
| sun block | **bloqueador solar** *blokeador solar* |
| suntan cream/lotion | **crema bronceadora/loción** *krema bronseadora/loseeyon* |
| tampons | **unos tampones** *oonos tampones* |
| tissues | **unos kleenex ®** *oonos kleeneks* |
| toilet paper | **un rollo de papel higiénico** *oon rol-yo deh papel eekheeyeneeko* |
| toothpaste | **una pasta [crema] de dientes** *oona pasta [krema] deh deeyentes* |

## Haircare

| | |
|---|---|
| comb | **el peine [la peinilla]** *el peyneh [la peyneel-ya]* |
| conditioner | **el acondicionador** *el akondeeseeonador* |
| hair mousse | **la espuma moldeadora para el cabello** *la espooma moldeadora para el kabel-yo* |
| hair spray | **la laca** *la laka* |
| shampoo | **el champú** *el champoo* |

## For the baby

| | |
|---|---|
| baby food | **comida para bebés** *komeeda para bebes* |
| baby wipes | **pañuelos húmedos para bebé** *pañwelos oomedos para bebeh* |
| diapers [nappies] | **los pañales** *los pañales* |
| sterilizing solution | **la solución esterilizante** *la solooseeyon estereeleesanteh* |

## CLOTHING

You'll find that airport boutiques offering tax-free shopping may have cheaper prices but less selection.

### General

| | |
|---|---|
| I'd like … | **Quisiera …** *keeseeyera* |
| Do you have any …? | **¿Tiene usted …?** *teeyeneh oosteth* |

| YOU MAY SEE | |
|---|---|
| **ROPA PARA DAMAS** | ladieswear |
| **ROPA PARA CABALLERO** | menswear |
| **ROPA PARA NIÑOS** | childrenswear |

### Color

| | |
|---|---|
| I'm looking for something in … | **Estoy buscando algo en …** *estoy booskando algo en* |
| beige | **beige** *beyeech* |
| black | **negro** *negro* |
| blue | **azul** *asool* |
| brown | **café** *kafeh* |
| green | **verde** *berdeh* |
| gray | **gris** *grees* |
| orange | **naranja [anaranjado]** *narankha [anarankhado]* |
| pink | **rosado** *rosado* |
| purple | **morado** *morado* |
| red | **rojo** *rokho* |
| white | **blanco** *blanko* |
| yellow | **amarillo** *amareel-yo* |
| light … | **claro …** *klaro* |
| dark … | **oscuro …** *oskooro* |
| I want a lighter shade. | **Quiero un matiz más claro.** *keeyero oon matees mas klaro* |
| Do you have the same in …? | **¿Lo tiene también en …?** *lo teeyeneh tambeeyen en* |

## Clothes and accessories

| | | |
|---|---|---|
| belt | **el cinturón** | *el seentooron* |
| blouse | **la blusa** | *la bloosa* |
| briefs *(man's/woman's)* | **los calzoncillos/las pantaletas** | |
| | *los kalsonseel-yos/las pantaletas* | |
| cap | **la gorra** | *la gorra* |
| coat | **el abrigo** | *el abreego* |
| dress | **el vestido** | *el besteedo* |
| handbag | **el bolso** | *el bolso* |
| hat | **el sombrero** | *el sombrero* |
| jacket | **la chaqueta** | *la chaketa* |
| leggings | **las leggings** | *las legeen* |
| pantyhose [tights] | **las pantimedias** | *las panteemedeeas* |
| raincoat | **el impermeable** | *el eempermeeyableh* |
| scarf | **la bufanda** | *la boofanda* |
| shirt | **la camisa** | *la kameesa* |
| shorts | **los shorts** | *los chors* |
| skirt | **la falda** | *la falda* |
| socks | **los calcetines** | *los kalseteenes* |
| stockings | **las medias** | *las medeeas* |
| suit *(man's/woman's)* | **el traje/el traje de sastre** | |
| | *el trakheh /el trakheh deh sastreh* | |
| sweater | **el suéter** | *el sweter* |
| sweatshirt | **la sudadera** | *la soodadera* |
| swimming trunks | **el pantalón de baño** | *el pantalon deh baño* |
| swimsuit | **el traje [vestido] de baño** | |
| | *el trakhe [besteedo] deh baño* | |
| T-shirt | **la camiseta** | *la kameeseta* |
| tie | **la corbata** | *la korbata* |
| trousers/pants | **los pantalones** | *los pantalones* |
| underpants | **los calzoncillos** | *los kalsonseel-yos* |
| with long/short sleeves | **de mangas largas/cortas** | |
| | *deh mangas largas/kortas* | |

### Shoes

| | |
|---|---|
| a pair of ... | **un par de ...** *oon par deh* |
| boots | **botas** *botas* |
| flip-flops | **chancletas** *chankletas* |
| running [training] shoes | **tenis** *tenees* |
| sandals | **sandalias** *sandaleeas* |
| shoes | **zapatos** *sapatos* |
| slippers | **pantuflas** *pantooflas* |

### Walking/Hiking gear

| | |
|---|---|
| knapsack | **mochila** *mocheela* |
| walking boots | **botas de montañismo** *botas deh montañeesmo* |
| waterproof jacket [anorak] | **chaqueta impermeable** *chakehta eempermeyableh* |
| windbreaker [cagoule] | **anorak impermeable** *anorak eempermeyableh* |

### Fabric

| | |
|---|---|
| I want something in ... | **Quiero algo de ...** *keeyero algo deh* |
| cotton | **algodón** *algodon* |
| denim | **tela vaquera** *tela bakera* |
| lace | **encaje** *enkakheh* |
| leather | **cuero** *kwero* |
| linen | **lino** *leeno* |
| wool | **lana** *lana* |
| Is this ...? | **¿Esto es ...?** *esto es* |
| pure cotton | **algodón puro** *algodon pooro* |
| synthetic | **sintético** *seenteteeko* |

## YOU MAY SEE

| | |
|---|---|
| **NO DESTEÑIBLE** | colorfast |
| **NO PLANCHAR** | do not iron |
| **LAVADO EN SECO SOLAMENTE** | dry clean only |
| **LAVADO A MANO SOLAMENTE** | handwash only |

## Does it fit?

| | |
|---|---|
| Can I try this on? | **¿Me lo puedo probar?** me lo _pwedo_ _probahr_ |
| Where's the fitting room? | **¿Dónde está el probador [vestier]?** _dondeh esta_ el _proba_dor [besteeyer] |
| It fits well. I'll take it. | **Me queda bien. Me lo llevo.** meh _keda beeyen._ meh lo _l-yebo_ |
| It doesn't fit. | **No me queda bien.** no meh _keda beeyen_ |
| It's too … | **Es demasiado …** es demasee_yado_ |
| short/long | **corto(-a)/largo(-a)** _korto_(-a)/_largo_(-a) |
| tight/loose | **ajustado(-a)/ suelto(-a)** akhoos_tado_(-a)/_swelto_(-a) |
| Do you have this in size …? | **¿Tiene este(-a) mismo(-a) en talla …?** teeyeneh esteh(-a) _mees_mo(-a) en _tal_-ya |
| What size is this? | **¿Qué talla es ésta?** keh _tal_-ya es _esta_ |
| Could you measure me, please? | **¿Podría tomarme las medidas, por favor?** podreeya tomarmeh las me_deedas_ por fa_bor_ |
| What size do you take? | **¿Cuál es su talla?** kwal es soo _tal_-ya |

## Size

| | Dresses/Suits | | | | | | Women's shoes | | | |
|---|---|---|---|---|---|---|---|---|---|---|
| **American** } | 8 | 10 | 12 | 14 | 16 | 18 | 6 | 7 | 8 | 9 |
| **British** | 10 | 12 | 14 | 16 | 18 | 20 | 4½ | 5½ | 6½ | 7½ |
| **Continental** | 36 | 38 | 40 | 42 | 44 | 46 | 37 | 38 | 39 | 40 |

| | Shirts | | | | Men's shoes | | | | | | | |
|---|---|---|---|---|---|---|---|---|---|---|---|---|
| **American** } | 15 | 16 | 17 | 18 | 6 | 7 | 8 | 8½ | 9 | 9½ | 10 | 11 |
| **British** | | | | | | | | | | | | |
| **Continental** | 38 | 41 | 43 | 45 | 38 | 39 | 41 | 42 | 43 | 43 | 44 | 44 |

| YOU MAY SEE | |
|---|---|
| **EXTRA GRANDE** | extra large (XL) |
| **GRANDE** | large (L) |
| **MEDIANO** | medium (M) |
| **PEQUEÑO** | small (S) |

## HEALTH AND BEAUTY

| | |
|---|---|
| I'd like a … | **Quisiera …** *keeseeyera* |
| facial | **un tratamiento facial** *oon tratameeyento faseeyal* |
| manicure | **una manicure** *oona maneekooreh* |
| massage | **un masaje** *oon masakheh* |
| waxing | **una depilación con cera** *oona depeelaseeyon kon sera* |

### Hairdresser

Tipping: the hairdresser usually receives 10–15% in Mexico; 10% is normal in Argentina, Chile and Colombia; 5–10% in Venezuela.

| | |
|---|---|
| I'd like to make an appointment for … | **Quisiera hacer una cita para …** *keeseeyera aser oona seeta para* |
| Can you make it a bit earlier/later? | **¿Podría dármela un poco más temprano/tarde?** *podreeya darmela oon poko mas temprano/tardeh* |
| I'd like a … | **Quisiera …** *keeseeyera* |
| cut and blow-dry | **un corte y secado** *oon korteh ee sekado* |
| shampoo and set | **un champú y fijador** *oon champoo ee feekhador* |
| I'd like my hair … | **Quisiera que me … el pelo** *keeseeyera keh meh … el pelo* |
| colored/tinted | **tinture/tiña** *teentooreh/teeña* |
| highlighted/permed | **haga unos rayitos/una permanente** *aga oonos rayeetos/oona permanenteh* |
| Don't cut it too short. | **No lo quiero demasiado corto.** *no lo keeyero demaseeyado korto* |
| back/front | **atrás/al frente** *atras/al frenteh* |
| neck/sides | **en el cuello/a los lados** *en el kwel-yo/a los lados* |
| top | **en la coronilla** *en la koroneel-ya* |
| That's fine, thanks. | **Así está bien, gracias.** *asee esta beeyen graseeas* |

146

## HOUSEHOLD ARTICLES

| | |
|---|---|
| I'd like a(n) … | **Quisiera …** *keeseeyera* |
| alumin[i]um foil | **un rollo de papel aluminio** |
| | *oon rol-yo deh papel aloomeeneeo* |
| battery | **una pila** *oona peela* |
| bottle opener | **un destapador** *oon destapador* |
| can [tin] opener | **un abrelatas** *oon abrelatas* |
| candles | **unas velas** *oonas belas* |
| clothes pins [pegs] | **unos ganchos para colgar la ropa** |
| | *oonos ganchos para kolgar la ropa* |
| corkscrew | **un descorchador** *oon deskorchador* |
| lightbulb | **un foco [un bombillo]** |
| | *oon foko [oon bombeel-yo]* |
| napkins | **unas servilletas** *oonas serbeel-yetas* |
| plastic wrap [cling film] | **un rollo de plástico para envolver** |
| | *oon rol-yo deh plasteeko para enbolber* |

### Cleaning items

| | |
|---|---|
| bleach | **el blanqueador** *el blankeador* |
| dish cloth | **el paño [limpión]** *el paño [leempeeyon]* |
| dishwashing [washing-up] liquid | **el detergente para los platos** |
| | *el deterkhenteh para los platos* |
| garbage [refuse] bags | **bolsas para la basura** |
| | *bolsas para la basoora* |
| laundry soap [washing powder] | **el jabón para lavadora** |
| | *el khabon para labadora* |

### Dishes/Utensils [Crockery/Cutlery]

| | |
|---|---|
| cups | **las tazas [pocillos]** *las tasas [poseel-yos]* |
| forks/knives | **los tenedores/los cuchillos** |
| | *los tenedores/os koocheel-yos* |
| glasses/mugs | **los vasos/las tazas** *los basos/las tasas* |
| plates | **los platos** *los platos* |
| spoons/teaspoons | **las cucharas/las cucharitas** |
| | *las koocharas/as koochareetas* |

## JEWELER

| | |
|---|---|
| Could I see …? | **¿Puedo ver …?** _pwedo behr_ |
| this/that | **esto/eso** _esto/eso_ |
| It's in the window/ display cabinet. | **Está en la vitrina [el aparador]/ el escaparate.** _esta en la beetreena [el aparador]/el eskaparateh_ |
| I'd like a(n) … | **Quisiera …** _keeseeyera_ |
| bracelet/chain | **una pulsera/una cadena** _oona poolsera/oona kadena_ |
| brooch | **un prendedor** _oon prendedor_ |
| earrings | **unos aretes** _oonos aretes_ |
| necklace | **un collar** _oon kol-yar_ |
| ring | **un anillo** _oon aneel-yo_ |
| watch | **un reloj de pulsera** _oon relokh deh poolsera_ |

## Materials

| | |
|---|---|
| Is this real silver/gold? | **¿Es plata verdadera/oro verdadero?** _es plata berdadera/oro berdadero_ |
| Is there any certification for it? | **¿Tiene algún documento que lo certifique?** _teeyeneh algoon dokoomento keh lo serteefeekeh_ |
| Do you have anything in …? | **¿Tiene algo de …?** _teeyeneh algo deh_ |
| copper | **cobre** _kobreh_ |
| crystal/cut glass | **cristal/cristal tallado** _kreestal/kreestal tal-yado_ |
| diamond | **diamante** _deeamanteh_ |
| enamel | **esmalte** _esmalteh_ |
| gold/gold plate | **oro/chapado en oro** _oro/chapado en oro_ |
| pearl | **perla** _perla_ |
| pewter | **peltre** _peltreh_ |
| platinum | **platino** _plateeno_ |
| silver plate | **plata/chapado en plata** _plata/chapado en plata_ |
| stainless steel | **acero inoxidable** _asero eenokseedableh_ |

## NEWSSTAND [NEWSAGENT]/TOBACCONIST

Foreign newspapers can usually be found at rail stations or airports, or on newsstands in major cities.

| | |
|---|---|
| Do you sell English-language books/newspapers? | **¿Vende usted libros/periódicos en inglés?** _bendeh oosteth leebros/pereeyodeekos en eengles_ |
| I'd like a(n)/some … | **Quisiera …** _keeseeyera_ |
| book | **un libro** _oon leebro_ |
| candy [sweets] | **un dulce** _oon doolseh_ |
| chewing gum | **un chicle** _oon chikleh_ |
| chocolate bar | **un chocolate [una chocolatina]** _oon chokolateh [oona chokolateena]_ |
| cigarettes (pack of)/cigars | **una cajetilla de cigarrillos/unos cigarros [unos puros]** _oona kakheteel-ya deh seegarreel-yos/oonos seegarros [oonos pooros]_ |
| dictionary | **un diccionario** _oon deekseeonareeo_ |
| English-Spanish | **Inglés-Español** _eengles-español_ |
| envelopes | **unos sobres** _oonos sobres_ |
| guidebook for … | **una guía de …** _oona geeya deh_ |
| lighter | **un encendedor** _oon ensendedor_ |
| magazine | **una revista** _oona rebeesta_ |
| map of the town | **un mapa de la ciudad/del pueblo** _oon mapa deh la seeoodath/del pweblo_ |
| matches | **unos fósforos** _oonos fosforos_ |
| newspaper | **un periódico** _oon pereeyodeeko_ |
| American/English | **estadounidense [de Estados Unidos]/ de Inglaterra** _estado-ooneedenseh [deh los estados ooneedos]/deh eenglaterra_ |
| paper/pen | **una hoja de papel/una pluma [un bolígrafo]** _oona okha de papel/oona plooma [oon boleegrafo]_ |
| postcard | **una postal** _oona postal_ |
| road map of … | **un mapa de carreteras** _oon mapa deh karreteras_ |
| stamps | **unas estampillas** _oonas estampeel-yas_ |

## PHOTOGRAPHY

| | |
|---|---|
| I'm looking for a(n) … camera. | **Estoy buscando una cámara …** *estoy booskando oona kamara* |
| automatic | **automática** *aootomateeka* |
| compact | **compacta** *kompakta* |
| disposable | **desechable** *desechableh* |
| SLR (single lens reflex) | **de reflejo sencillo** *deh reflekho senseel-yo* |
| I'd like a(n) … | **Quisiera …** *keeseeyera* |
| battery | **la pila** *la peela* |
| camera case | **el estuche [la funda] de la cámara** *el estoocheh [la foonda] deh la kamara* |
| electronic flash | **el flash** *el flach* |
| filter | **el filtro** *el feeltro* |
| lens | **el objetivo** *el obkheteebo* |
| lens cap | **la tapa del objetivo** *la tapa del obkheteebo* |

## Film/Processing

| | |
|---|---|
| I'd like a … film. | **Quisiera un rollo …** *keeseeyera oon rol-yo* |
| black and white | **en blanco y negro** *en blanko ee negro* |
| color | **a color** *a kolor* |
| 24/36 exposures | **de 24/36 revelaciones** *deh beyntee-kwatro/ treynta ee seys rebelaseeyones* |
| I'd like this film developed, please. | **Quisiera que me revelara este rollo, por favor.** *keeseeyera keh meh rebelara esteh rol-yo por fabor* |
| Would you enlarge this, please? | **¿Podría ampliarme esta fotografía, por favor?** *podreeya ampleeyarmeh esta fotografeeya por fabor* |
| How much do … exposures cost? | **¿Cuánto cuesta el revelado de …?** *kwanto kwesta el rebelado deh* |
| When will the photos be ready? | **¿Cuándo estarán listas las fotografías?** *kwando estaran leestas las fotografeeyas* |
| I'd like to pick up my photos. Here's the receipt. | **Vengo a reclamar mis fotografías. Aquí está el recibo.** *bengo a reklamar mees fotografeeyas. akee esta el reseebo* |

## POLICE

Beware of pickpockets, particularly in crowded places. Report all thefts to the local police within 24 hours for your own insurance purposes. In Mexico, a 24-hour hotline is run by **SECTUR**, to help tourists in emergencies (5) 250-01-23/51 in Mexico City, 800-9-03-92 outside.

| | |
|---|---|
| Where's the nearest police station? | **¿Dónde está la estación de policía más cercana?** _dondeh esta la estaseeyon deh poleeseeya mas serkana_ |
| Does anyone here speak English? | **¿Hay alguien aquí que hable inglés?** _eye algeeyen akee keh ableh eengles_ |
| I want to report a(n) … | **Quiero denunciar …** _keeyero dehnoonseeyahr_ |
| accident | **un accidente** _oon akseedenteh_ |
| mugging/rape | **un asalto/una violación** _oon asalto/oona beeolaseeyon_ |
| My child is missing. | **Mi hijo(-a) ha desaparecido.** _mee eekho(-a) a desapareseedo_ |
| I need an English-speaking lawyer. | **Necesito un abogado que hable inglés.** _neseseeto oon abogado keh ableh eengles_ |
| I need to make a phone call. | **Necesito hacer una llamada telefónica.** _neseseeto aser oona l-yamada telefoneeka_ |
| I need to contact the Consulate. | **Necesito comunicarme con el consulado.** _neseseeto komooneekarmeh kon el konsoolado_ |
| American/British | **norteamericano/británico** _norteamereekano/breetaneeko_ |

### YOU MAY HEAR

| | |
|---|---|
| **¿Puede describirlo(-la)?** | Can you describe him/her? |
| **hombre/mujer** | male/female |
| **rubio(-a)/moreno(-a)** | blond(e)/brunette |
| **pelirrojo(-a)/de cabello gris** | red-headed/gray-haired |
| **de cabello largo/corto** | long/short hair |
| **calvo(a)** | balding |
| **estatura aproximada …** | approximate height … |
| **edad aproximada …** | aged (approximately) … |
| **Vestía [Llevaba puesto(-a)] …** | He/She was wearing … |

## LOST PROPERTY/THEFT

| | |
|---|---|
| I want to report a theft/break-in. | **Quiero denunciar sobre un robo/asalto.** *keeyero dehnoonseeyahr sobre oon robo/asalto* |
| I've been robbed/mugged. | **Me han robado/atracado.** *meh an robado/atrakado* |
| I've lost my … | **Se me perdió/perdieron …** *seh meh perdeeyo/perdeeyeron* |
| My … has been stolen. | **Me robaron …** *meh robaron* |
| camera | **mi cámara** *mee kamara* |
| (rental) car | **el carro (que había alquilado)** *el karro (keh abeeya alkeelado)* |
| credit cards | **mis tarjetas de crédito** *mees tarkhetas deh kredeeto* |
| handbag | **mi bolso** *mee bolso* |
| money | **mi dinero** *mee deenero* |
| passport/ticket | **mi pasaporte/mi boleto [tiquete]** *mee pasaporteh/mee boleto [teeketeh]* |
| purse/wallet | **mi monedero/mi billetera** *mee monedero/mee beel-yetera* |
| I need a police report for my insurance claim. | **Necesito un informe de la policía para la demanda de seguro.** *neseseeto oon informeh deh la poleeseeya para la demanda deh segooro* |

### YOU MAY HEAR

| | |
|---|---|
| **¿Qué falta?** | What's missing? |
| **¿Cuándo sucedió?** | When did it happen? |
| **¿Dónde se hospeda?** | Where are you staying? |
| **¿De dónde se lo robaron?** | Where was it taken from? |
| **¿Dónde estaba usted en ese momento?** | Where were you at the time? |
| **Vamos a conseguirle un intérprete.** | We're getting an interpreter for you. |
| **Llene esta hoja, por favor.** | Please fill out this form. |

## POST OFFICE

Post offices carry the sign **Correos y Telégrafos**. Main offices are generally open from 8 a.m. to 7 p.m. The main post office in Mexico City is open from 7 a.m. to midnight, Monday through Friday; until 8 p.m. on Saturday; and until 4 p.m. on Sunday. Mailboxes are generally red, marked **Aéreo** for air-mail items, **D.F.** (for Mexico City), **Local** for local mail, or **Terrestre** for surface mail.

Stamps are also sold at newsstands, stationery stores, souvenir stands, and from stamp machines.

### General queries

Where is the nearest post office?

**¿Dónde queda la oficina de correo más cercana?** _dondeh keda la ofeeseena deh korreyo mas serkana_

What time does the post office open/close?

**¿A qué hora abre/cierra el correo?** _a keh ora abre/seeyera el korreyo_

Does it close for lunch?

**¿Cierra el correo al mediodía?** _seeyera el korreyo al medeeodeeya_

Where's the mailbox [postbox]?

**¿Dónde está el buzón?** _dondeh esta el booson_

### Buying stamps

A stamp for this postcard/ letter, please.

**Un sello [estampilla] para esta postal/ carta, por favor.** _oon sel-yo [estampeel-ya] para esta postal/karta por fabor_

A … pesos stamp, please.

**Una estampilla de … pesos, por favor.** _oona estampeel-ya deh … pesos por fabor_

What's the postage for a postcard/letter to …?

**¿Cuál es la tarifa de correo para una postal/carta para …?** _kwal es la tareefa deh korreyo para oona postal/karta para_

### IN A POST OFFICE

**Quiero enviar estas postales.** _keeyero enbeeyar estas postales_ (I'd like to send these postcards.)
**Son quinientos pesos.** _son keeneeyentos pesos_ (That's 500 pesos.)
**Aquí tiene.** _akee teeyeneh_ (Here you are.)

153

### Sending packages

| | |
|---|---|
| I want to send this package [parcel] by … | **Quiero enviar este paquete por …** *keeyero enbeeyar esteh paketeh por* |
| airmail | **correo aéreo** *korreyo ayereo* |
| special delivery [express] | **entrega inmediata** *entrega inmedeeyata* |
| It contains … | **Contiene …** *konteeyeneh* |

---

## YOU MAY HEAR

| | |
|---|---|
| **Por favor, llene la declaración de aduana.** | Please fill out the customs declaration form. |
| **¿Cuál es el valor aproximado del contenido del paquete?** | What's the value of the contents? |

---

### Telecommunications

| | |
|---|---|
| I'd like a phone card. | **Quisiera una tarjeta de teléfono.** *keeseeyera oona tarkheta deh telefono* |
| 50/120 units | **de cincuenta/ciento veinte unidades** *deh seenkwenta/seeyento beynteh ooneedades* |
| I'd like to send a message… | **Quisiera enviar un mensaje …** *keeseeyera enbeeyar oon mensakheh* |
| by e-mail/fax | **por "e-mail"/fax** *por "e-mail"/fax* |
| Can I access the Internet here? | **¿Me puedo conectar con el "Internet" aquí?** *meh pwedo konektar kon el "Internet" akee* |
| What are the charges per hour? | **¿Cuánto se cobra por hora?** *kwanto seh kobra por ora* |
| How do I log on? | **¿Cómo hago la conexión?** *komo ago la konekseeyon* |

---

## YOU MAY SEE

| | |
|---|---|
| **TELEGRAMAS** | telegrams |
| **LISTA DE CORREO** | general delivery [poste restante] |
| **PRÓXIMA RECOLECCIÓN** | next collection |
| **GIRO POSTAL** | money matters |
| **PAQUETES** | parcels |

## SOUVENIRS

Mexico and the rest of Latin America are rich in handicrafts (**artesanías**) of all kinds. Shopping can be a real delight, with something new and exciting around every corner. Ceramics, silverware, papier-mâché articles, textiles, and a host of other handmade or handworked local products all exude a sense of history, tradition, talent, and imagination.

In Mexico, look for embroidered traditional Indian costumes, such as **huipil** (sleeveless tunic), **quechquémitl** (cape), **rebozo** (long shawl); rugs and wall hangings, yarn paintings, embroidered cloths.

Pottery: **animalitos** (small animals), **Talavera**-style plates, bowls, and tiles. Masks and head dresses; gourd drinking vessels, lacquered trays, dolls; musical instruments like the maracas, tambourines, drums. Bark paintings; leatherware including sandals (**huaraches**); silver and gold jewelry; crafted tinplate; religious paintings (**retablo**); hammocks; baskets. **Piñata** (candy-filled papier-mâché stars) for children's parties and festivities.

### Gifts

| | | |
|---|---|---|
| carpets | **tapetes [alfombras]** | *tapetes [alfombras]* |
| copperware | **cobres** *kobres* | |
| embroidery | **bordados** *bordados* | |
| hand-blown glass | **vidrio soplado** *beedreeo soplado* | |
| jewelry | **joyas** *khoyas* | |
| masks | **máscaras** *maskaras* | |
| onyx | **ónix** *oneeks* | |
| painted gourds | **calabazas pintadas** | |
| | *kalabasas peentadas* | |
| papier mâché | **papel maché** *papel macheh* | |
| poncho | **jorongo [poncho]** | |
| | *khorongo [poncho]* | |
| pottery | **cerámica** *serameeka* | |
| saddle | **silla de montar** *seel-ya deh montar* | |
| sandals | **huaraches** *waraches* | |
| shawl *(woman's)* | **rebozo** *reboso* | |
| silver | **plata** *plata* | |
| sun hat | **sombrero** *sombrero* | |

## Music

| | |
|---|---|
| I'd like a … | **Quisiera …** <br> *keeseeyera* |
| cassette | **un cassette** <br> *oon kaset* |
| compact disc | **un compact disc** <br> *oon kompak deesk* |
| record | **un disco** <br> *oon deesko* |
| video cassette | **un video** <br> *oon beedeo* |
| Who are the popular native singers/bands? | **¿Cuáles son los cantantes/las orquestas populares de la región?** *kwales son los kantantes/las orkestas popoolares deh la rekheeyon* |

## Toys and games

| | |
|---|---|
| I'd like a toy/game … | **Quisiera un juguete/juego …** <br> *keeseeyera oon khoogeteh/khwego* |
| for a boy | **para un niño** <br> *para oon neeño* |
| for a girl | **para una niña** <br> *para oona neeña* |
| for a 5-year-old girl | **para una niña de cinco años** <br> *para oona neeña deh seenko años* |
| chess set | **un juego de ajedrez** <br> *oon khwego deh akhedres* |
| doll | **una muñeca** <br> *oona mooñeka* |
| electronic game | **un juego electrónico** <br> *oon khwego elektroneeko* |
| pail and shovel [bucket and spade] | **la cubeta y la palita [el balde y la pala]** <br> *oona koobeta ee la paleeta [el balde ee la pala]* |
| teddy bear | **un oso de peluche** <br> *oon oso deh peloocheh* |

156

### Antiques

It's illegal to take antiques out of Mexico; check before purchasing.

How old is this? **¿Cuántos años tiene esto?**
*kwantos años teeneh esto*

Can you send it to me? **¿Podría enviármelo?** *podreeya enbeeyarmelo*

Will I have problems **¿Tendré problemas con la aduana?**
with customs? *tendreh problemas kon la adwana*

## SUPERMARKET/MINIMART

### At the supermarket

Where can I find ...? **¿Dónde puedo encontrar ...?**
*dondeh pwedo enkontrar*

Do I pay for this here **¿Dónde pago esto, aquí o en la caja?**
or at the checkout? *dondeh pago esto akee o en la kakha*

Where are the carts **¿Dónde están los carritos/las canastas?**
[trolleys]/baskets? *dondeh estan los karreetos/las kanastas*

Is there a ... here? **¿Hay ... aquí?** *eye ... akee*

delicatessen **un delicatessen [una tienda de
especialidades]** *oon deleekatesen
[oona teeyenda deh espeseealeedades]*

pharmacy **una farmacia [una droguería]**
*oona farmaseea [oona drogereeya]*

| YOU MAY SEE | |
|---|---|
| **ALIMENTOS CONGELADOS** | frozen foods |
| **ARTÍCULOS PARA EL HOGAR** | household goods |
| **CARNE FRESCA** | fresh meat |
| **FRUTAS Y VERDURAS ENLATADAS** | canned fruit/vegetables |
| **PAN Y PASTELES [TORTAS]** | bread and cakes |
| **PESCADO FRESCO** | fresh fish |
| **POLLOS** | poultry |
| **PRODUCTOS DE LIMPIEZA** | cleaning products |
| **PRODUCTOS FRESCOS** | fresh produce |
| **PRODUCTOS LÁCTEOS** | dairy products |
| **VINOS Y LICORES** | wines and spirits |

## Food hygiene

### At the minimart

| | |
|---|---|
| I'd like some of that/those. | **Quisiera un poco de eso/unos cuantos.** *keeseeyera oon poko deh eso/oonos kwantos* |
| this one/those | **éste/estos** *esteh/estos* |
| over there/here | **por allá/por aquí** *por al-ya/por akee* |
| That's all, thanks. | **Eso es todo, gracias.** *eso es todo graseeas* |
| I'd like … | **Quisiera …** *keeseeyera* |
| a kilo of apples | **un kilo de manzanas** *oon keelo deh mansanas* |
| half a kilo of tomatoes | **medio kilo de tomates** *medeeo keelo deh tomates* |
| 100 grams of cheese | **cien gramos de queso** *seeyen gramos de keso* |
| a liter of milk | **un litro de leche** *oon leetro deh lecheh* |
| half-dozen eggs | **media docena de huevos** *medeea dosena deh webos* |
| … slices of ham | **… rebanadas de jamón** *… rebanadas deh khamon* |
| a piece of cake | **una rebanada [un pedazo] de pastel [torta]** *oona rebanada [oon pedaso] deh pastel [torta]* |
| a bottle of wine | **una botella de vino** *oona botel-ya de beeno* |

## IN A SUPERMARKET

¿Dónde puedo encontrar azúcar? _dondeh pwedo enkontrar ahzoogahr_ (Where can I find sugar?)
Ahí, a la derecha. _aee ala dehrecha_ (Over there, to the right.)

### Snacks/Picnic

| | |
|---|---|
| butter | **la mantequilla** _la mantekeel-ya_ |
| cheese | **el queso** _el keso_ |
| fries [chips] | **las papas a la francesa/fritas** _las papas a la fransesa/freetas_ |
| cookies [biscuits] | **los galletas** _los ga-yetas_ |
| eggs | **los huevos** _los webos_ |
| grapes | **las uvas** _las oobas_ |
| ice cream | **el helado** _el elado_ |
| instant coffee | **el café instantáneo** _el kafeh instantaneo_ |
| loaf of bread | **el pan de molde** _el pan deh moldeh_ |
| margarine | **la margarina** _la margareena_ |
| milk | **la leche** _la lecheh_ |
| rolls | **los bolillos [panecillos]** _los boleel-yos [paneseel-yos]_ |
| sausages | **las salchichas** _las salcheechas_ |
| six-pack of beer | **el paquete de seis latas de cerveza** _el paketeh deh seys latas de serbesa_ |
| soft drinks | **los refrescos [las gaseosas]** _los refreskos [las gaseosas]_ |
| tea bags | **las bolsas de té** _las bolsas de teh_ |
| wine | **el vino** _el beeno_ |

## CONVERSION CHARTS

The following conversion charts contain the most commonly used measures.

| | | |
|---|---|---|
| **1 Gramo (g)** | = 1000 milligrams | = 0.35 oz. |
| **1 Libra (lb)** | = 500 grams | = 1.1 lb |
| **1 Kilogramo (kg)** | = 1000 grams | = 2.2 lb |
| **1 Litro (l)** | = 1000 milliliters | = 1.06 U.S / 0.88 Brit. quarts |
| | | = 2.11 /1.8 US /Brit. pints |
| | | = 34 /35 US /Brit. fluid oz. |
| | | = 0.26 /0.22 US /Brit. gallons |
| **1 Centímetro (cm)** | = 100 millimeter | = 0.4 inch |
| **1 Metro (m)** | = 100 centimeters | = 39.37 inches/3.28 ft. |
| **1 Kilómetro (km)** | = 1000 meters | = 0.62 mile |
| **1 Metro cuadrado (m²)** | = 10.8 square feet | |
| **1 Hectárea (qm)** | = 2.5 acres | |
| **1 Km cuadrado (km²)** | = 247 acres | |

Not sure whether to put on a bathing suit or a winter coat? Here is a comparison of Fahrenheit and and Celsius/Centigrade degrees.

| | | |
|---|---|---|
| -40°C  –  -40°F | 5° C  –  41°F | **Oven Temperatures** |
| -30°C  –  -22°F | 10°C  –  50°F | 100° C – 212° F |
| -20°C  –  -4°  F | 15°C  –  59°F | 121° C – 250° F |
| -10°C  –  14°  F | 20°C  –  68°F | 154° C – 300° F |
| -5° C  –  23°  F | 25°C  –  77°F | 177° C – 350° F |
| -1°  C  –  30°  F | 30°C  –  86°F | 204° C – 400° F |
| 0°  C  –  32°  F | 35°C  –  95°F | 260° C – 500° F |

| When you know | Multiply by | To find |
|---|---|---|
| ounces | 28.3 | grams |
| pounds | 0.45 | kilograms |
| inches | 2.54 | centimeters |
| feet | 0.3 | meters |
| miles | 1.61 | kilometers |
| square inches | 6.45 | sq. centimeters |
| square feet | 0.09 | sq. meters |
| square miles | 2.59 | sq. kilometers |
| pints (US/Brit) | 0.47 / 0.56 | liters |
| gallons (US/Brit) | 3.8 / 4.5 | liters |
| Fahrenheit | 5/9, after subtracting 32 | Centigrade |
| Centigrade | 9/5, then add 32 | Fahrenheit |

# HEALTH

Before you leave, make sure your health insurance policy covers any illness or accident while on vacation [holiday]. Mexico has no reciprocal health arrangements, so travel insurance is a must. Every Mexican town has a health center (**centro de salud**). Your nearest consulate should have a list of English-speaking doctors.

It is advisable for tourists to drink bottled water only. Be wary of foods served outdoors as hygiene standards are variable. Eat lightly until your stomach has adapted to local food (particularly tropical fruit), and avoid unwashed salads and raw seafood, or you may fall victim to Montezuma's revenge!

In mosquito-infested areas, wear loose-fitting light-colored clothing, and sleep beneath mosquito nets.

## DOCTOR (GENERAL)

| | |
|---|---|
| Where can I find a doctor/ dentist? | **¿Dónde puedo encontrar un doctor/ dentista?** _dondeh pwedo enkontrar oon doktor/denteesta_ |
| Where's there a doctor who speaks English? | **¿Dónde hay un doctor que hable inglés?** _dondeh eye oon doktor keh ableh eengles_ |
| What are the office [surgery] hours? | **¿Cuáles son las horas de consulta?** _kwales son las oras deh konsoolta_ |
| Could the doctor come to see me here? | **¿Podría el doctor venir a examinarme aquí?** _podreeya el doktor beneer a eksameenarmeh akee_ |
| Can I make an appointment for …? | **¿Me puede dar una cita para …?** _meh pwedeh dar oona seeta para_ |
| today/tomorrow | **hoy/mañana** _oy/mañana_ |
| as soon as possible | **cuanto antes** _kwanto antes_ |
| It's urgent. | **Es urgente.** _es oorkhenteh_ |

## Accident and injury

| | |
|---|---|
| My ... is injured. | **Mi ... está herido(-a).** mee ... esta ereedo(-a) |
| husband/wife | **esposo/esposa** esposo/esposa |
| son/daughter/baby | **hijo/hija/bebé** eekho/eekha/bebeh |
| He/She is ... | **Él/Ella está ...** el/el-ya esta |
| unconscious | **inconsciente** eenkonseeyenteh |
| bleeding (heavily) | **sangrando (mucho)** sangrando (moocho) |
| (seriously) injured | **(gravemente) herido(-a)** (grabementeh) ereedo(-a) |
| I've got a(n) ... | **Tengo ...** tengo |
| bruise | **un moretón** oon moreton |
| burn | **una quemadura** oona kemadoora |
| cut | **una cortadura** oona kortadoora |
| graze | **un arañazo** oon arañaso |
| insect bite | **una mordedura de insecto** oona mordedoora deh eensekto |
| rash | **un salpullido** oon salpool-yeedo |
| sprained muscle | **un músculo torcido** oon mooskoolo torseedo |
| swelling | **una inflamación** oona inflamaseeyon |

## Symptoms

| | |
|---|---|
| I've been feeling ill for ... days. | **He estado enfermo(-a) desde hace ... días.** eh estado enfermo(-a) desdeh aseh ... deeyas |
| I feel ... | **Tengo ...** tengo |
| dizzy/faint | **mareo** mareyo |
| feverish | **fiebre** feeyebreh |
| I've been vomiting. | **He estado vomitando.** eh estado bomeetando |
| I have diarrhea. | **Tengo diarrea.** tengo deeareya |
| It hurts here. | **Me duele aquí.** meh dweleh akee |
| I have (a/an) ... | **Tengo ...** tengo |
| cold | **un resfriado** oon resfreeyado |
| cramps | **calambres** kalambres |
| headache | **dolor de cabeza** dolor deh kabesa |

| sore throat | **dolor de garganta** *dolor deh garganta* |
| stiff neck | **tortícolis** *torteekolees* |
| stomachache | **dolor de estómago** *dolor deh estomago* |

## Conditions

| I have arthritis. | **Tengo artritis.** *tengo artreetees* |
| I have asthma. | **Tengo asma.** *tengo asma* |
| I am … | **Soy** *soy* |
| diabetic | **diabético(-a)** *deeabeteeko(-a)* |
| epileptic | **epiléptico(-a)** *epeelepteeko(-a)* |
| handicapped | **incapacitado(-a) [minusválido(-a)]** *eenkapaseetado(-a) [meenoosbaleedo(-a)]* |
| I have a heart condition. | **Sufro del corazón.** *soofro del korason* |
| I have high blood pressure. | **Tengo la presión alta.** *tengo la preseeyon alta* |

## Parts of the body

| | | | |
|---|---|---|---|
| appendix | **el apéndice** *el apendeeseh* | knee | **la rodilla** *la rodeel-ya* |
| arm | **el brazo** *el braso* | leg | **la pierna** *la peeyerna* |
| back | **la espalda** *la espalda* | lip | **el labio** *el labeeo* |
| bladder | **la vejiga** *la bekheega* | liver | **el hígado** *el eegado* |
| bone | **el hueso** *el weso* | mouth | **la boca** *la boka* |
| breast | **el seno** *el seno* | muscle | **el músculo** *el mooskoolo* |
| chest | **el pecho** *el pecho* | neck | **el cuello** *el kwel-yo* |
| ear | **el oído** *el oyeedo* | nose | **la nariz** *la narees* |
| eye | **el ojo** *el okho* | rib | **la costilla** *la kosteel-ya* |
| face | **la cara** *la kara* | shoulder | **el hombro** *el ombro* |
| finger | **el dedo** *el dedo* | skin | **la piel** *la peeyel* |
| foot | **el pie** *el peeyeh* | stomach | **el estómago** *el estomago* |
| gland | **la glándula** *la glandoola* | thigh | **el muslo** *el mooslo* |
| hand | **la mano** *la mano* | throat | **la garganta** *la garganta* |
| head | **la cabeza** *la kabesa* | thumb | **el dedo pulgar** *el dedo poolgar* |
| heart | **el corazón** *el korason* | toe | **el dedo del pie** *el dedo del peeyeh* |
| jaw | **la mandíbula** *la mandeeboola* | tongue | **la lengua** *la lengwa* |
| joint | **la articulación** *la arteekoolaseeyon* | tonsils | **las amígdalas** *las ameegdalas* |
| kidney | **el riñón** *el reeñon* | vein | **la vena** *la bena* |

## Doctor's inquiries

| | |
|---|---|
| ¿Cuánto tiempo hace que se siente así? | How long have you been feeling like this? |
| ¿Es la primera vez que le sucede eso? | Is this the first time you've had this? |
| ¿Está tomando alguna otra medicina? | Are you taking any other medication? |
| ¿Es alérgico(-a) a algo? | Are you allergic to anything? |
| ¿Ha perdido el apetito? | Have you lost your appetite? |

## Examination

| | |
|---|---|
| Voy a tomarle la temperatura/ la presión arterial. | I'll take your temperature/ blood pressure. |
| Súbase la manga, por favor. | Roll up your sleeve, please. |
| Desvístase hasta la cintura. | Please undress to the waist. |
| Acuéstese, por favor. | Please lie down. |
| Abra la boca. | Open your mouth. |
| Respire profundo [hondo]. | Breathe deeply. |
| Tosa, por favor. | Cough please. |
| ¿Dónde le duele? | Where does it hurt? |
| ¿Le duele aquí? | Does it hurt here? |

## Diagnosis

| | |
|---|---|
| Quiero que le tomen una radiografía. | I want you to have an X-ray. |
| Quiero una muestra de sangre/ heces [materias fecales]/orina. | I want a specimen of your blood/stool/urine. |
| Quiero que consulte a un especialista. | I want you to see a specialist. |
| Quiero que vaya al hospital. | I want you to go to the hospital. |
| Está roto(-a)/torcido(-a). | It's broken/sprained. |
| Está dislocado(-a)/desgarrado(-a). | It's dislocated/torn. |
| Tiene ... | You have (a/an) ... |

| | |
|---|---|
| apendicitis | appendicitis |
| cistitis | cystitis |
| gripe | flu |
| una fractura | fracture |
| gastritis | gastritis |
| una hernia | hernia |
| el/la …. inflamado(-a) | inflammation of … |
| sarampión | measles |
| neumonía | pneumonia |
| ciática | sciatica |
| amigdalitis | tonsilitis |
| un tumor | tumor |
| una enfermedad venérea | venereal disease |
| Está intoxicado(-a). | You have food poisoning. |
| Está infectado(-a). | It's infected. |
| Es contagioso(-a). | It's contagious. |

## Treatment

| | |
|---|---|
| Le daré … | I'll give you … |
| un antiséptico | an antiseptic |
| un analgésico | a painkiller |
| Le voy a recetar [formular] … | I'm going to prescribe … |
| un tratamiento de antibióticos | a course of antibiotics |
| unos supositorios | some suppositories |
| ¿Es alérgico(-a) | Are you allergic |
| a alguna medicina? | to any medication? |
| Tome una píldora … | Take one pill … |
| cada … horas | every … hours |
| antes/después de cada comida | before/after each meal |
| en caso de dolor | in case of pain |
| para … días | for … days |
| Consulte a un médico cuando regrese a casa. | Consult a doctor when you get home. |

## GYNECOLOGIST

| | |
|---|---|
| I have … | **Tengo …** _tengo_ |
| abdominal pains | **dolores abdominales [cólicos]** <br> _dolores abdomeenales [koleekos]_ |
| period pains | **cólicos menstruales** <br> _koleekos menstrooales_ |
| a vaginal infection | **una infección vaginal** <br> _oona infekseeyon bakheenal_ |
| I haven't had my period for … months. | **Hace … meses que no tengo la regla [la menstruación].** _aseh … meses keh no tengo la regla [la menstrooaseeyon]_ |
| I'm on the Pill. | **Tomo la píldora.** _tomo la peeldora_ |

## HOSPITAL

| | |
|---|---|
| Please notify my family. | **Avísele a mi familia, por favor.** <br> _abeeseleh a mee fameeleea por fabor_ |
| I'm in pain. | **Tengo mucho dolor.** _tengo moocho dolor_ |
| I can't eat/sleep. | **No puedo comer/dormir.** <br> _no pwedo komer/dormeer_ |
| When will the doctor come? | **¿Cuándo vendrá el doctor?** <br> _kwando bendra el doktor_ |
| Which section [ward] is … in? | **¿En qué sala está …?** <br> _en keh sala esta_ |
| I'm visiting … | **Estoy visitando …** _estoy beeseetando_ |

## OPTICIAN

| | |
|---|---|
| I'm near- [short-] sighted far- [long-] sighted. | **Soy miope/hipermétrope.** <br> _soy meeyopeh/eepermetropeh_ |
| I've lost … | **Se me perdió …** _seh meh perdeeyo_ |
| one of my contact lenses | **uno de mis lentes de contacto** <br> _oono deh mees lentes deh kontakto_ |
| my glasses | **mis gafas [anteojos]** <br> _mees gafas [anteokhos]_ |
| a lens | **un lente** _oon lenteh_ |
| Could you give me a replacement? | **¿Podría darme uno(-as) nuevo(-as)?** <br> _podreeya darmeh oono(-as) nwebo(-as)_ |

## DENTIST

| | |
|---|---|
| I have a toothache. | **Tengo dolor de muela.** _tengo dolor de mwela_ |
| This tooth hurts. | **Me duele este diente.** _meh dweleh esteh deeyenteh_ |
| I've lost a filling/a tooth. | **Se me cayó un empaste [una calza]/ un diente.** _seh meh kayo oon empasteh [oona kalsa]/oon deeyenteh_ |
| Can you repair this denture? | **¿Me puede arreglar esta dentadura?** _meh pwedeh arreglar esta dentadoora_ |
| I don't want it extracted. | **No quiero que me la saque.** _no keeyero keh meh la sakeh_ |

### YOU MAY HEAR

| | |
|---|---|
| **Le voy a poner una inyección/ anestesia local.** | I'm going to give you an injection/a local anesthetic. |
| **Usted necesita un empaste/ una calza.** | You need a filling/cap (crown). |
| **Voy a tener que sacarla.** | I'll have to take it out. |
| **Sólo la puedo arreglar temporalmente.** | I can only fix it temporarily. |
| **No coma nada durante … horas.** | Don't eat anything for … hours. |

## PAYMENT AND INSURANCE

| | |
|---|---|
| I have insurance. | **Tengo seguro. [Estoy afiliado(-a) al seguro.]** _tengo segooro. [estoy afeeleeyado(-a) al segooro]_ |
| Can I have a receipt for my health insurance? | **¿Podría darme un recibo para mi seguro médico?** _podreeya darmeh oon reseebo para mee segooro medeeko_ |
| Would you fill out this health insurance form, please? | **¿Podría llenar este formulario de seguro médico, por favor?** _podreeya l-yenar este formoolareeo deh segooro medeeko por fabor_ |
| Can I have a medical certificate? | **¿Me puede dar un certificado médico?** _meh pwedeh dar oon serteefeekado medeeko_ |

# DICTIONARY
# ENGLISH-SPANISH

## A

**a few** unos(-as) pocos(-as)
**a little** un poquito
**a lot** mucho
**a, an** un(a)
**a.m.** a.m.
**able, to be** (*also* ➤ **can, could**) poder
**about** (*approximately*) cerca de, alrededor de
**above** (*place*) arriba
**abroad** en el extranjero
**abscess** absceso m
**accept, to** aceptar; **do you accept...?** ¿aceptan...?
**access** (*noun*) entrada f
**accessories** accesorios mpl
**accident** accidente m
**accidentally** por accidente
**accommodation** alojamiento m
**accompany, to** acompañar
**accountant** contador(a) m/f
**ace** (*cards*) as m
**across** al otro lado
**activities** actividades f
**actor/actress** actor m, actriz f
**adaptor** adaptador m
**address** dirección f
**adjoining room** habitación f [cuarto m] contiguo(-a)
**admission charge** precio m de la entrada
**adult** adulto m/f
**advance, in** por adelantado
**aerial** (*car/TV*) antena f
**after** (*time*) después; (*place*) después de
**aftershave** loción f para después de la afeitada
**after-sun lotion** loción f para después del sol
**afternoon, in the** por la tarde
**age: what age?** ¿qué edad?
**aged, to be** tenía... años

**ago** hace...
**agree: I agree** estoy de acuerdo
**air conditioning** aire m acondicionado
**air freshener** aerosol m de ambiente
**air mattress** colchón inflable m
**air pump** bomba f de aire
**airline** aerolínea f
**airmail** correo m aéreo
**airplane** avión m
**airport** aeropuerto m
**alarm clock** reloj m despertador
**alcoholic drink** bebida f alcohólica
**all** todo(-a), todos(-as)
**all-night pharmacy** farmacia f de veinticuatro horas
**allergic, to be** ser alérgico(-a)
**allergy** alergia f
**allowed: is it allowed?** ¿está permitido?
**almost** casi
**alone** solo(-a)
**already** ya
**also** también
**alter, to** arreglar
**alumin[i]um foil** papel m aluminio
**always** siempre
**am: I am** soy
**ambassador** embajador(a)
**ambulance** ambulancia f
**American** (*noun/adj.*) estadounidense m/f; norteamericano(-a); ~ **football** fútbol m americano
**amount** cantidad f
**amusement arcade** local m de maquinitas/juegos electrónicos
**anesthetic** anestesia f
**anchor, to** anclar
**and** y
**angling** pesca f con caña
**animal** animal m
**anorak** anorak m
**another** otro(-a); ~ **time** a otra hora/en otra ocasión
**antibiotic** antibiótico m
**antique** antigüedad f; ~ **shop** almacén m de antigüedades
**antiseptic** antiséptico m; ~ **cream** crema f antiséptica
**any** algún(a)

anyone else alguien más
anything cheaper algo más barato
anything else? ¿algo más?
apartment departamento
[apartamento] m
apologize: I apologize ¡Perdóneme!
apples manzanas f
appointment cita f; to make an ~
pedir una cita
approximately aproximadamente
April abril
archery tiro con arco m
architect arquitecto m/f
architecture arquitectura f
are there…? ¿hay…?
are you…? ¿es usted…?
area área f; ~ code código m
Argentina Argentina
Argentinian (noun/adj.) argentino(-a)
arm brazo m
armband (swimming) brazalete m
around (time) cerca de [alrededor de];
(place) alrededor
arrange: can you arrange it? ¿puede
organizarlo(-a)?
arrest, to be under estar arrestado(-a)
arrive, to llegar
art arte m; ~ gallery galería f
de arte
artery arteria m
arthritis, to have tener artrítis
artist artista m/f
as soon as possible cuanto antes
ashore, to go desembarcar
ashtray cenicero m
ask, to: please ask her to call me
back dígale que me llame, por favor
asleep, to be estar dormido(-a)
aspirin aspirina f
asthmatic, to be ser asmático(-a)
at (time) a la(s); (place) en
at least por lo menos
attack (crime) atentado m; (medical)
ataque m
attendant asistente m/f
attractive atractivo(-a)
August agosto
aunt tía f

Australia Australia
Australian (noun/adj.) australiano(-a)
authenticity autenticidad f
automatic (car) carro m automático
automatic camera cámara f
automática
automobile carro m
autumn otoño m
avalanche avalancha f
away lejos
awful horrible

B

baby bebé m/f; ~ bottle biberón m del
bebé [tetero m del bebé]; ~ food comida
f para bebés; ~ seat asiento m para
bebé; ~sitter niñera f; ~ wipes pañuelos
m húmedos para bebés
back (body) espalda f
backache dolor m de espalda
backpacking de mochila [con morral]
bad malo(-a)
baggage check depósito m de equipaje
baggage reclaim recogida f de equipaje
bakery panadería f
balance of account balance m de
cuenta
ball pelota f
ballet ballet m
band (musical group) banda f
bandage venda f
bank banco m; ~ account cuenta f
bancaria; ~ card tarjeta f del banco; ~
loan préstamo m bancario
bar bar m [taberna f]
barbecue barbacoa f [asador m]
barber shop barbería [peluquería] f
barge (narrowboat)
barcaza [lancha] f
basement sótano m
basin lavamanos m
basket canasta f
bath towel toalla f
bath: to take a darse un baño
bathroom baño m
battery pila f; (car) batería f
battle site campo de batalla m

**be, to** (*also* ➤ **am, are**) ser/estar
**beach** playa f
**beard** barba f
**beautiful** hermoso(-a)
**because** porque; ~ **of** por [debido a]
**bed** cama f; ~ **and breakfast**
habitación f con desayuno incluido; **I'm
going to ~** me voy a la cama [me voy a
dormir]
**bedding** ropa f de cama
**bee** abeja f
**beer** cerveza f
**before** (*time*) antes (de)
**begin, to** (*also* ➤ **start**) empezar
**beginning** principio [comienzo] m
**beige** beige m
**belt** cinturón m
**beneath** debajo de
**berth** litera f
**best** mejor m/f
**better** mejor
**between** entre
**bib** babero m
**bicycle** bicicleta f; ~ **hire** alquiler de
bicicletas m; ~ **parts**; ~ **route** ruta f
para tránsito de bicicletas
**bidet** bidet m
**big** grande
**bikini** bikini m
**bill** factura f; cuenta f; **put it on the ~**
inclúyalo en la cuenta
**binoculars** binoculares mpl
**bird** pájaro m
**birthday** cumpleaños mpl
**biscuits** galletas fpl; bizcochos m
**bishop** (*chess*) alfil m
**bite** (*insect*) mordedura f
**bitten: I've been bitten by a dog** me
mordió un perro
**bitter** amargo(-a)
**black** negro(-a); ~ **and white film** (*camera*) rollo en blanco y negro m
**blanket** manta f
**bleeding** hemorragia f; **to be ~** estar
sangrando
**bless you** ¡salud!
**blind** (*window*) persiana f
**blister** ampolla f

**blocked, to be** tapado(-a); **the road is
~** la carretera está bloqueada
**blood** sangre f; ~ **group** grupo m
sanguíneo; ~ **pressure** presión f arterial
**blouse** blusa f
**blow-dry** secado m
**blue** azul m
**blusher** (*rouge*) rubor m
**boarding card** tarjeta f de embarque
**boat** bote m; ~ **trip** viaje m en barco
**body: parts of the body** partes del
cuerpo
**boil** (*ailment*) furúnculo m
**boiler** caldera f
**Bolivia** Bolivia
**Bolivian** (*noun/adj.*) boliviano(-a)
**bone** hueso m
**book** libro m
**book, to** reservar
**booked up, to be** estar todo reservado;
no quedar nada libre
**booking** reservación f; ~ **office** oficina
f de reservaciones
**bookstore** librería f
**boots** botas f
**border** (*country*) frontera f
**boring** aburrido(-a)
**born: I was born in** nací en
**borrow: may I borrow your...?** ¿me
presta su...?
**botanical garden** jardín m botánico
**bottle** botella f; ~ **bank** banco m de
botellas; ~ **opener** destapador m
**bow** (*ship*) proa f
**bowel** intestino m
**box of chocolates** caja f de chocolates
**box office** boletería [taquilla] f
**boxing** boxeo m
**boy** niño m
**boyfriend** novio m
**bra** brassiere m
**bracelet** pulsera f
**brass** latón m
**Brazil** Brasil
**Brazilian** (*n/adj*) brasileño(-a)
**bread** pan m
**break, to** romper
**break-in** asalto m

**breakage** ruptura f
**breakdown** *(mechanical)* avería f; *(mechanical)* **to have a ~** estar descompuesto
**breakfast** desayuno m
**breast** seno m
**breathe, to** respirar
**bridge** puente m; *(cards)* bridge m
**briefcase** maletín [portafolio] m
**briefs** *(man's)* calzoncillos mpl, *(woman's)* pantaletas fpl
**brilliant** brillante
**bring, to** traer
**Britain** la Gran Bretaña
**British** *(noun/adj.)* británico(-a)
**brochure** folleto m
**broken** roto(-a); **to be ~** estar roto(-a)
**bronchitis** bronquitis f
**bronze** bronce m
**brooch** prendedor m
**brother** hermano m
**brown** café m
**browse, to** mirar
**bruise** moretón m
**brush** cepillo m
**bucket** cubeta m [balde m]
**build, to** construir
**building** edificio m
**built** construido(-a)
**bulletin board** cartelera f de anuncios
**bureau de change** oficina f [casa f] de cambio
**burger** hamburguesa f; **~ stand** puesto de hamburguesas m
**burglary** *(also ➤ theft)* robo m (de casa)
**burn** quemadura f; **it's burned** *(food)* está quemado(-a)
**burst pipe** tubo m roto
**burst tire [tyre]** llanta f pinchada
**bus** autobús m; **~ route** ruta f de buses f; **~ station** estación f de autobuses; **~ stop** parada f del autobús; **~ terminal** parada f [paradero m]
**business class** clase f ejecutiva
**business trip** viaje m de negocios
**business, on** en viaje de negocios

**businessman/woman** negociante m/f
**busy, to be** estar ocupado(-a)
**but** pero
**butane gas** gas m butano
**butcher** carnicería f
**butter** mantequilla f
**button** botón m
**buy, to** comprar
**by** *(time)* antes de …; **~ car** en carro; **~ credit card** con tarjeta de crédito
**bye!** ¡adiós!
**bypass** carretera f de circunvalación; by-pass m

## C

**cabaret** cabaret m
**cabin** cabina f
**cable car** funicular m
**café** café m [cafetería f]
**cagoule** anorak m impermeable
**cake** pastel m; **~ shop** pastelería f
**calendar** calendario m
**call, to** *(phone)* llamar (por teléfono); **~ for someone** ir a recoger a alguien; **I'll call back** volveré a llamar; **call collect, to** llamar por cobro revertido; **call the police!** ¡llame a la policía!
**camcorder** videocámara f
**camera** cámara f; **~ case** funda f [estuche m]de la cámara; **~ store** almacén de fotografía m
**campbed** cama plegable f
**camping** campamento [camping] m; **~ equipment** equipo m de campamento
**campsite** zona de campamento
**can I?** ¿podría?
**can I have?** ¿puede traerme?
**can you help me?** ¿puede ayudarme?
**can you recommend?** ¿puede recomendarme?
**can** lata f; **~ opener** abrelatas m
**can opener** abrelatas m
**Canada** Canadá
**Canadian** *(person/adj.)* canadiense m/f
**canal** canal m
**cancel, to** cancelar
**cancer** *(disease)* cáncer m

candles velas f
candy dulces mpl [caramelos] m
canoe canoa f
canoeing piragüismo m
cap gorra f; (dental) calza f
capital city capital f
captain (boat) capitán m
car (automobile) carro m; (train) coche [vagón] m
car alarm alarma f del carro
caravan casa f móvil
car ferry transbordador m de carros [ferry]
car parts repuestos m
car rental local m alquiler de carros
car wash servicio m de lavado de carros
car, by en carro
carafe jarra f
careful: be careful! ¡ten cuidado!
carpet (rug) alfombra f; (fitted) alfombra f fija
carrier bag bolsa f
carry-on equipaje m de mano
carton caja f [cartón m]
cash efectivo m; ~ card tarjeta f del cajero automático; ~ desk caja f; ~ machine (ATM) cajero m automático
cash, to cambiar un cheque
cassette cassette m
castle castillo m
cat gato m
catch, to (bus) coger [tomar]
cathedral catedral f
cause, to ocasionar
cave cueva f
CD CD m; ~-player grabadora f con CD
cemetery cementerio m
central heating calefacción f
center of town centro m
ceramics cerámica f
certificate certificado m
certification documento m que certifique algo
chair silla f
change (coins) cambio [suelto, sencillo] m; keep the ~ guardar el cambio

change, to (money) cambiar; (reservation); (bus, train); (clothes) cambiarse; ~ lanes cambiar de carril; where can I change the baby? ¿dónde puedo cambiar al bebé?
changing facilities lugar m para cambiar a los bebés
changing rooms vestuario m
channel (sea) canal m
chapel capilla f
charge precio m [tarifa f]
charter flight vuelo m chárter
cheap barato(-a)
cheaper más barato(-a)
check, to revisar
checkbook chequera f
check guarantee card tarjeta f de garantía de cheques
check in, to presentarse [registrarse]
check-in desk ventanilla f
check out, to (hotel) desocupar
checked (patterned) a cuadros
checkers (game) damas chinas fpl
checkout caja f
cheers! ¡salud!
cheese queso m
chemical toilet baño portátil m
chemist farmacia [droguería] f
chess ajedrez m; ~ set juego m de ajedrez
chest (body) pecho m
chickenpox varicela f
child niño(-a)
child's seat asiento m para niños
childcarer [childminder] niñera f
children niños m
children's meals comida f para niños
Chile Chile
Chilean (person/adj.) chileno(-a)
chips (U.K.) papas fpl fritas/a la francesa
chocolate chocolate m; ~ bar chocolatina f; box of chocolates caja f de chocolates
chocolate ice cream helado m de chocolate
christian (adj) cristiano(-a)
Christmas navidad f

church iglesia f
cigarette cigarrillo m; **pack of ~**
cajetilla f de cigarrillos; **~ machine**
máquina f expendedora de cigarrillos
cigars cigarros [puros] m
cinema cine m
circle *(theater)* balcón m
city wall muro m de la ciudad
civil-servant miembro m/f del servicio
civil
claim check etiqueta f de reclamo
class: first class primera clase
clean limpio(-a)
clean, to lavar
cleaned: I'd like my shoes cleaned
quiero que me limpie los zapatos
cleansing lotion loción f limpiadora
cliff acantilado [precipicio] m
clinic clínica f
cloakroom guardarropa m
clock reloj m
close *(near)* cerca
close, to cerrar
clothes ropa f
clothes pins [pegs] ganchos mpl para
colgar la ropa
clothing store almacén m de ropa
cloudy: it's cloudy está nublado **clubs**
*(golf)* palos mpl de golf
coach *(train)* coche [vagón] m
coast costa f
coat abrigo m; **~check** guardarropa m
coathanger percha f
cockroach cucaracha f
code *(area/dialling)* código m
coffee café m
coffee filter papel m de filtro
coil *(contraceptive)* espiral f
intrauterina
coin moneda f
cold frío(-a); *(flu)* resfriado m
collapse: he's collapsed él sufrió un
colapso
collect, to reclamar
college universidad f
Colombia Colombia
Colombian *(person/adj.)*
colombiano(-a)

color color m
color film rollo m a color
comb peine m [peinilla f]
come back to *(return)* volver;
regresar
commission comisión f
communion comunión f
compact disc compact disc m
company *(business)* compañía f
compartment *(train)* coche [vagón] m
compass brújula f
complaint, to make a hacer un
reclamo [presentar una queja]
complaint *(in hotel/store)* reclamo m;
*(statement of dissatisfaction)* queja f
computer computadora f
concert concierto m
concert hall sala f de conciertos
concession *(reduction)* concesión f
concussion, to have tener una
conmoción cerebral
conditioner acondicionador m
condoms condones m
conference conferencia f
confirm, to confirmar
confirmation confirmación f
congratulations! ¡felicitaciones!
connection *(transport)* conexión f
conscious, to be estar consciente
constipated, to be tener estreñimiento
constipation estreñimiento m
consulate consulado m
consult, to consultar
consultant *(medical)* especialista m/f
contact, to localizar
contact lens lentes de contacto m;
**~ fluid** líquido m para lentes
contagious, to be ser contagioso (-a)
contain, to contener
contemporary dance danza
contemporánea f
contraceptive anticonceptivo m
convenient conveniente
convertible *(car)* convertible
cook, to cocinar
cook cocinero(-a)
cookbook libro m de recetas de cocina
cookies galletas fpl; bizcochos m

**cooking** (cuisine) cocina f
**copper** cobre m
**copy** copiar
**corduroy** pana f
**corkscrew** descorchador m
**corner** esquina f
**correct** (also ➤ **right**) bien [correcto(-a)]
**cosmetics** cosméticos m
**Costa Rica** Costa Rica
**Costa Rican** (person/adj.) costarricense m/f
**cot** (child's) cuna para bebé f; (campbed) cama plegable f
**cottage** cabaña f
**cotton** algodón m; ~ [**wool**] paquete de algodón m
**cough, to** toser
**cough** tos f; ~ **syrup** jarabe m para la tos
**could I have …?** ¿podría traerme…?
**counter** mostrador m
**country** (nation) país m
**countryside** campo m
**course** (meal) plato m
**cousin** primo(-a)
**cover** (lid) tapa f
**cover charge** consumo mínimo m
**craft shop** tienda f de artesanías
**cramps** calambres mpl
**crash: I've had a crash** me estrellé
**creche** guardería f infantil
**credit card** tarjeta f de crédito
**credit card number** número m de tarjeta de crédito
**credit status** capacidad f de crédito
**credit, in** estar en números negros
**crib** (child's) cuna para bebé f
**crockery** loza [vajilla] f
**cross** (crucifix) cruz f
**cross, to** (road) cruzar
**crossing** (boat) travesía f; cruce f
**crossroad** cruce m de carreteras
**crowded: it's crowded** hay mucha gente
**crown** (dental) corona f
**cruise** crucero m
**crutches** muletas fpl
**Cuba** Cuba

**Cuban** (person/adj.) cubano(-a)
**cuisine** comida f
**cup** taza f [pocillos m]
**cupboard** armario m
**curlers** tubos [rulos] m
**currency** moneda f
**currency exchange (office)** oficina f de cambio [casa f de cambio]
**cushion** almohadón [cojín] m
**customs** (control) aduana f
**customs declaration form** declaración f de aduana
**cut** cortadura f
**cutlery** cubiertos m
**cycle helmet** casco m para bicicleta
**cycle path** carril m de bicicleta
**cycling** ciclismo m
**cyclist** ciclista m/f
**cystitis** cistitis f

## D

**daily** diariamente
**damaged, to be** no funcionar; se dañó
**damp** (noun) humedad f; (adj.) húmedo(-a)
**dance** (performance) baile [danza] f
**dancing, to go** ir a bailar
**dangerous** peligroso(-a)
**dark** oscuro(-a)
**darts, to play** jugar a los dardos
**daughter** hija f
**day** día m
**day trip** viaje m de un día
**dead** muerto(-a); (battery) descargado(-a)
**deaf, to be** ser sordo(-a)
**dear** (greeting) querido(-a)
**December** diciembre
**decide: we haven't decided yet** no hemos decidido todavía
**deck** (ship) cubierta f
**deck chair** silla f de lona
**declare, to** declarar
**deep** profundo(-a)
**deep-freeze** congelador m
**defrost, to** descongelar
**degrees** (temperature) grados m
**delay** retraso m

**delicate** delicado(-a)
**delicatessen** delicatessen m [tienda f de especialidades]
**delicious** delicioso(-a)
**deliver, to** entregar
**denim** tela f vaquera
**dental floss** hilo m dental
**dentist** dentista m/f
**dentures** dentadura f
**deodorant** desodorante m
**depart, to** *(train, bus)* salir
**department** *(store)* departamento m [sección f]
**department store** almacén m
**departure** *(train, etc.)* salida f
**departure lounge** sala de embarque f
**depend: it depends on** depende de
**deposit** depósito m
**describe, to** describir
**destination** destino m
**details** detalles mpl
**detergent** detergente m
**develop, to** *(photos)* revelar
**diabetes** diabetes f
**diabetic, to be** ser diabético(-a)
**diagnosis** diagnóstico m
**dialling code** código m
**diamonds** *(cards)* diamantes m
**diapers** pañales mpl
**diarrhea** diarrea f
**dice** dado m
**dictionary** diccionario m
**diesel** diesel
**difficult** difícil
**dine, to** cenar
**dinghy** bote m [barca] f
**dining car** coche comedor m
**dining room** comedor m
**dinner, to have** cenar
**dinner jacket** esmoquin m
**direct** directo(-a)
**direct-dial telephone** teléfono dial m
**direction** dirección f; **in the ~ of …** en dirección a …
**director** *(film)* director m; *(company)* gerente m
**directory** *(telephone)* directorio m; *(store)* guía f del almacén

**Directory Enquiries** Información f
**dirty** sucio(-a)
**disabled** personas fpl incapacitadas
**disco** discoteca f
**discount** descuento m; **can you offer me a ~** ¿puede ofrecerme un descuento?
**dish** *(meal)* plato m [especialidad f]; **~ cloth** paño [limpión] m
**dishes** loza [vajilla] f
**dishwashing liquid** detergente para los platos m
**dislocated, to be** estar dislocado(-a)
**display cabinet/case** escaparate m
**disposable camera** cámara f desechable
**distilled water** agua f destilada
**district** distrito m
**disturb: don't disturb** no interrumpir
**dive, to** bucear
**diversion** desvío m
**diving equipment** equipo m de buceo
**divorced, to be** ser divorciado(-a)
**dizzy, to feel** tener mareo
**doctor** doctor(a)
**dog** perro m
**do-it-yourself store** almacén m de bricolaje
**doll** muñeca f
**dollar** dólar m
**door** puerta f
**dosage** dosis f
**double** doble
**double bed** cama f matrimonial [doble]
**double room** habitación f doble [cuarto m doble]
**downstairs** abajo
**downtown area** centro m (de la ciudad)
**dozen** docena f
**draft [draught]** *(beer)* de barril *(wind)* corriente f de aire
**drain** desagua-dero [desagüe] m
**drama** drama m
**draughts** *(game)* damas chinas fpl
**dress** vestido m
**drink** copa f; bebida f
**drinking water** agua potable f

**drive, to** conducir [manejar]
**driver** conductor [chofer] m
**driver's license** licencia de conducir f
**drop off, to** *(someone)* dejar
**drowning: someone is drowning** alguien se está ahogando
**drugstore** farmacia [droguería] f
**drunk** borracho(-a)
**dry cleaner** tintorería [lavandería] f
**dry cut** corte m en seco
**dry-clean, to** lavar en seco
**dual freeway** autopista f
**dubbed** *(film)* doblada
**due, to be** *(payment)* vencer
**dummy** chupón [chupo] m
**during** durante
**dustbin** bote m de la basura [caneca f]
**dusty** que tiene polvo
**duty: to pay duty** pagar impuestos
**duty-free goods** artículos fpl libres de impuestos
**duty-free store** tienda f libres de impuestos
**duvet** edredón m

## E

**each: how much each?** ¿cuánto vale cada uno?
**ear** oído m
**earache** dolor de oído m
**earlier** más temprano
**early** temprano
**earrings** aretes m
**east** oriente
**Easter** semana santa f
**easy** fácil
**eat, to** comer; **places ~** sitios para ir a comer; **have you eaten?** ¿ha comido?; **we've already eaten** ya hemos comido
**economical** económico(-a)
**economy class** clase económica [de turista]
**Ecuador** Ecuador
**Ecuadorian** *(person/adj.)* ecuatoriano(-a)
**eight** ocho
**either... or** ... o ...
**elastic** *(adj)* elástico(-a)

**electrician** electricista m/f
**electric blanket** cobija [manta] f eléctrica
**electric fire** fuego m eléctrico
**electric meter** medidor m eléctrico [contador eléctrico]
**electric shaver** afeitadora f eléctrica
**electrical store** almacén m de instalaciones eléctricas
**electricity** electricidad f
**electronic flash** flash m
**eleven** once
**elevator** ascensor m
**else, something** algo más
**embark, to** *(boat)* embarcar
**embassy** embajada f
**emergency** emergencia f; **~ exit** salida de emergencia f; **it's an ~** es una emergencia
**emergency [casualty] deptartment** *(hospital)* sección f de accidentes
**empty** desocupado(-a)
**end, to** terminar
**end: at the end** al final
**engaged, to be** estar comprometido(-a)
**engine** motor m
**engineer** ingeniero m/f
**England** Inglaterra
**English** *(language)* inglés m
**English-speaking** que hable inglés
**enjoy, to** gustar [disfrutar]
**enlarge, to** *(photos)* ampliar
**enough** suficiente
**enquiry desk** puesto m de información
**ensuite bathroom** con baño adjunto
**entertainment guide** guía de diversiones f
**entrance fee** entrada f
**entry visa** visa f de entrada al país
**envelope** sobre m
**epileptic, to be** ser epiléptico(-a)
**equipment** *(sports)* equipo deportivo m
**error** error m
**escalator** escalera eléctrica f
**essential** indispensable

estate agent  agencia f de bienes raíces
estate car  camioneta f
EU  Unión Europea f
Eurocheque  eurocheque m
evening dress  traje m de noche
evening, in the  por la noche
events  eventos f
every day  todos los días
every week  todas las semanas
examination  *(medical)* exámen m médico
example, for  por ejemplo
except  excepto
excess baggage  exceso de equipaje m
exchange, to  cambiar
exchange rate  tasa de cambio f
excursion  excursión f
excuse me  *(apology)* disculpe [perdón]; *(attention)* ¡disculpe!
exhausted, to be  estar muy cansado(-a)
exhibition  exposición f
exit  salida f; **at the ~**  a la salida
expected, to be  se exige
expensive  caro(-a)
expiration [expiry] date  fecha de vencimiento f
expire, to: when does it expire?  ¿cuándo vence?
extension  extensión f
extension cord [lead]  extensión f
extra  *(additional)* adicional
extracted, to be  *(tooth)* sacar
extremely  demasiado [extremadamente]
eye  ojo m
eyeliner  delineador m de ojos
eyeshadow  sombra f de ojos

## F

fabric  *(material)* tela f
face  cara f
facilities  servicios m
factor  *(suntan)* factor m
faint, to feel  tener mareo
fairground  parque m de atracciones
fall  *(season)* otoño m

fall: he's had a fall  él se cayó
family  familia f
famous  famoso(-a)
fan  *(air)* ventilador m
fan: I'm a fan of  soy fan [seguidora] de
far  lejos; **how ~ is it?**  ¿a qué distancia está…?; **is it ~?**  ¿está lejos?
fare  tarifa f
far-sighted  hipermétrope
farm  finca f
fashionable, to be  estar de moda
fast  rápido(-a)
fast, to be  *(clock)* estar adelantado
fast food  comida rápida f; **~ restaurant**  restaurante m de comidas rápidas
fat  *(food)* grasa f
father  padre m
faucet  llave f [grifo m]
fault: it's my fault  es mi culpa
faulty  defectuoso(-a)
favorite  favorito(-a)
fax  *(machine)* fax m; **~ bureau/facilities**  servicio m de fax
February  febrero
feed, to  alimentar
feeding bottle  mamila f biberón m
feel ill, to  estar enfermo(-a)
feel sick, to  estar mareado(-a)
female  *(noun)* mujer f
ferry  transbordador m
festival  festival m
feverish, to feel  tener fiebre
few  poco(-a)
fiancé(e)  prometido(-a) m/f [novio(-a)]
field  campo m
fifth  quinto(-a)
fight  *(brawl)* pelea f
fill out, to  *(form)* llenar
filling  *(dental)* empaste m [calza f]; *(sandwich)* relleno m
film  *(camera)* rollo m; *(movie)* película f
filter  filtro m
fine  *(well)* bien; *(penalty)* multa f
finger  dedo m
fire: there's a fire!  ¡hay un incendio!

**fire alarm** alarma f de incendios
**fire department [brigade]** bomberos m
**fire escape** escalera f de incendios
**fire extinguisher** extinguidor m de incendios
**fireplace** chimenea f
**firewood** leña f
**first** primero(-a)
**first class** primera clase
**first [ground** *(U.K.)***] floor** planta baja f
**first-aid kit** botiquín m de primeros auxilios
**fishing rod** caña f de pescar
**fishing, to go** pescar
**fish store [fishmonger]** pescadería f
**fit, to** *(clothes)* quedar bien
**fitting room** probador [vestier] m
**five** cinco
**fix: can you fix it?** ¿puede repararlo (-la)?
**flash** *(photo)* flash m
**flashlight** antorcha f
**flat** *(tire)* pinchada m
**flea** pulga f
**flea market** mercado m de las pulgas
**flight** vuelo m; **~ number** número m de vuelo; pasaje; **~ attendant** auxiliar m/f de vuelo
**flip-flops** chancletas f
**flood** inundación f
**floor** *(level)* piso m
**floor mop** trapeador m
**floor show** espectáculo m
**florist** floristería f
**flower** flor f
**flu** gripe f
**fluent: to speak fluent Spanish** hablar bien el español
**fly** *(insect)* mosca
**fly, to** volar
**foggy: it's foggy** hay niebla
**folding chair/table** silla/mesa f plegable
**follow, to** seguir
**follow, to** *(pursue)* perseguir
**food** alimento m; comida f
**food poisoning** intoxicación f
**foot** pie m

**football** fútbol m
**footpath** sendero m
**for a day** para un día
**for a week** para una semana
**for ... hours** por ... horas
**forecast** predicción f
**foreign** extranjero(-a); **~ currency** moneda extranjera f
**forest** selva f
**forget, to** olvidar
**fork** tenedor m; *(in the road)* empalme m [bifurcación f]
**form** formulario m
**formal dress** traje f formal
**fortnight** dos semanas fpl
**fortunately** afortunadamente
**forty** cuarenta
**forwarding address** dirección f donde remitir la correspondencia
**foundation** *(make-up)* base f
**fountain** fuente f
**four** cuatro
**four-door car** carro m de cuatro puertas
**four-wheel drive** tracción f a cuatro ruedas
**fourth** cuarto(-a)
**foyer** *(hotel/theater)* vestíbulo m
**frame** *(glasses)* montura f
**free** *(available)* disponible [libre]; *(of charge)* gratis
**freezer** congelador m
**French** *(language)* francés
**frequently** frecuentemente
**fresh** fresco(-a)
**Friday** viernes m
**friend** amigo(-a)
**friendly** amistoso(-a)
**fries** papas fpl fritas/a la francesa
**from** *(place)* de; *(time)* de
**front door** puerta f principal; **~ key** llave f de la puerta principal
**frozen** congelado(-a)
**fruit juice** jugo de fruta m
**frying pan** sartén f
**fuel** *(petrol)* gasolina f
**full** lleno(-a)

**full board (American Plan [A.P.])**
pensión f completa
**fun, to have** divertirse
**funny** *(amusing/odd)* raro(-a)
**furniture** muebles mpl
**fuse** fusible m
**fuse box** caja f de fusibles

## G

**gallon** galón m
**gamble, to** jugar (juegos de azar)
**game** *(sport)* partido m; *(toy)* juego m
**garage** garaje/estacionamiento cubierto
[parqueadero cubierto] m; **~ repairs** taller
m de mecánica
**garbage bags** bolsas fpl para
la basura
**garden** jardín m
**gardening** jardinería f
**gas: I smell gas!** ¡huele a gas!
**gas bottle** cilindro m de gas [la bom-
bona f]
**gas permeable lenses** lentes m de gas
permeable
**gas station** gasolinera f
[estación de servicio]
**gasoline** gasolina f
**gastritis** gastritis f
**gate** *(airport)* puerta f
**gauze** *(bandage)* venda f
**gay club** club de gays m
**general delivery** lista f de correo
**genuine** original [auténtico(-a)];
genuino(-a)
**get by: may I get by?** ¿puedo pasar?
**get off/out of, to** *(transport)* bajar(se)
**get to, to** llegar a; **how do I get to…?**
¿cómo se llega a…?
**gift** regalo m; **~ shop** almacén f de
regalos
**girl** niña f
**girlfriend** novia f
**give, to** dar
**glass** vaso m; **a ~ of wine** una copa de
vino f
**glasses** *(optical)* gafas fpl [anteojos m]
**gliding** planeo m
**glossy finish** *(photos)* acabado brillante

**glove** guante m
**go, to** ir; **~ back** *(turn around)*
regresar; **~ for a walk** dar un paseo; **~
out** *(in evening)* salir; **~ shopping** ir de
compras; **go away!** ¡váyase!; **where
does this bus go?** ¿adónde va este bus?
**goggles** gafas fpl de natación [gafas
para deportes] f
**gold** oro m
**gold plate** chapado(-a) en oro
**golf** golf m
**golf course** campo de golf m
**good** bueno(-a); **~ afternoon** buenas
tardes; **~ evening** buenas noches; **~
morning** buenos días; **~ night** buenas
noches [hasta mañana]; **~-bye** adiós
**got: have you got any …?** ¿tiene …?
**grade** *(fuel)* grado m
**gram** gramo m
**grandparents** abuelos mpl
**grass** pasto m
**gratuity** propina f
**gray** gris
**greasy** *(hair)* grasoso(-a)
**green** verde
**greengrocer** verdulería [tienda] f
**grey** gris
**grocery store** abarrotes mpl [tienda f]
**ground floor** planta f baja
**group** grupo m
**guarantee** garantía f; **is it
guaranteed?** ¿tiene garantía?
**Guatemalan** *(person/adj.)*
guatemalteco(-a)
**guide** *(tour)* guía m/f
**guidebook** guía f (turística)
**guided tour** tour m con guía
**guitar** guitarra f
**gum** *(mouth)* encía f
**gynecologist** ginecólogo(-a)

## H

**hair** cabello [pelo] m; **~ brush** cepillo
m para el pelo; **~ dryer** secador m; **~
gel** gel m para el pelo; **~ mousse**
espuma f moldeadora para el cabello; **~
spray** laca f
**haircut** corte m de pelo

**hairdresser** *(person)* peluquero(-a) m/f; *(salon)* **hairdresser** salón m de belleza
**hairstylist** estilista m/f
**half, a** una mitad
**half board (Modified American Plan [M.A.P.])** media pensión f
**half fare** medio pasaje m
**half past** … y media
**hammer** martillo m
**hand** mano f: **~ cream** crema f de manos; **~ luggage** equipaje m de mano; **~ towel** toalla f para las manos; **~ washable** que se puede lavar a mano
**handbag** bolso m
**handicapped, to be** ser incapacitado (-a) [minusválido(-a)]
**handicrafts** artesanías f
**handkerchief** pañuelo m
**handle** manija f
**hang-gliding** vuelo m ala delta
**hanger** percha f
**hangover** cruda f [resaca f, guayabo m]
**happen: what happened?** ¿qué pasó?
**happy: I'm not happy with the service** no estoy satisfecho con el servicio
**harbor** puerto m
**hard shoulder** *(road)* arcén m
**hardware store** ferretería m
**hat** sombrero m
**hatchback** puerta trasera f
**have, to** tener
**have to, to** *(must)* tener que
**head** cabeza f
**head waiter** jefe m/f de meseros
**headache** dolor m de cabeza
**health food shop/store** tienda f de alimentos naturales
**health insurance** seguro m médico
**hear, to** oír
**hearing aid** audífono m
**heart** corazón m: **~ attack** ataque m cardiaco; **I have a heart condition** sufro del corazón
**hearts** *(cards)* corazones m
**heater** calentador m
**heating** calefacción f
**heavy** pesado(-a)

**height** *(altitude)* altura f, *(person)* estatura f,
**helicopter** helicóptero m
**hello** hola
**help** ayuda f
**help, to** ayudar; **can you help me?** ¿puede ayudarme?
**helper** asistente m/f
**hemorrhoids** hemorroides f
**her** *(adj.)* su(s); *(pronoun)* la
**here** aquí
**hers** suya(s); de ella
**hi!** ¡qué tal!
**high** alto(-a); **~ tide** marea f alta
**highlight, to** hacer rayitos
**highway** autopista f
**hike** *(walk)* caminata
**hiking** excursionismo m
**hill** colina f
**him** *(pronoun)* lo
**hire, to** alquilar
**his** *(pronoun)* suyo(s), de él; *(adj.)* su(s)
**history** historia f
**hitchhike, to** hacer autostop
**hitchhiking** autostop m
**HIV-positive, to be** tener el virus del SIDA
**hobby** hobby m [pasatiempo m favorito]
**hockey** *(field)* hockey m
**hold, to** *(contain)* contener
**hold on, to** *(wait)* esperar un momento
**hole** *(clothes)* agujero m
**holiday, on** de vacaciones
**holiday resort** sitio m de veraneo
**home: to go home** irse a casa
**homosexual** *(adj.)* homosexual
**honeymoon, to be on** estar de luna de miel
**hopefully!** ¡ojalá!
**horse** caballo m; **~ racing** carreras fpl de caballos
**horseback trip** viaje m a caballo
**hospital** hospital m
**hot** muy caliente [hirviendo]
**hot dog** hot dog m [perro m caliente]

**hot water** agua f caliente; **~ bottle** botella f de agua caliente
**hotel** hotel m; **~ reservation** reservación de hotel
**hour** hora f; **in an ~** dentro de una hora
**house** casa f
**housewife** ama f de casa
**hovercraft** hidrodeslizador m
**how?** ¿cómo?; **~ are you?** cómo está?
**how far?** ¿a qué distancia?
**how long?** ¿cuánto tiempo? ,
**how many?** ¿cuántos(-as)?
**how much is it?** ¿cuánto es?, ¿cuánto cuesta?
**how often?** ¿cuántas veces al día?
**how old?** ¿qué edad? [cuántos años]
**however** sin embargo
**hundred** cien
**hungry, to be** tener hambre
**hurry, to be in a** estar de prisa [tener prisa]
**hurt, to be** estar herido(-a); estar lastimado(-a); **it hurts** duele
**husband** esposo m

## I

**I'd like ...** quisiera ...
**ice** hielo m
**ice cream** helado m; **~ parlor** heladería f; **~ cone** cono m de helado
**ice pack** bolsa f de hielo
**ice rink** pista f de hielo
**identification** documento m de identificación
**ill, to be** estar enfermo(-a)
**illegal, to be** ser ilegal
**illness** enfermedad f
**imitation** imitación f
**immediately** inmediatamente
**impressive** impresionante
**in** *(place)* en; *(time)* dentro de
**in-law: mother/father-in-law** suegra f/suegro m
**included: is... included?** ¿está incluido(-a)...?
**indicate, to** poner las direccionales
**indigestion** indigestión f

**indoor pool** piscina f cubierta
**inexpensive** barato(-a)
**infected, to be** estar infectado(-a)
**infection** infección f
**inflammation** inflamación f
**informal dress** ropa informal f
**information** información f; **~ desk** oficina [ventanilla] f de información; **~ office** oficina f de información
**injection** inyección f
**injured, to be** estar herido(-a)
**innocent** inocente m/f
**insect** insecto m; **~ bite** mordedura f de insecto; **~ repellent/spray** repelente contra insectos m
**inside** a dentro
**insist, to** insistir
**insomnia** insomnio m
**instead of** en vez de
**instructions** instrucciones fpl
**instructor** instructor(a)
**insulin** insulina f
**insurance** seguro m; **~ certificate** certificado m del seguro; **~ claim** demanda f de seguro; **~ company** compañía f de seguros
**interest** interés m
**interest rate** tasa de interés f
**interesting** interesante
**international** internacional
**International Student Card** credencial m [tarjeta f] internacional de estudiante
**interpreter** intérprete m/f
**intersection** cruce m de carreteras
**interval** intervalo m [periodo]
**into** dentro
**introduce oneself, to** presentarse
**invitation** invitación m
**invite, to** invitar
**involved, to be** estar involucrado(-a)
**Ireland** Irlanda
**Irish** *(person/adj.)* irlandés(-esa)
**iron** *(electrical)* plancha f
**iron, to** *(press clothes)* planchar
**is there...?** ¿hay...?
**island** isla f
**it is** esto es/está

**Italian** *(adj.)* italiano(-a)
**itemized bill** factura f [recibo m detallado]

## J

**jack** *(cards)* valet m, sota f
**jacket** chaqueta f
**jammed, to be** estar atascado(-a)
**January** enero
**jar** frasco m
**jaw** mandíbula f
**jeans** jeans m
**jellyfish** medusa f
**jet lag: I have** estoy sintiendo el desfase de horarios
**jet-ski** jet-ski m [moto f acuática]
**jeweler** joyería f
**job: what's your job?** ¿a qué se dedica?
**jogging, to go** trotar
**joint** *(body part)* articulación f; *(meat)* trozo m
**joint passport** pasaporte m conjunto
**joke** chiste m
**joker** *(cards)* joker m
**journalist** periodista m/f
**journey** viaje m
**jug** jarra f
**July** julio
**jumper cables [jump leads]** cables mpl de emergencia
**jumper** suéter [saco] m
**junction** *(intersection)* cruce m [entronque m]
**June** junio

## K

**kaolin** caolín m
**keep: keep the change** guarde el cambio
**kettle** tetera f
**key** llave f; ~ **ring** llavero m
**kiddie pool** piscina f para niños
**kidney** riñón m
**kilo(gram)** kilo m
**kilometer** kilómetro m
**kind** *(pleasant)* amable

**kind: what kind of...?** ¿qué clase de...?
**king** *(cards, chess)* rey m
**kiosk** quiosco m
**kiss, to** dar un beso, besar
**kitchen paper** papel m de cocina
**knapsack** mochila f
**knave** *(cards)* valet m, sota f
**knee** rodilla f
**knickers** pantaletas f [pantalones m]
**knife** cuchillo m
**knight** *(chess)* caballo m
**knocked down, to be** ser derribado (-a)
**know: I don't know** no lo sé

## L

**label** etiqueta f
**lace** encaje m
**ladder** escalera f
**ladies** *(toilet)* baño m para damas
**lake** lago m
**lamp** lámpara f
**land, to** aterrizar
**landlord/landlady** dueño(-a) de la casa
**lane** carril m
**language course** curso m de idiomas
**large** *(adj.)* grande
**last** último(-a)
**last, to** *(time)* durar
**late** *(adv.)* tarde; **late** *(delayed)* retrasado(-a)
**later** más tarde
**laugh, to** reír
**laundromat** lavandería f
**laundry service** servicio m de lavandería
**lavatories** baños mpl públicos
**lawn** césped m
**lawyer** abogado(-a)
**laxative** laxante m
**lead-free** *(gas [petrol])* sin plomo
**leaflet** folleto m
**leak, to** *(car)* botar; *(roof/pipe)* gotear
**learn, to** *(language, sport)* aprender
**learner** *(driver)* aprendiz(-a) m/f
**least expensive** el/la menos caro(-a)

**leather** cuero m
**leave, to** *(place)* salir; *(drop off)* dejar;
**leave me alone!** ¡déjeme tranquilo(-a)!; **are there any left?** ¿queda(n) algún(-os/-as)?
**left, on the** a la izquierda
**left-hand side** lado m izquierdo
**left-handed** zurdo(-a)
**left-luggage office** depósito m de equipaje
**leg** pierna f
**legal, to be** ser legal
**leggings** leggings f
**lemon** limón m
**lemonade** limonada f
**lend: could you lend me...?** ¿puede prestarme...?
**length** longitud f
**lens** *(camera)* objetivo m; *(optical)* lentes m
**lesbian club** club m de lesbianas
**less** menos
**let: please let me know** avíseme
**letter** carta f
**library** biblioteca f
**license plate number** número m de matrícula
**lie down, to** acostarse
**lifeboat** bote m salvavidas
**lifeguard** salvavidas m/f
**life jacket** chaqueta f salvavidas
**life preserver [belt]** cinturón m salvavidas
**lift** ascensor m; *(hitchhiking)* aventón m
**light** *(color)* claro(-a); *(weight)* liviano (-a); *(cigarette)* lumbre f [encendedor m]; *(electric, bicycle)* luz f
**lightbulb** foco [bombillo] m
**lighter** *(cigarette)* encendedor m
**lighthouse** faro m
**lighting** iluminación f [alumbrado m]
**like: I'd like ...** quisiera ...
**like this** *(similar)* como esto
**limousine** limosina f
**line** *(metro)* línea f; *(queue)* cola [fila] f; *(profession)* especialidad f; *(telephone)*
**an outside ~** una línea externa

**linen** lino m
**lip** labio m
**lipsalve** cacao m para los labios [manteca f de cacao]
**lipstick** lápiz m de labios
**liqueur** licor m
**liquor store** vinetería [licorería] f
**litre/liter** litro m
**little** pequeño(-a)
**live, to** vivir; **~ together** vivir juntos
**liver** hígado m
**lobby** *(theater/hotel)* sala de espera f
**local** de la región
**local anesthetic** anestesia f local
**local road** carretera f comarcal [camino m vecinal]
**lock** *(door)* cerradura f; *(canal)* esclusa f
**lock oneself out, to** quedarse por fuera de la habitación
**locked, to be** estar cerrado(-a) con llave
**locker** casillero [lócker] m
**long** largo(-a)
**long** *(time)* mucho tiempo; **how ~?** ¿cuánto tiempo?; **how much longer?** ¿cuánto tiempo más?
**long-distance bus** autocar m
**long-distance call** llamada de larga distancia f
**long-sighted** hipermétrope
**look, to have a** *(check)* revisar
**look: I'm just looking** sólo estoy mirando
**look after: please look after my case for a minute** cuídeme mi maleta un momento, por favor
**look for, to** buscar
**loose** suelto(-a)
**lose, to** perder
**lost-and-found [lost property office]** oficina f de objetos perdidos
**lost, to be** estar perdido(-a); **I've lost...** se me perdió
**lotion** loción m
**lots** muchos(-as)
**loud, it's too** está demasiado alto(-a)
**love: I love you** te amo

**low-fat** bajo en grasa
**lower** *(berth)* inferior
**luck: good luck** buena suerte
**luggage** equipaje m;
**~ allowance (baggage allowance)**, cantidad de equipaje permitido f;
**~ lockers** casilleros [lóckers] m; **~ tag** etiqueta f de equipaje; **~ carts [trolleys]** carritos m de equipaje
**lump** protuberancia f
**lumpy** *(mattress)* lleno de bultos
**lunch** comida f [almuerzo m]
**lung** pulmón m
**luxury** lujo m

## M

**machine washable** que se puede lavar en la lavadora
**madam** *(dear)* señora f
**made: what is it made of?** ¿de qué está hecho?
**magazine** revista f
**magnetic north** norte m magnético
**magnificent** suntuoso(-a) [majestuoso(-a)]
**maid** empleado(-a) m/f; *(cleaner)* aseador(a) m/f
**maiden name** apellido m de soltera
**mail, to** llevar al correo
**mail** *(post)* carta f [correspondencia f]; **by ~** por escrito
**mailbox** buzón m
**main** principal; **~ course** plato m principal; **~ rail station** estación f (principal) de tren; **~ street** calle f principal
**mains** *(electricity)* red f eléctrica
**make** *(brand)* marca f
**make an appointment, to** pedir una cita
**make-up** *(cosmetics)* maquillaje m
**male** hombre m
**mall** zona f de tiendas
**man** hombre m
**manager** gerente m
**manicure** manicure m
**many** muchos(-as)
**map** mapa m
**March** marzo m

**margarine** margarina f
**market** mercado m
**market day** día m de mercado
**married, to be** ser casado(-a)
**mascara** rímel m [pestañina f]
**mask** *(diving)* gafas fpl de bucear
**mass** misa f
**massage** masaje m
**match** *(sport)* partido m
**matches** fósforos m
**matinée** función f de matiné
**matte finish** *(photos)* acabado mate
**matter: it doesn't matter** no importa;
**what's the matter?** ¿qué pasa?
**mattress (air)** colchón m (inflable)
**May** mayo
**may I ...?** ¿puedo ...?
**maybe** tal vez
**me** me
**meal** comida f; cena f
**mean: what does that mean?** ¿qué significa eso?
**measles** sarampión m
**measure, to** tomar las medidas
**measurement** medida f
**meat** carne f
**medical certificate** certificado m médico
**medication** medicina f [remedio m]
**medium** *(regular)* mediano(-a); *(steak)* a medio cocinar
**meet, to** encontrarse; **pleased to meet you** mucho gusto
**meeting place [point]** sitio m de reunión
**member** *(of club)* miembro m
**men** *(toilets)* baños mpl para caballeros
**mend, to** remendar
**mention: don't mention it** no es nada [no hay de qué]
**menu** menú m [carta f]
**message** recado m [razón f]; mensaje m
**metal** metal m
**meter** *(taxi)* taxímetro m
**methylated spirits** alcohol m desnaturalizado/metilado
**Mexican** *(person/adj.)* mexicano(-a)

**Mexican peso** peso m mexicano
**Mexico** México
**microwave** *(oven)* horno m microondas
**midday** mediodía m
**midnight** medianoche f
**migraine** migraña f
**mileage** kilometraje m
**milk** leche f: **with ~** con leche;
**~ of magnesia** leche de magnesia f
**million** millón m
**mind: do you mind?** ¿le molesta?; **I've changed my mind**
he cambiado de opinión
**mine** mío(-a); **it's ~** es mío(-a)
**mineral water** agua f mineral
**minibar** mini-bar m
**minibus** minibús m [buseta f]
**minimart** súper [minimercado] m
**minimum** mínimo
**minister** ministro m
**minor road** carretera f secundaria
**minute** minuto m
**mirror** espejo m
**miss, to** pasar(se); perder
**missing, to be** faltar; *(person)* estar desaparecido(-a)
**mistake** equivocación f [error m]
**misunderstanding: there's been a ~**
ha habido un mal entendido
**modern** moderno(-a); **~ art** arte moderno m
**moisturizer** *(cream)* crema f hidratante
**monastery** monasterio m
**Monday** lunes m
**money** dinero m,; **~ order** giro m postal; **~-belt** cinturón m para llevar el dinero
**month** mes m
**monument** monumento m
**moor, to** amarrar
**mooring** amarradero m
**moped** ciclomotor m; velomotor m
**more** más; **I'd like some more**
quisiera un poco más
**morning, in the** por la mañana
**morning-after pill** píldora del día siguiente
**moslem** *(adj.)* musulmán(a)

**mosquito** mosquito m; **~ bite** picadura de mosquito f
**mother** madre f
**motorbike** motocicleta f; **~ parts**
**motorboat** lancha de motor f
**motorway** autopista f
**mountain** montaña f; **~ bike** bicicleta de montaña f; **~ pass** cruce m de montaña; **~ range** cordillera f
**mountaineering** montañismo m
**mousetrap** ratonera f
**moustache** bigote m
**mouth** boca f
**mouth ulcer** llaga f en la boca
**move, to** trasladarse; *(house)* mudar;
**don't move him!** ¡no lo mueva!
**movie theater** cine m
**Mr.** señor m
**Mrs.** señora f
**much** mucho(-a)
**mugged, to be** ser asaltado(-a) [atracado(-a)]
**mugging** asalto m
**mugs** tazas fpl
**multiplex cinema** cinema m múltiple
**mumps** paperas f
**muscle** músculo m
**museum** museo m
**music** música f; **~ box** caja de música f;
**~ store** almacén m de discos
**musician** músico(-a)
**must: I must ...** tengo que ...
**my** mi(s)

## N

**nail polish** esmalte m
**nail scissors** tijeras para uñas f
**name** nombre m; **my name is ...** me llamo ...; **what's your name?** ¿cómo te llamas?
**napkin** *(serviette)* servilleta f
**nappies** pañales mpl
**narrow** angosto(-a)
**national** nacional m/f
**national health** seguro m social
**nationality** nacionalidad f
**nature reserve** reserva f natural
**nature trail** ruta f ecológica

**nausea** náusea f
**navy blue** azul m marino
**near** cerca
**nearby** cerca de aquí; por aquí
**nearest** el/la más cercano(-a)
**near-sighted** miope
**necessary** necesario(-a)
**neck** cuello m
**necklace** collar m
**need: I need to...** necesito
**needle** aguja f
**negative** *(photo)* negativo m
**neighbor** vecino(-a)
**nephew** sobrino m
**nerve** nervio m
**never** nunca
**new** nuevo(-a)
**New Year** año nuevo m
**New Zealand** Nueva Zelanda
**newspaper** periódico m
**newsstand [newsagent]** puesto
[kiosko, quiosco] m de periódicos
**next** próximo(-a); **~ stop!** ¡próximo
paradero!
**next to** al lado de
**Nicaragua** Nicaragua
**Nicaraguan** *(person/adj.)*
nicaragüense
**niece** sobrina f
**night, at** de noche; por la noche
**night porter** portero m nocturno
**nightclub** club m nocturno
**nightdress** camisón
**nine** nueve
**nipple** *(for baby's bottle)* seno [pezón] m
**no** no
**noisy** ruidoso(-a)
**non-alcoholic** sin alcohol
**non-smoking** *(adj.)* no fumadores;
*(area)* sección f de no fumadores
**none** *(thing)* ninguno(-a)
**noon** mediodía m
**no one** nadie
**north** norte m
**Northern Ireland** Irlanda del Norte
**nose** nariz f
**nosebleed** hemorragia f nasal
**not that one** ése(-a) no

**note** billete m
**notebook** cuaderno m
**nothing** nada; **~ to declare** nada que
declarar; **~ else** nada más; **~ for me**
nada para mí
**notice board** cartelera f de anuncios
**notify, to** avisar
**November** noviembre
**now** ahora
**nudist beach** playa nudista f
**number** *(telephone)* número; **sorry,**
**wrong ~** disculpe, número equivocado
**nurse** enfermera f
**nursery slope** *(skiing)* pista f para prin-
cipiantes
**nylon** nylon m

---
O
---

**o'clock: it's ... o'clock** son las ... en
punto
**observatory** observatorio m
**occupied** ocupado(-a)
**October** octubre
**odds** *(betting)* probabilidades f
**of** de
**of course** por supuesto [claro que sí]
**off-licence** vinetería [licorería] f
**off-road (multipurpose) vehicle** jeep m
**office** oficina f
**often** a menudo
**oil** aceite m
**oil lamp** lámpara f de aceite
**okay** de acuerdo [bueno]
**old** viejo(-a); **~ fashioned** pasado(-a)
de moda [anticuado(-a)]; **~ town** ciudad
f vieja
**on: on board** *(ship)* a bordo; **on foot**
a pie; **on the left** a la izquierda; **on the**
**other side** al otro lado; **on the right** a
la derecha
**on, to be** *(showing)* presentar
**on/off switch** interruptor de prender y
apagar
**once** una vez
**once a week** una vez a la semana
**one** uno(-a); **~ like that** uno(-a)
como ése
**one-way ticket** boleto m de ida

**open** abierto(-a); **~ to the public**
abierto(-a) al público
**open, to** abrir
**open-air pool** piscina f al aire libre
**opening hours** horarios m
**opera** ópera f; **~ house**
teatro m de la ópera
**operation** operación f
**operator** *(tel.)* operador m
**opposite** enfrente de
**optician** oculista
**or** o
**orange** naranja [anaranjado] m *(fruit)*
naranja f
**orchestra** orquesta f
**order, to** pedir; encargar
**organized walk** caminata f
**others** otros(-as)
**our(s)** nuestro(s)(-a(s))
**out: he's out** él no se encuentra
**outdoor** al aire libre; **~ pool**
una piscina al aire libre
**outside** fuera de; afuera
**oval** ovalado(-a)
**oven** horno m
**over** por encima de; **~ there** por allá
**overdone** *(adj)* demasiado asado(-a)
**overheated** recalentado(-a)
**overnight** durante la noche
**owe: how much do I owe you?**
¿Cuánto le debo?
**own: on my own** solo (-a)
**owner** propietario(-a) m/f

## P

**pacifier** chupón [chupo] m
**pack of cards**
baraja [las cartas] f
**pack, to** empacar
**package** paquete m
**packed lunch** almuerzo m
[lonchera f]
**pack[et]** paquete m; **~ of cigarettes**
cajetilla f de cigarrillos
**paddling pool** piscina f para niños
**padlock** candado m
**pail** cubeta f [balde m]
**pain, to be in** tener mucho dolor

**pain killer** analgésico m
**paint, to** pintar
**painter** pintor(a)
**painting** pintura f
**pair of, a** un par m de
**pajamas** piyama f
**palace** palacio m
**palpitations** palpitaciones f
**Panama** Panamá
**Panamanian** *(person/adj.)*
panameño(-a)
**panorama** panorama f
**pantomime** pantomima f
**pants (U.S.)** pantalones mpl
**paper** hoja f de papel; **~ napkins**
servilletas f
**paraffin** parafina f
**Paraguay** Paraguay
**Paraguayan** *(person/adj.)*
paraguayo(-a)
**paralysis** parálisis f
**parcel** paquete m
**pardon?** ¿perdón?
**parents** padres mpl
**park** parque m
**park, to** estacionar
**parking** estacionamiento [parqueo] m;
**~ meter** parquímetro m [contador m de
estacionamiento ]; **~ lot** estacionamiento
[parqueadero] m
**partner** *(boyfriend/girlfriend)*
compañero(-a)
**parts** *(components)* repuestos m
**party** *(social)* fiesta f
**pass, to** pasar
**pass through, to** estar de paso
**passenger** pasajero m
**passport** pasaporte m
**pastry shop** pastelería f
**patch, to** poner un parche
**path** camino m
**patient** paciente m
**pavement, on the** andén m [acera f]
**pay, to** pagar; **~ a fine** pagar una
multa; **~ by credit card** pagar con
tarjeta de crédito
**pay phone** teléfono público m
**paying** pagar

**payment** pago m
**peak** pico m
**pearl** perla f
**pedestrian crossing**
cruce m peatonal; **~ zone [precinct]**
zona f peatonal
**pedicure** pedicura f
**pen** pluma f [bolígrafo m]
**pencil** lápiz m
**penicillin** penicilina f
**penknife** navaja f
**penpal [penfriend]** amigo(-a) por
correspondencia
**pensioner** pensionado(-a)
**people** personas f; gente f
**pepper** pimienta f
**per day** por día
**per hour** por hora
**per night** por noche
**per week** por semana
**performance** función f
**perhaps** quizá [tal vez]
**period** periodo m; *(menstrual)* regla
[menstruación] f; **~ pains** cólicos mpl
menstruales
**perm** permanente f
**permit** permiso m
**personal stereo** walkman m
[radio/grabadora m con audífonos]
**Peru** Perú
**Peruvian** *(person/adj)* peruano(-a)
**peso** peso m
**pet** animal doméstico m
**petrol** gasolina f; **~ can** bidón de
gasolina; **~ station** gasolinera f [estación
de servicio]
**pharmacy** farmacia [droguería] f
**phone** teléfono m; **~ call** llamada f
telefónica; **~ card** tarjeta f de teléfono
*(also* ➤ **telephone***)*
**photo, to take a** tomar una fotografía
**photo: passport-sized** fotografía f
tamaño pasaporte
**photocopier** fotocopiadora f
**photographer** fotógrafo(-a) m/f
**photography** fotografía f
**phrase** frase f; **~ book** libro m
de frases

**piano** piano m
**pick up, to** reclamar
**picnic** picnic m
**picnic area** zona f de picnic
**piece** *(portion)* rebanada f [pedazo m]
**pill: to be on the pill** tomar la
píldora f
**pillow** almohada f; **~ case** funda f
**pilot light** piloto m
**pink** rosado
**pipe** *(water)* tubería f; *(smoking)* pipa f
**~ cleaners** limpiadores mpl de pipa; **~
tobacco** tabaco m de pipa
**pitch** *(camping)* terreno m de camping;
**~ charge** precio m por el terreno de
camping
**pity: it's a pity** ¡qué lástima!
**place** *(space)* cupo m, lugar m
**place a bet, to** hacer una apuesta
**plain** *(not patterned)* sin adornos
**plane** avión m
**plans** *(intentions)* planes mpl
**plant** planta f
**plastic bags** bolsas fpl plásticas
**plate** plato m
**platform** andén m
**play, to** jugar; *(music)* tocar
**play group** guardería f
**playground** patio de recreo [patio de
juego]
**playing cards** naipes mpl
[juego m de cartas]
**playing field** campos m deportivo
**playwright** autor m
**pleasant** agradable
**please** por favor
**pliers** alicates mpl
**plug** *(sink, basin)* tapón m
**plumber** plomero m
**p.m.** p.m.
**pneumonia** neumonía f
**point to, to** señalar [mostrar]
**poison** veneno m
**poisonous** venenoso(-a)
**police** policía f; **~ certificate** certifi-
cación de la policía f; **~ station** estación
f de policía
**pollen count** recuento m polínico

**pond** laguna m
**pony ride** paseo en pony m
**pop music** música pop f
**popcorn** palomitas fpl de maíz [maíz f pira]
**popular** popular
**port** *(harbor)* puerto m
**porter** señor m; portero m
**portion** porción f
**possible: as soon as ~** cuanto antes
**possibly** posiblemente
**post, to** llevar al correo
**post** correo m
**post office** oficina f de correo
**postcard** postal f
**poste restante** lista f de correo
**poster** afiche m
**postman** cartero m
**pottery** *(objects)* cerámica f, *(craft)* alfarería f
**pound** *(sterling)* libra f esterlina
**power cut** apagón m [corte de corriente]
**power point** toma f de corriente
**pregnant, to be** estar embarazada
**premium** *(gas)* súper
**prescribe, to** recetar [formular]
**prescription** receta [fórmula] f
**present** *(gift)* regalo m
**press, to** *(iron)* planchar
**pretty** bonito(-a)
**priest** sacerdote m
**prison** prisión [cárcel] f
**private bathroom** baño m privado
**probably** probablemente
**produce store** abarrotes mpl [tienda f]
**program** programa m
**program of events** programa m de eventos
**prohibited: is it prohibited?** ¿está prohibido?
**promenade deck** cubierta f de paseo
**pronounce, to** pronunciar
**properly** apropiadamente
**Protestant** protestante m/f
**public bulding** edificio m público
**public holiday** día m festivo
**pullover** suéter m

**pump** *(gas [petrol])* bomba f
**puncture** pinchada m
**puppet show** función f de títeres
**pure** puro(-a)
**purple** morado
**purpose** motivo m
**purse** monedero m
**put by, to** *(keep)* guardar
**put up: can you put me up for the night?** ¿me puede alojar esta noche?
**putting course** campo de golf pequeño para entrenamiento m

## Q

**quality** calidad f
**quantity** cantidad f
**quarantine** cuarentena f
**quarter, a** un cuarto
**quarter past ...** *(after)* ... y cuarto
**quarter to ...** *(before)* un cuarto para las ...
**quay** muelle m
**queen** *(cards, chess)* reina f
**question** pregunta f
**queue** *(line)* cola [fila] f
**queue, to** hacer cola [fila]
**quick** rápido(-a)
**quickly** rápidamente
**quiet** tranquilo(-a)
**quieter** más tranquilo

## R

**rabbi** rabino m
**race** *(cars/horses)* carrera f; **~track [~course]** pista f de carreras
**racket** *(tennis, squash)* raqueta f
**radio** radio m
**railroad** ferrocarril m
**rail station** estación de tren f
**railway** ferroca-rril m
**rain, to** llover
**raincoat** impermeable m
**rape** violación f
**rapids** rápidos mpl
**rare** *(unusual)* raro(-a); *(steak)* poco hecho(-a)
**rarely** rara vez

**rash** *(ailment)* salpullido m
**razor** máquina f de afeitar; **~ blades** hojas de afeitar [máquinas de afeitar desechables]
**re-enter, to** volver a entrar
**reading** *(interest)* lectura f; **~ glasses** anteojos para la lectura m
**ready** listo(-a)
**real** *(genuine)* verdadero(-a) [auténtico(-a)]
**real estate agent** agencia f de bienes raíces
**receipt** recibo m
**reception** *(desk)* recepción f
**receptionist** recepcionista f
**reclaim tag** etiqueta f de reclamo
**reclaim, to** reclamar
**reclining seat** silla f reclinable
**recommend, to** recomendar; **can you recommend** ¿qué me/nos recomienda?
**record** *(LP)* disco m; **~ store** almacén m de discos
**recovery service** *(car breakdown)* servicio m de rescate
**red** rojo m; **~ wine** vino tinto m
**reduction** descuento m
**refrigerator** nevera f
**refund** devolución f del dinero
**refuse bags** bolsas fpl para la basura
**regards to ...** recuerdos [saludos] a
**region** región m
**register receipt** recibo de caja m
**registered mail** correo certificado m
**registration form** hoja de registro f
**registration number** número m de matrícula
**regular** mediano(-a); *(gas)* normal
**regulations: I didn't know the regulations** yo no conocía las reglas
**religion** religión f
**remember: I don't remember** no me acuerdo
**rent, to** alquilar
**rent: for rent** se alquila
**rental car** carro m alquilado
**repair, to** reparar; arreglar
**repairs** reparaciones f

**repeat, to** repetir; **please repeat that** repítamelo por favor
**replacement** uno(-a) nuevo(-a); **~ part** repuesto m
**report, to** informar sobre
**representative** representante m/f
**required, to be** exigir(se)
**rescue service** *(car breakdown)* servicio m de rescate
**reservation** reservación f
**reservations desk** taquilla f [ventanilla f]
**reserve, to** reservar
**rest, to** descansar
**restaurant** restaurante m
**retired, to be** estar retirado(-a)
**return ticket** boleto [tiquete] de ida y vuelta m
**return, to** *(come back)* regresar; *(take back)* devolver
**reverse the charges, to** llamar por cobro revertido
**revolting** asqueroso(-a)
**rheumatism** reumatismo m
**rib** costilla f
**right** *(correct)* bien [correcto(-a)]; apropiado(-a)
**right of way** derecho a la vía m
**right, on the** a la derecha;
**to drive ~** conducir por la derecha
**right-handed** diestro(-a)
**right: that's right** muy bien [correcto]
**ring** anillo m
**rip-off** estafa f
**river** río m; **~ cruise** crucero m por el río
**road** carretera f; **~ accident** accidente m de tráfico; **~ map** mapa m de carreteras; **~ signs** señales fpl de ca-rretera
**robbed, to be** ser robado(-a)
**robbery** robo m
**rock** *(stone)* roca f
**rock climbing** alpinismo m
**rock concert** concierto m de rock
**roller blades/skates** patines mpl de ruedas
**romantic** romántico(-a)
**roof** *(house/car)* techo m

**roof-rack** portaequipajes m
**rook** *(chess)* torre f
**room** habitación f [cuarto m];
**~ service** servicio m a la habitación
**rope** cuerda f
**round** *(shape)* redondo(-a);
*(of golf)* ronda f
**roundabout** glorieta f
**round-trip ticket** boleto m
de ida y vuelta
**route** ruta f
**rowing** remo m
**rubbish** basura f [caneca f]
**rucksack** mochila f
**rude, to be** ser grosero(-a)
**rugby** rugby m
**ruins** ruinas f
**run into, to** *(crash)* chocar
**running shoes** tenis m
**run out, to** *(fuel)* acabarse
**rush hour** hora f pico [hora de
mayor congestión]

## S

**safe** caja de seguridad [caja fuerte f] f;
*(not dangerous)* seguro(-a); **to feel ~**
sentir(se)
**safety** seguridad f; **~ pins** seguros
[ganchos] m
**sailboard** tabla f a vela
**sailboarding** hacer windsurf
**sailing boat** barco m de vela
**salad** ensalada f
**sales representative** representante
de ventas m/f
**sales tax** IVA m; **~ receipt** recibo m
del IVA
**salt** sal f
**Salvadorian** *(person/adj.)*
salvadoreño(-a)
**same** el/la mismo(-a); **the same**
**again** lo mismo otra vez
**sand** arena f
**sandals** sandalias fpl
**sandwich** sandwich m
**sandy** *(beach)* de arena
**sanitary napkins** toallas fpl higiénicas
**satellite TV** televisión f satélite

**satisfied: I'm not satisfied with this**
no estoy satisfecho(-a) con esto
**Saturday** sábado m
**sauna** sauna m
**sausage** salchicha f
**say: how do you say...?** ¿cómo se
dice...?; **what did he say?** ¿qué
dijo él?
**scarf** bufanda f
**scenic route** ruta f pintoresca
**scheduled flight** vuelo m regular
**school** colegio m
**scientist** científico m
**scissors** tijeras fpl
**scooter** motoneta f
**Scotland** Escocia
**Scottish** *(person/adj.)* escocés(a)
**scouring pad** estropajo m
**screw** tornillo m
**screwdriver** destornillador m
**scrubbing brush** cepillo m de fregar
**sculptor** escultor(a)
**sea** mar m
**seafront** malecón f
**seasick, I feel** estoy mareado(-a)
**season ticket** boleto [tiquete] m de
temporada
**seat** asiento m
**second** segundo(-a); **~ class** segunda
clase; **~ [first *(U.K.)*] floor** primer m
piso
**secondhand** de segunda mano; **~ shop**
almacén m de artículos de segunda
mano
**secretary** secretaria f
**security guard** guardia m de seguridad
[celador]
**sedative** sedante m
**see, to** ver; **~ someone again** ver (a
alguien) de nuevo
**self-employed, to be** ser
independiente
**self-service** autoservicio m
**sell, to** vender
**send, to** enviar
**senior citizen** anciano m
**separated, to be** estar separado(-a)
**separately** *(adv)* por separado

**September** septiembre
**serious** grave
**served, to be** *(meal)* servirse
**service** servicio m; *(religious)* oficio m;
**~ charge** gastos mpl de servicio; **is ~
included?** ¿está incluido el servicio?
**set menu** menú m del día
**seventy** setenta
**sex** *(act)* acto m sexual
**shady: it's too shady** hay demasiada
sombra
**shallow** poco profundo(-a)
**shampoo** champú m
**shape** modelo f
**share, to** *(room)* compartir
**sharp** afilado(-a)
**shaver** máquina de afeitar eléctrica
[afeitadora eléctrica]; **~ brush** brocha f
de afeitar; **~ cream** crema f de afeitar;
**~ socket** toma f [enchufe m] para
máquinas de afeitar
**she** ella
**sheet** *(bedding)* sábana f
**shelf** estante m
**ship** barco m
**shivery, to feel** tener escalofríos
**shock** *(electric)* descarga f eléctrica
**shoe** zapato m; **~ laces** cordones
[lazos] m de los zapatos; **~ polish** betún
m; **~ repair** zapatería f [zapatero
remendón] m; **~ store** almacén m de
zapatos m
**shoemaker** zapatero
**shop** tienda f; **~ assistant**
vendedor(a) [dependiente] m/f
**shopkeeper** tendero(-a)
**shopping area** zona f comercial
**shopping basket** canasta f
**shopping center** zona f de tiendas
**shopping list** lista f de compras
**shopping trolley** carro m del
supermercado
**shopping, to go** ir de compras
**shore** *(sea/lake)* orilla f
**short** corto(-a)
**shorts** shorts m
**short-sighted** miope
**shoulder** hombro m

**show** espectáculo m
**show, to** mostrar; **can you show me?**
¿puede mostrarme?
**shower** ducha f; **~ gel** gel m para la
ducha
**shrunk: they've shrunk** se encogieron
**shut** cerrado(-a); **when do you shut?**
¿a qué hora cierran?
**shutter** contraventana f
**shy** tímido(-a)
**sick, to feel** tener ganas de vomitar
**sick: I'm going to be** voy a vomitar
**side** *(of road)* lado [costado] m
**side street** calle lateral f
**sidewalk, on the** andén m
**sightseeing, to go** hacer un viaje
de turismo
**sightseeing tour** recorrido m por los
lugares turísticos
**sign** señal f
**signpost** señalización f
**silk** seda f
**silver** plata f
**silver plate** chapado(-a) en plata
**singer** cantante m/f
**single** *(room, etc.)* sencillo(-a);
**~ room** habitación sencilla f [cuarto
individual m]; **to be ~** ser soltero(-a)
**single ticket** boleto [tiquete] de ida m
**sister** hermana f
**sit, to** sentarse; **sit down** siéntese
**six** seis
**six-pack of beer** paquete m de seis
latas de cerveza
**size** talla f
**skating rink** pista f de patinaje
**ski, to** esquiar
**ski** esquí m
**ski instructor** instructor(a) m/f
de esquí
**ski suit** traje m de esquí
**ski trousers** pantalones m de esquí
**skin** piel f
**skirt** falda f
**slalom** slalom m
**sleep, to** dormir
**sleeping bag** saco m de dormir/
sleeping

**sleeping car** coche m cama
**sleeping pill** pastilla f para dormir [somnífero m]
**sleeve** manga f
**slice** rebanada f
**slide film** diapositiva [filmina] f
**slip** *(undergarment)* combinación f
**slippers** pantuflas f
**slot machine** máquina f automática
**slow** lento(-a); **slow down!** ¡disminuya la velocidad!
**slow, to be** *(clock)* estar retrasado
**slowly** lentamente; despacio
**small** pequeño(-a)
**small change** cambio [suelto] m
**smoke, to** fumar; **I don't smoke** yo no fumo
**smokers** fumadores
**smoky: it's too smoky** hay demasiado humo
**snack bar** cafetería f
**snacks** golosinas f
**sneakers** zapatillas de lona f
**snorkel** esnórkel m
**snow, to** nevar
**snowed in, to be** estar encerrado por la nieve
**snowplow** quitanieves m
**soap** jabón m; **~ powder** jabón m en polvo
**soccer** fútbol m
**socket** enchufe m
**socks** calcetines m
**sofa** sofá f
**sofabed** sofá-cama m
**soft drink** *(soda)* refresco m [gaseosa f]
**solarium** solario m
**sole** *(shoes)* suela f
**soluble aspirin** aspirina f efervecente
**some** un poco de
**someone** alguien
**something** algo
**sometimes** algunas veces
**son** hijo m
**soon** pronto; **as ~ as possible** cuanto antes
**sore throat** dolor de garganta m

**sorry!** perdón
**sort** clase f; **a ~ of** una clase de
**sound-and-light show** concierto de luz y sonido m
**sour** ácido(-a)
**south** sur m
**souvenir** recuerdo m; **~ store** almacén m de recuerdos [souvenirs]
**spa** aguas termales fpl
**space** *(room)* sitio m
**spade** *(shovel)* pala f
**spades** *(cards)* picas fpl
**Spain** España
**Spanish** *(language)* español m
**Spanish** *(person/adj.)* español(a)
**spare** *(extra)* de repuesto
**speak, to** hablar; **do you speak English?** ¿habla usted inglés?
**special rate** precio m especial
**specialist** especialista m/f
**specimen** muestra f
**spectacles** gafas f
**speed, to** conducir a gran velocidad
**speed limit** límite m de velocidad
**spell, to** deletrear
**spend, to** gastar
**spin-dryer** secadora f (centrífugadora)
**spine** *(body)* columna f vertebral
**sponge** esponja f
**spoon** cuchara f
**sports** deportes mpl; **~ club** club m deportivo; **~ ground** campos m deportivo
**sporting goods store** almacén m de artículos deportivos
**sprained, to be** estar torcido(-a)
**spring** *(water)* manantial f; *(season)* primavera f
**square** *(shape)* cuadrado(-a)
**squash** squash m
**stain** mancha f
**stainless steel** acero m inoxidable
**stairs** escaleras fpl
**stale** rancio(-a) [pasado(-a)]
**stall: the engine stalls** el motor se apaga
**stalls** *(orchestra)* luneta, platea f
**stamp** sello m [estampilla f]

**stamp machine** máquina f expendedora de sellos [estampillas]
**stand in line, to** hacer cola [fila]
**standby ticket** boleto [tiquete] m de stand-by
**start, to** (begin) empezar; (car) arrancar
**starter** entrada f
**statement** (legal) declaración f
**station** estación f
**station wagon** camioneta f
**stationer** papelería f
**statue** estatua f
**stay, to** hospedarse; quedar(se)
**steak house** restaurante m especializado en carnes
**stereo** estéreo [equipo de sonido] m
**stiff neck** tortícolis f
**still: I'm still waiting** todavía estoy esperando
**sting** picadura f
**stockings** medias fpl
**stomach** estómago m; ~ache dolor m de estómago
**stool** (faeces) feces [materias fecales] fpl
**stop** (bus, subway) parada f [paradero m]; **which stop?** ¿qué parada f [paradero m]?
**stop, to** parar; **please stop here** pare aquí, por favor
**stop over, to** pasar la noche
**stopcock** (water valve) llave f de cierre
**store** tienda f; ~ **assistant** vendedor(a) [dependiente] m/f; ~ **guide** guía f del almacén; ~keeper tendero(-a)
**stove** estufa f
**straight ahead** derecho
**strained muscle** músculo m torcido
**strange** raro(-a)
**straw** (drinking) popote m [pajita f]
**stream** arroyo m
**streetcar** tranvía m
**string** cuerda f
**striped** (patterned) a rayas
**strong** (potent) fuerte
**stuck: the key's stuck** la llave está atascada

**student** estudiante m/f
**study, to** estudiar
**stunning** sensacional
**stupid: that was stupid!** ¡qué estupidez!
**sturdy** resistente
**style** estilo m
**styling mousse** espuma f moldeadora para el cabello
**subtitled, to be** tener subtítulos
**subway** metro m; ~ **station** estación f de metro; (U.K.) pasadizo m subterráneo
**sugar** azúcar f
**suggest, to** sugerir
**suit** (man's) traje [vestido] m
**suitable, to be** es apropiado(-a) [recomendable]
**summer** verano m
**sun block** bloqueador m solar
**sunbathe, to** tomar el sol [asolearse]
**sunburn** insolación f
**Sunday** domingo m
**sundeck** (ship) cubierta f para tomar el sol
**sunglasses** gafas f de sol
**sun lounger** silla f reclinable para tomar el sol
**sunshade** (umbrella) sombrilla f
**sunstroke** insolación f
**suntan cream/lotion** crema/loción f bronceadora
**superb** magnífico(-a)
**supermarket** supermercado m
**supervision** vigilancia f
**supplement** sobrecargo [recargo] m
**suppositories** supositorios mpl
**sure: are you sure?** ¿está seguro(-a)?
**surfboard** tabla f de surf
**surgery** consultorio m
**surname** apellido m
**suspicious** sospechoso(-a)
**swallow, to** tragar [pasar]
**sweater** suéter m
**sweatshirt** sudadera f
**sweet** (taste) dulce
**sweets** (candy) dulces mpl
**swelling** inflamación f
**swim, to** nadar
**swimming** natación f; ~ **pool** piscina f;

**~ trunks** pantalón m de baño
**swimsuit** traje [vestido] m de baño
**switch** interruptor m
**switch off, to** apagar
**switch on, to** prender
**swollen, to be** estar inflamado(-a)
**symptoms** síntomas m
**synagogue** sinagoga f
**synthetic** sintético(-a)

## T

**T-shirt** camiseta f
**table** mesa f; **~ cloth** mantel m; **~ tennis** ping pong [tenis de mesa] m
**tablet** pastilla f
**take, to** *(carry, accept)* llevar; *(medicine)* tomar; *(time)* durar
**take away, to** para llevar
**take pictures/photos** tomar fotografías
**take someone home, to** llevar (a alguien) hasta su casa
**takeaway** restaurante m de comidas rápidas
**taken** *(occupied)* ocupado(-a)
**talcum powder** talco m
**talk, to** hablar
**tall** alto(-a)
**tampons** tampones m
**tan, to** broncearse
**tap** *(faucet)* llave f [grifo m]
**taste** sabor m
**taxi** taxi m; **~ driver** conductor de taxi [taxista] m/f; **~ [stand] rank** parada de taxi f
**tea** té m; **~ bags** bolsas fpl de té
**teacher** profesor(a) m/f
**team** equipo m
**teaspoon** cucharita f
**teat** *(for baby)* seno [pezón] m
**teenager** joven de a años [adolescente] m/f
**telephone** teléfono m; **~ bill** cuenta de teléfono f; **~ booth** teléfono m público [cabina f de teléfono]; **~ calls** llamadas fpl telefónicas; **~ directory** directorio m telefónico; **~ kiosk** cabina f telefónica; **~ number** número m de teléfono (*also* ➤ **phone**)

**telephone, to** llamar por teléfono
**television** televisión f
**tell, to** decir; **tell her/him** cuéntele a él/ella; **tell me** cuénteme (a mí); decir(me); *(warn)* avisar
**temperature** temperatura f
**temporarily** temporalmente
**temporary** temporal
**ten** diez
**tendon** tendón m
**tennis** tenis m; **~ ball** pelota f de tenis; **~ court** cancha f de tenis
**tent** tienda f (de campaña); **~ pegs** estacas fpl de la tienda; **~ pole** poste m de la tienda
**terminus** terminal m
**terrible** terrible
**tetanus** tétano m
**thank you** gracias
**thanks for your help** gracias por su ayuda
**that** eso(-a); **~ one** ése(-a); **that's all** eso es todo
**thawing snow** nieve f derretida
**theater** teatro m
**theft** robo m
**their** su(s)
**theirs** suyo(s), de ellos(as)
**theme park** parque m temático
**then** *(time)* luego
**there** allá
**there is/are ...** hay ...
**thermometer** termómetro m
**thermos flask** termo m
**these** estos(-as)
**they** ellos(-as)
**thick** grueso(-a)
**thief** ladrón m
**thigh** muslo m
**thin** delgado(-a) [flaco(-a)]
**think: I think that ...** creo que ...
**think about it, to** pensarlo
**third** tercero(-a)
**third party insurance** seguro m contra terceros
**third, a** un tercio [una tercera parte]
**thirsty: I am thirsty** tengo sed
**this** éste(-a)

**those** ésos(-as)
**thousand** mil
**thread** hilo m
**three** tres
**throat** garganta f
**throat lozenges** pastillas fpl para la garganta
**thrombosis** trombosis f
**through** a través de
**thumb** dedo pulgar m
**Thursday** jueves m
**ticket** boleto [tiquete] m; **~ office** venta f de boletos [tiquetes]
**tie** corbata f; **~ pin** prendedor [broche] m de la corbata
**tight** ajustado(-a)
**tights** pantimedias fpl
**till receipt** recibo de caja m
**time** *(of day)* hora f; **on ~** a tiempo; **free ~** tiempo m libre
**timetable** horario m
**tin can** lata f; **~ opener** abrelatas m
**tin foil** papel m aluminio
**tinted** *(glass/lens)* de colores
**tip** propina f
**tire [tyre]** llanta f
**tired, to be** estar cansado(-a)
**tissues** *(paper)* unos kleenex® m
**to** *(place)* hacia/a
**to be** ser
**toaster** tostadora f
**tobacco** tabaco m
**tobacconist** tabaquería [cigarrería] m
**tobogganing** deslizarse en tobogán
**today** hoy
**toe** dedo del pie m
**toilet(s)** baño(s) m
**toilet paper** papel m higiénico
**toiletries** artículos mpl de tocador
**tomorrow** mañana
**tongue** lengua f
**tonight** esta noche ; **for ~** para esta noche
**tonsillitis** amigdalitis f
**tonsils** amígdalas fpl
**too** *(extreme)* demasiado; *(also)* también
**too much** demasiado(-a)

**tooth** diente m [muela f]
**toothache** dolor m de muela
**toothbrush** cepillo m de dientes
**toothpaste** pasta [crema] f de dientes
**top floor** último piso m
**torch** antorcha f
**torn, to be** *(muscle)* estar desgarrado(-a)
**totally** totalmente
**tough** *(food)* duro(-a)
**tour** tour [recorrido] m; **~ guide** guía turística m/f; **~ operator** operador(a) de viajes; **~ representative** representante m/f de viaje
**tourist** turista m/f
**tourist office** oficina f de turismo
**tow rope** cable m de remolque
**tow, to** remolcar
**toward** en dirección a
**towel** toalla f
**toweling** felpa f para toallas
**tower** torre f
**town** ciudad m; pueblo m; **~ hall** casa f del ayuntamiento [consejo m municipal]
**toy** juguete m; **~ and game store** juguetería f
**track** senda f
**tracksuit** ropa f de entrenamiento
**traditional** tradicional
**traffic** tráfico m; **~ jam** embotellamiento [trancón] m; **~ violation [offence]** infracción f de tránsito
**trail** camino m
**trailer** casa f móvil; **~ park** camping m para casas móviles
**train** tren m; **~ station** estación de tren f; **~ times** horarios mpl de trenes
**training shoes** tenis m
**tram** tranvía m
**translate, to** traducir
**translation** traducción f
**translator** traductor(a)
**trash** basura f; **~ can** bote m de la basura [caneca f]; **~ can liner** bolsa f de la basura
**travel, to** viajar

**travel agency** agencia f de viajes
**travel iron** plancha f portátil
**travel sickness** mareo m
**traveler's check [cheque]** cheque m de viajero
**tray** bandeja f
**tree** árbol m
**tremendous** tremendo(-a)
**trip** viaje m
**trolley** *(shopping)* carrito m
**trouser press** prensa f para pantalones
**trousers** pantalones mpl
**truck** camión m
**true: that's not true** no es cierto
**true north** polo m norte magnético
**try on, to** *(sample)* medir
**Tuesday** martes m
**tumor** tumor m
**tunnel** túnel m
**turn, to** girar
**turn down, to** *(volume, heat)* bajar
**turn off, to** apagar
**turn on, to** encender
**turn up, to** *(volume, heat)* subir
**turning** *(road)* giro m
**TV** televisión f; **~ room** sala f de televisión
**TV-listings** *(magazine)* programación f de televisión
**tweezers** pinzas f
**twelve** doce
**twice** dos veces
**twin bed** dos camas f
**twist: I've twisted my ankle** me he torcido el tobillo
**two** dos
**two-door car** carro m de dos puertas
**type: what type?** ¿qué clase?
**typical** típico

# U

**ugly** feo(-a)
**U.K.** Reino m Unido
**ulcer** úlcera f
**umbrella** *(sunshade)* sombrilla f
**uncle** tío m
**unconscious, to be** estar inconsciente
**under** *(place)* debajo

**underdone** *(adj.)* poco hecho(-a) [cruda]
**underground** metro m; **~ station** estación f de metro
**underpants** calzoncillos m
**underpass** pasadizo m subterráneo
**understand, to** entender [comprender]; **I don't understand** no entiendo [no comprendo]
**undress, to** desvestirse
**unfortunately** desafortunadamente
**uniform** uniforme m
**unit** unidad f
**university** universidad f
**unleaded gasoline** gasolina f sin plomo
**unlimited mileage** kilometraje m ilimitado
**unlock, to** abrir (con llave)
**unpleasant** desagradable
**unscrew, to** desatornillar
**until** hasta
**upper** *(berth)* superior
**upset stomach** trastorno [malestar] m estomacal
**upstairs** arriba
**up to** hasta
**urgent** urgente
**urine** orina f
**Uruguay** Uruguay
**Uruguayan** *(person/adj.)* uruguayo(-a)
**us** nosotros
**U.S.** los Estados Unidos
**use, to** utilizar
**useful** útil m/f
**utensils** cubiertos m

# V

**vacancies** habitaciones disponibles/libres
**vacant** libre [disponible]
**vacate, to** *(room, etc.)* desocupar
**vacation** vacaciones f
**vaccination** vacunación f
**vaginal infection** infección f vaginal
**valet service** servicio m de planchado
**valid** válido(-a)
**validate, to** *(ticket)* convalidar

**valley** valle m
**valuable** valioso(-a)
**value** valor m
**VAT** *(sales tax)* IVA m; **~ receipt** recibo m del IVA
**vegetable store** verdulería f
**vegetables** verduras f
**vegetarian** vegetariano(-a)
**vehicle** vehículo m
**vehicle registration document** documento m de matriculación del vehículo
**vein** vena f
**vending machine** vendedora f automática
**venereal disease** enfermedad f venérea
**Venezuela** Venezuela
**Venezuelan** *(person/adj)* venezolano(-a)
**very** muy
**vest** camiseta f
**veterinarian** veterinario(-a) m
**video** video m; **~ game** juego m de video; **~ recorder** videograbadora f
**view: with a ~ of the sea** con vista al mar
**viewpoint** mirador m
**village** aldea f
**vineyard** viña f
**visa** visa f
**visit** visita f
**visit, to** visitar
**visiting hours** horas fpl de visita
**visitor center** oficina f de información
**vitamins** vitaminas f
**voice** voz f
**volleyball** voleibol
**voltage** voltaje m
**vomit, to** vomitar

W

**waist** cintura f
**wait, to** esperar; **wait!** ¡un momento!
**waiter!** ¡mesero! m
**waiting room** sala f de espera
**waitress!** ¡mesera! f
**wake, to** *(self)* despertarse; *(someone)* despertar a alguien
**wake-up call** llamada f
**Wales** (País de) Gales

**walk home, to** caminar hasta la casa
**walk: to go for a walk** salir a dar una vuelta [un paseo]
**walking** caminata f; **~ boots** botas f de montañismo; **~ gear** equipo m de montañismo; **~ route** rutas f peatonal
**wall** pared f
**wallet** billetera f
**want, to** desear [querer]
**ward** *(hospital)* sala f
**warm** *(weather)* caliente m/f
**warm, to** calentar
**wash, to** lavar
**wash basin** lavamanos m
**washer** *(for tap/faucet)* arandela f
**washing: to do ~** lavar; **~ machine** lavadora f; **~ instructions** instrucciones de lavado f; **~ powder** jabón para lavadora f
**washing-up liquid** detergente para los platos m
**wasp** avispa f
**watch** reloj m de pulsera; **~ strap** pulsera [correa] f del reloj
**watch television, to** ver televisión
**watchmaker** relojero m
**water** agua f; **~ bottle** botella f de agua; **~ heater** calentador m; **~skis** esquíes mpl acuáticos
**waterfall** cascada [catarata] f
**waterproof jacket** chaqueta f impermeable
**wave** ola f
**waxing** depilación con cera f
**way** *(direction)* camino m, ruta f;
**I've lost my ~** estoy perdido(-a);
**on the ~** en la vía
**we** nosotros(as)
**weak** *(coffee)* suave
**weak: I feel weak** me siento débil
**wear, to** vestir [llevar puesto(-a)]
**weather** tiempo m ; **~ forecast** el tiempo meteorológico [la predicción del tiempo]
**wedding** boda f
**wedding ring** anillo m de bodas
**Wednesday** miércoles m
**week** semana f

**weekend** fin de semana m; **on [at] the ~** en el fin de semana; **~ rate** precio m de fin de semana

**weight: my weight is ...** peso ...

**welcome to ...** bienvenido(-a) a ...

**Welsh** *(person/adj.)* galés(a)

**west** occidente m

**wetsuit** vestido m térmico

**what?** ¿qué?

**what kind of ...?** ¿qué clase de ...?

**what time?** ¿a qué hora?

**what's the time?** ¿qué hora es?

**wheelchair** silla f de ruedas

**when?** ¿cuándo?

**where?** ¿dónde?; **~ are you from?** ¿de dónde es usted?

**which?** ¿cuál? *(sing.)*/¿cuáles? *(plur.)*

**while** mientras

**white** blanco(-a); **~ wine** vino blanco m

**who?** ¿quién?

**whole: the whole day** todo el día

**whose** ¿de quién?

**why?** ¿por qué?

**wide** ancho(-a)

**wife** esposa f

**wildlife** fauna f

**windbreaker** anorak m impermeable

**window** ventana f; *(shop)* vitrina [aparador m]

**window seat** asiento m cerca a la ventana/ventanilla m

**windshield [windscreen]** parabrisas m

**windsurfing** windsurfing

**windy: it's windy** hace viento

**wine** vino m; **~box** caja f de vino [cartón m de vino]; **~ list** lista de vinos f; **winery** viña f

**wine and spirits merchant** *(liquor store)* vinetería [licorería] f

**winter** invierno m

**wishes: my/our best wishes** mis/nuestros mejores deseos

**with** con

**withdraw, to** *(money)* retirar

**without** sin

**witness** testigo m

**wood** *(forest)* bosque m; *(material)* madera f

**wool** lana f

**work, to** trabajar; *(function)* funcionar

**worry: I'm worried** estoy preocupado(-a)

**worse** peor; **it's gotten [got] worse** está empeorando

**worth: is it worth seeing?** ¿vale la pena verlo(-a)?

**wound** herida f

**wrap up, to** envolver

**write: write soon!** *(familiar)* ¡escribe pronto!

**write down, to** escribir

**writing pad** libreta de notas f

**wrong** *(not right)* mal; **~ number** número equivocado

XYZ

**x-ray** radiografía f

**yacht** yate m

**year** año m

**yellow** amarillo m

**yes** sí

**yesterday** ayer

**yogurt** yogur m

**you** usted(es); *(familiar)* tú

**young** joven

**your** su(s); *(familiar)* tu(s)

**yours** suyo(-a)(s)/de usted(es), *(familiar)* tuyo

**youth hostel** albergue m juvenil

**zebra crossing** paso m de cebra

**zero** cero m

**zip(per)** cremallera f [cierre m]

**zoo** zoológico m

# DICTIONARY
# SPANISH-ENGLISH

This Spanish–English Dictionary covers all the areas where you may need to decode written Spanish: hotels, public buildings, restaurants, stores, ticket offices, and on transportation. It will also help with understanding forms, maps, product labels, road signs, and operating instuctions (for telephones, parking meters, etc.).

## A

**a elegir** at your choice
**a la carta** a la carte
**a la medida** made to measure
**los andenes** to the platforms
**a prueba de choques** shockproof
**abierto(-a)** open
**abono mensual** monthly ticket
**abono semanal** weekly ticket
**abordar** to board
**abordar por la puerta delantera** enter by the front door
**ábrase por aquí** open here
**abril** April
**abroche su cinturón de seguridad** fasten your seatbelt
**acantilado** cliff
**accesorios para automóvil** car accessories/spares store
**accesorios para baño** bathroom accessories
**accesorios para cuartos** bedroom accessories
**aceptamos (todas las) tarjetas de crédito** we accept (all) credit cards
**acrílico** acrylic
**actualizado(-a)** updated
**acueducto** aqueduct
**adentro** indoors
**admisiones** admissions
**aduana** customs control
**advertencia** warning

**aeropuerto** airport
**aerobismo** aerobics
**aerodeslizador** hovercraft/hydrofoil
**afuera** outdoor
**agencia de viajes** travel agent
**agítese bien antes de usar** shake well before use
**agosto** August
**agua para beber** drinking water
**al aire libre** open-air/outdoor
**al estilo ...** ... style
**ala delta** gliding
**alberca** swimming pool
**albergue juvenil** youth hostel
**algodón** cotton
**alimentos congelados** frozen foods
**alpinismo** mountaineering
**alquilan cuartos** rooms to let
**alto** stop
**alto voltaje** high voltage
**altura** altitude
**altura máxima ...** low bridge (maximum height ...)
**altura sobre el nivel del mar** height above sea level
**aluminio** alumin[i]um
**ambulancia** ambulance
**amperes** amps
**ampliación** enlargement service
**ancho libre** horizontal clearance
**Año Nuevo** New Year's Day
**antes de las comidas/los alimentos** before meals
**anticipe su bajada** request stop
**antigüedades** antiques
**antojitos** snacks
**apague su motor** turn off your engine
**aquí está usted** you are here
**arcada** arcade
**área de servicio** service area
**arena movediza** quick sand
**arquería** archery
**arte** art
**artículos libres de impuestos** duty-free goods
**artículos extraviados** lost property

**8 artículos o menos** 8 items or less
**artículos que declarar** goods to declare
**ascensor** elevator/lift
**asegurador** insurance agent
**asiento de ventanilla** window seat
**asiento en el pasillo** aisle seat
**asiento número** seat number
**atletismo** athletics
**atracción turística** tourist feature
**auditorio** auditorium
**auto** car
**auto-cinema** drive-in *(movie)*
**auto-servicio** self-service
**autobús** bus, coach
**automóvil** car
**avenida** avenue
**avenida principal** main road/
principal highway
**avión** plane
**ayuntamiento** town hall
**azúcar** sugar

### B

**bahía** bay
**bahía de carga** loading bay
**bahía de descanso** rest area
**bailar** dance
**bailarín(a)** dancer
**bajo su propio riesgo/su
responsabilidad** at the owner's risk
**balcón** balcony
**baloncesto** basketball
**banco** bank
**barata** clearance [sale]
**barco** ship
**barco de vapor** steamer
**barco ultra-rápido** jetfoil
**base** terminus
**baños** restrooms/toilets; baths;
washing facilities
**bebidas incluidas** drinks included
**bebidas sin alcohol** soft drinks
**biblioteca** library
**bicicleta** bicycle
**bicicleta de montaña** mountain bike
**bienes raíces** real estate agent
**¡bienvenidos!** welcome!

**bloqueador solar** sunblock
**boletería** box office
**boleto de temporada** season ticket
**boletos** tickets
**boletos agotados** sold out
**boletos para hoy** tickets for today
**boliche** bowling
**bomba de aire** pump
**bomberos** fire department [brigade]
**bosque** forest
**botas de esquí** ski boots
**bote de vapor** steamboat
**botes salvavidas** lifeboats
**botica** pharmacy
**botiquín** medicine box
**boxeo** boxing
**buceo** deep water diving
**butacas** stalls

### C

**caballeros** gentlemen *(toilets)*
**cada ... horas** every ... hours
**cadena montañosa** mountain range
**café** coffee
**caja** checkout
**caja de ahorro** savings bank
**caja rápida** express checkout
**cajero automático** automated teller
(ATM) [cash machine]
**calcio** calcium
**calidad estándar** quality standard
**calle** street
**calle peatonal** walkway
**calle principal** main [high] street
**callejón/calle cerrada** cul-de-sac
**calorías** calories
**camarotes** cabins *(ship)*; sleeping car
[sleeper] *(train)*
**camine** walk
**camino** road/path
**camino angosto** narrow road
**camino cerrado** road closed
**camino de terracería** unpaved road
**camino derrapante** slippery road
**camino en construcción** road under
construction
**camino estrecho** narrow road

**camino irregular** poor road surface
**camión** bus/coach; truck
**campo** field
**campo de aterrizaje** airfield
**campo de batalla** battle site
**canal** canal
**cancelado** canceled
**canoa** canoe
**canotaje** canoeing
**caña de pescar** fishing rod
**cañón** canyon
**capilla** chapel
**cápsulas** capsules
**característico** typical
**cargo por servicio** service charge
**carnaval** carnival
**carne** meat
**carnicería** butcher shop
**carrera de galgos** greyhound racing
**carretera** highway [motorway]; road
**carretera de cuota** toll road
**carril** lane
**carril exclusivo para autobuses** bus lane
**carril exclusivo para ciclistas** bicycle path/lane
**carro** car
**casa** house
**casa de bolsa** stock exchange
**casa de cambio** currency exchange office [bureau de change]
**casa de huéspedes** guest house
**casa de la ópera** opera house
**cascada** waterfall
**casco** crash helmet
**caseta de cobro** toll booth
**casimir** cashmere
**castillo** castle
**casualidad** chance
**catador de vinos** winetasting
**catedral** cathedral
**ceda el asiento a ancianos e inválidos** please give up this seat to the elderly or handicapped
**cementerio** cemetery
**centro** downtown area

**centro comercial** shopping mall [arcade]
**centro deportivo y de recreación** sports center
**cerrado** closed
**cereal** cereal
**cerrado (por hoy)** closed (today)
**cerrado a vehículos pesados** closed to heavy vehicles
**cerrado al tránsito en general** closed to traffic
**cerrado hasta ...** closed until ...
**cerrado por remodelación/reparación** closed for repairs
**cerrado por vacaciones** closed for holiday/vacation
**cerrado, regresamos a las ...** closed until ...
**cerveza** beer
**chaleco salvavidas** lifejacket
**charco** pond
**chifón** chiffon
**ciclismo** cycling
**ciclistas solamente** cyclists only
**ciclo de secado** spin dry
**cine** movie theater [cinema]
**cinturón de seguridad** safety belt
**circo** circus
**clasificación A** universal (*film classification*)
**clasificación B** parental guidance (*film classification*)
**clínica** health clinic
**club de campo** country club
**club de recreación** sports center
**cobros por comisión** bank charges
**coche** car
**coche comedor** buffet/dining car
**cocina** cooking [cookery]
**cocínese congelado** cook frozen
**código de larga distancia** area code
**colina** hill
**comedia** comedy
**comedor** dining room
**comenzando a las ...** beginning at ...
**comida del día** menu of the day
**comida saludable/sana** health foods

**compartimiento de (no) fumadores** (non)smoking compartment
**compra de divisa** foreign exchange
**con baño (en el cuarto)** with (ensuite) bathroom
**con el estómago vacío** on an empty stomach
**con las comidas** with meals
**con plomo** leaded *(gas [petrol])*
**con vista al mar** with sea view
**concierto pop** pop concert
**concurso** contest
**congelado** frozen
**conserje** night porter
**conservas** preserves
**conserve su derecha** keep right
**consulta externa** outpatients
**consulte a su médico antes de usarse/administrarse** consult your doctor before use
**consultorio** consulting room/ doctor's office [surgery]
**consúmase antes del …** best before …
**contenido de grasa** fat content
**contorno** contour
**control de pasaportes** passport control
**convento** convent
**copias e impresiones** printing and copying
**correo** post office
**corte** court house
**corte aquí** cut here
**costa** coast
**costurera** dressmaker
**cruce** intersection [junction]
**cruce de tren** grade [level] crossing
**crucero** cruise liner; cruise
**cuadra** square
**cuartos vacantes/disponibles** accommodations available
**cuatro estrellas** four-star
**cubierta** car deck
**cubierta superior** sun/upper deck
**cubierto(-a)** indoor
**cuero** leather
**cueva** cave

**cuidad intensivo** intensive care
**cuidado** caution
**cuidado con el perro** beware of the dog
**cuidado con los ladrones** beware pickpockets
**cuide su equipaje** do not leave baggage unattended
**cuota** toll
**curva peligrosa** dangerous bend
**córtese aquí** tear here

## D

**damas** ladies *(toilets)*
**de … a …** from … to …
**de lunes a viernes** weekdays only
**de parte de …** sender …
**de temporada** in season
**deje rebasar** yield [give way]
**deje salir antes de entrar** let passengers off first
**deje su automóvil en primera (velocidad)** leave your car in first gear
**delicioso(-a)** delicious
**delta** delta
**demorado** delayed
**demoras posibles** delays likely
**dentista** dentist
**departamento** department
**departamento en renta/alquiler** apartment to let
**deporte** sport
**deportivo de recreación** sports center
**deposite su dinero y tome su boleto** insert money in machine and remove ticket
**depósitos** deposits
**depósitos y retiros** deposits and withdrawals
**derrumbes** falling rocks
**desayunador** breakfast room
**desayuno** breakfast
**desconectado** disconnected
**desconéctese completamente antes de mover** disconnect from mains before moving
**descuentos** reductions
**desechable** disposable

**desierto** desert
**deslizando** gliding
**despacio** slow
**después de las comidas/los alimentos**
after meals
**no desteñible** colorfast
**destino** destination
**desviación** detour [diversion]
**devoluciones** refund
**diciembre** December
**dieta** diet
**diócesis** diocese
**dique** dam
**dirección** address
**directo** direct *(service)*
**director** conductor
**directorio telefónico** telephone directory
**discos compactos** CDs
**disminuya su velocidad** slow down
**disolver en agua** dissolve in water
**doblada** dubbed
**doble circulación/sentido** two-way
traffic
**domicilio particular** home address
**domingo** Sunday
**Domingo de Ramos** Palm Sunday
**Domingo de Pascua** Easter Sunday
**domingos solamente** Sundays only
**dos estrellas** two-star
**dosis para adultos** adult dose
**dosis para niños** child dose
**duchas** showers
**duna** dune
**durante ... días** for ... days

## E

**edificio público** public building
**el próximo tour es a las...**
next tour at ...
**el servicio no está incluido** service not
included
**elevador** elevator [lift]
**elija destino** select destination/zone
**embajada** embassy
**emergencia** emergency
**empieza a las ...** begins at ...
**empuje** push

**en construcción** under
construction/proposed
**en renta** for hire
**en temporada** in season
**encienda sus luces** switch on headlights
**enero** January
**enfermería** infirmary
**entrada** entrance/way in
**entrada exclusiva de residentes**
access to residents only
**entrega de equipaje**
baggage claim [reclaim]
**entronque** interchange [junction]
**equipaje olvidado**
baggage check [left-luggage office]
**equipo de buceo** diving equipment
**equipo de cocina** kitchen equipment
**equitación** horseback riding
**es obligatorio usar gorra de natación**
bathing caps must be worn
**escalada en roca** rock climbing
**escalera eléctrica** escalator
**escuela** school
**especialidad de la casa** specialty of
the house
**especialidades regionales**
local specialties
**espectadores** spectators
**espectáculo** spectacle
**esquí** skiing
**esquí a campo traviesa** cross-country
skiing
**esquí acuático** waterskiing
**esquís** skis
**esta máquina no da cambio** this
machine does not give change
**esta noche** this evening
**estación de ambulancias** ambulance
station
**estación de metro** subway
[metro] station
**estación de servicio** service station
**estación de tren** train station
**estacionamiento** parking lot [car park]
**estacionamiento exclusivo para**
**clientes** customer parking

**estacionamiento gratuito** free parking
**estacionamiento permitido** parking permitted
**estacionamiento público** public parking lot [car park]
**estacionamiento subterráneo** underground parking [car park]
**estacione bajo su responsabilidad** park at your own risk
**estadio** stadium
**estampillas** stamps
**estatua** statue
**estuario** estuary
**evento** event
**exclusivo para adultos** adults only
**explosivo** explosive
**extinguidor** fire extinguisher

**fábrica** factory
**fácil acceso al mar/a la playa** within easy reach of the sea
**factor de protección 8** factor 8 *(sunscreen)*
**familiar** family section
**farmacia** pharmacy [chemist]
**faro** lighthouse
**favor de cerrar la puerta** please shut the door
**favor de dejar sus bolsas aquí** please leave your bags here
**favor de entrar sin alimentos** no food in the room
**favor de esperar atrás de la marca/línea** please wait behind barrier/line
**favor de hacer el aseo** please make up the room
**favor de mantenerse atrás de este punto** stand behind this point
**favor de mostrar sus bolsas antes de salir** please show your bags before leaving
**favor de pagar antes de consumir** please pay for gas [petrol] before filling car
**favor de pagar en el mostrador** please pay at counter
**favor de pagar la tarifa exacta** please have exact change ready
**favor de respetar este lugar sagrado** please respect this place of worship
**favor de tocar el timbre** please ring the bell
**fax público** faxes sent
**febrero** February
**fecha de nacimiento** date of birth
**fecha en que expira su tarjeta de crédito** credit card expiration [expiry] date
**feriado nacional/oficial** national holiday
**ferry de pasajeros** passenger ferry
**ficción** fiction
**fiesta nacional/oficial** national holiday
**fila** row/tier
**fin de reglamento de carretera** end of highway [motorway] regulation
**firma** signature
**florería** florist
**formal** formal wear
**fortaleza** fortress
**fotografía** photography
**frágil – vidrio** fragile – glass
**freno de emergencia** emergency brake
**fresco** fresh
**frontera** border crossing
**fruta** fruit
**fuegos artificiales** fireworks
**fuente** fountain
**función nocturna** evening performance
**funicular** cable car
**fútbol** soccer [football]

**galería de arte** art gallery
**galletas** biscuits
**ganado** cattle/livestock
**gasolina** gas [petrol]
**gasolinera** gas [petrol] station
**genuino(-a)** genuine
**gerente** manager
**gimnasio** fitness room
**giros** money orders
**giros postales** postal orders

**glorieta (a ... metros)** traffic circle [roundabout] (... meters ahead)

**glutamato monosódico** monosodium glutimate

**gotas** drops

**gratis** free

**grava suelta** loose gravel

**guardarropa/guardarropía** coatcheck [cloakroom]

**guarnición de verduras** choice of vegetables

**guía de la tienda/de ofertas** store directory [guide]

**guía telefónica** telephone directory

## H

**hasta terminar el tratamiento** finish the course

**hay cuartos vacantes/disponibles** accommodations available

**hay lugares arriba** seats upstairs

**hay refrescos** refreshments available

**hecho a mano** handmade

**hecho en casa** homemade

**helicóptero** helicopter

**hielo** icy *(snow)*

**hipermercado** supermarket

**hipódromo** racetrack [racecourse] *(horses)*

**hockey sobre hielo** ice hockey

**hombres** men *(toilets)*

**homeópata** homeopath

**horario** opening hours/timetable

**horario de recolección** times of collection

**horario de verano/invierno** summer/winter timetable

**horas de oficina** business hours

**horas de visita** visiting hours

**hospicio** hospice

**hospital** hospital

**hoy/hoy día** today

## I

**I.V.A. (impuesto al valor agregado)** sales tax [VAT]

**iglesia** church

**impuesto incluido** sales tax [VAT] included

**incluido en el precio** included in the price

**incluye** inclusive

**incluye una bebida** includes 1 complimentary drink

**incluido** included

**inflador** pump

**información** information desk

**información al cliente** customer information

**información nutricional** nutritional information

**informal** informal wear

**ingredientes** ingredients

**inmigración** immigration control

**inserte moneda** insert coin

**inserte tarjeta de crédito** insert credit card

**instrucciones de uso** instructions for use

**invierno** winter

## J

**jale** pull

**jardín** garden

**jardín botánico** botanical garden

**jardín de iglesia** churchyard

**joyería** jeweler

**jueves** Thursday

**jugos de fruta** fruit juices

**juguetería** toy store

**julio** July

**junio** June

## K

**kilómetro** kilometer

## L

**la bajada es por atrás** exit by the rear door

**lago** lake

**laguna** pond

**lana** wool

**lancha** row boat
**lateral** secondary/minor road
**lavado de coches** car wash
**lavandería** laundry
**lávese a mano** hand wash only
**lávese a máquina** machine washable
**lectura de poesía** poetry reading
**lencería** lingerie
**lenguaje** language
**libre** for hire, vacant
**libre de grasa** fat-free
**libre de impuestos** duty-free *(shop)*
**librería** bookstore
**límite de carga** load limit
**llame sin costo** toll free number [freephone number]
**llave de agua** faucet [tap]
**llegadas** arrivals
**llévese ... de regalo** free gift
**lo mejor del mundo** world's best
**lo mismo servido con ...** the same served with ...
**lotería** lottery
**lugar de nacimiento** place of birth
**lugar número** seat number
**lugares arriba** seats upstairs
**lunes** Monday
**Lunes de Pascua** Easter Monday

## M

**madera** wood
**malecón** embankment/pier
**maneje con cuidado** drive carefully
**maneje despacio** drive slow
**mañana** tomorrow
**mantenga la puerta cerrada** keep gate shut
**mantenga su carrril** keep/get in lane
**mantenga su derecha** keep to the right
**mantenga su izquierda** keep to the left
**manténgase en congelación** keep frozen
**manténgase en refrigeración** keep refrigerated
**manténgase en un lugar fresco** keep in a cool place

**manténgase fuera** keep out
**manténgase fuera de los jardines/del pasto** keep off the grass
**manténgase lejos del alcance de los niños** keep out of reach of children
**mar** sea
**marina** marina
**marque ... para comunicarse a recepción** dial ... for reception
**marque ... para obtener línea** dial ... for an outside line
**martes** Tuesday
**marzo** March
**mascotas** pet store
**maternidad** maternity
**matiné** matinée
**mayo** May
**media pensión** half board (Modified American Plan [M.A.P.])
**medidor de electricidad** electricity meter
**mejorado(-a)** improved
**... menos en su próxima compra** ... off your next purchase
**menú del día** set menu
**menú para turistas** tourist menu
**mercado** market
**mercancía irregular** soiled goods
**metro** subway [metro]
**mientras espera** while you wait
**miércoles** Wednesday
**mimo** mime
**mina** mine
**mínimo** minimum
**mirador** viewpoint
**modista** dressmaker
**molino** mill
**molino de viento** windmill
**monasterio** monastery
**moneda extranjera** foreign currency
**montaña** mountain
**monumento** monument
**motel** motel
**moto acuática** jet ski
**mueblería** furniture warehouse
**muebles** furniture
**muebles de jardín** garden center

**mujeres** women *(toilets)*
**multicinemas** movie theater [multiplex cinema]
**multipack** multipack
**muralla** city wall
**museo** museum
**música** music
**música bailable** dance music
**música clásica** classical music
**música de órgano** organ music
**música folklórica** folk music
**música viva/en vivo** live music

## N

**nacionalidad** nationality
**nada que declarar** nothing to declare
**natación** swimming
**navegación** sailing
**Navidad** Christmas
**nevada fuerte** heavy snow
**nieve fresca** powdery snow
**nivel A** circle
**nivel B** dress circle
**niñas** women (bathrooms [toilets])
**niños** men (bathrooms [toilets])
**no acampar** no camping
**no anclar** no anchorage
**no bloquee la salida** do not block entrance
**no correr** no running
**no debe ingerirse** not for internal consumption
**no debe ingerirse por vía oral** not to be taken orally
**no deje objetos de valor en su automóvil** do not leave valuables in your car
**no destiñe** colorfast
**no distraiga al conductor** do not talk to the driver
**no ensuciar** do not litter
**no esperar** no waiting
**no estacionar (entre… y …)** no stopping (between … and …)
**no estacionar sin permiso autorizado se usará grúa** unauthorized vehicles will be towed away

**no estacionar se usará trampa** wheel booting [clamping] in operation
**no estacionarse** no parking
**no hay cambio** exact fare
**no hay cambios** goods cannot be exchanged
**no hay descuentos** no discounts
**no hay devoluciones** no refunds
**no hay entrada** no entry
**no hay paso** no entry
**no hay salida** no exit
**no hay vacantes/ cuartos disponibles** no vacancies
**no incluye** exclusive
**no interrumpir/molestar** do not disturb
**no obstruir (el paso)** keep clear
**no pise/pisar el pasto** keep off the grass
**no planchar** do not iron
**no rebase** no passing/overtaking
**no residentes** non-residents
**no retornable** non-returnable
**no se aceptan cheques** no checks [cheques]
**no se aceptan tarjetas de crédito** no credit cards
**no se aleje de la pista** keep on the trail [no off-track skiiing]
**no se da cambio** no change given
**no se exponga al sol** do not expose to sunlight
**no se pega** non-stick
**no se recargue en la puerta** do not lean against door
**no sirve** out of order
**no tirar basura** no dumping
**no tocar** do not touch
**no tocar bocina/claxon** use of horn prohibited
**no tomar fotografías** no photography
**no usar flash/trípode** no flash/tripod
**nombre** name
**nombre de la cónyuge** name of spouse
**nombre de soltera** maiden name
**noviembre** November
**nuevo sistema de tráfico operando** new traffic system in operation

**nuevo(-a)** brand new
**número de afiliación al seguro social**
social security number
**número de asiento/lugar** seat number
**número de cuenta** credit card number
**número de pasaporte** passport
number
**número de registro de su automóvil**
car license plate [registration] number
**número de vuelo** flight number
**número gratuito** toll free number

## O

**obispo** bishop
**observatorio** observatory
**océano** ocean
**octubre** October
**oculista** optician
**ocupado** occupied/engaged
**oferta especial** special offer
**oficina de información** information
office
**oficina postal** post office
**operadora** operator
**óptica** optician
**oraciones** prayers
**oraciones vespertinas** evensong
**orilla del río** river bank
**oro** gold
**orquesta** orchestra
**orquesta sinfónica** symphony orchestra
**ortodoncista** orthodontist
**osteópata** osteopath
**otoño** fall [autumn]

## P

**pabellón** pavilion
**páginas amarillas** yellow pages
**pague 2 y llévese 3** buy 2 get 1 free
**pague aquí** please pay here
**pague en el parquímetro** pay at the
meter
**palacio** palace
**palos de esquí** ski poles/sticks
**pan** bread

**panadería** bakery
**pantano** marsh/swamp
**papel reciclado** recycled paper
**papelería** stationary store/stationer
**papeles de registro** registration papers
**paquetes** packages [parcels]
**para asistencia en carretera llame al**
**…** in case of breakdown, phone/
contact …
**para cabello graso/grasoso** for oily
[greasy] hair
**para cabello normal** for normal hair
**para cabello seco** for dry hair
**para después del sol** aftersun
**para dos (personas)** for two
**para llevar** take-away
**para vegetarianos** suitable for
vegetarians/vegans
**paracaídismo** parachuting
**parada (de autobuses)** bus stop
**paradas fijas** stopping service *(bus)*
**pared** wall
**parlamento** parliament building
**parque** park
**parque de diversiones** amusement
park
**parque ecológico** country park
**parque nacional** national park
**parrilla** barbeque
**parroquia** parish
**partido** game [match]
**pasadizo** alley
**pasaje** flight
**pasarlas enteras** swallow whole
**Pascua** Easter
**paso** gorge/pass
**paso a desnivel** fly-over
**paso cerrado** (mountain) pass closed
**paso de peatones** pedestrian crossing
**paso peatonal** pedestrian crossing
**paso subterráneo** underpass [subway]
**pastelería** bakery/pastry shop
**pastillas** pills/tablets
**patinaje sobre hielo** ice skating
**patines** skates
**peatones** pedestrians
**pediatría** pediatric ward

**peligro** danger
**peligro de avalancha** avalanche danger
**peligroso** dangerous
**pelota de mano** handball
**peluquero** barber
**peluquería** hairdresser
**películas** movies [films]
**pendiente pronunciada** dangerous slope
**pensiones** pensions
**pensión completa** full board (American Plan {A.P.})
**permita bajar antes de subir (abordar)** let passengers off first
**pesca** fishing
**pesca con autorización/permiso** fishing by permit only
**pescadería** fish store [fishmonger]
**pescado** fish
**pico** peak
**piel** leather
**píldoras** pills/tablets
**pintura fresca** wet paint
**piscina** swimming pool
**pista cerrada** road closed
**pista de carreras** racetrack
**pista para esquiadores avanzados/intermedios/principiantes** for advanced/intermediate/beginner skiers
**plancha** iron
**plata** silver
**plataforma** platform
**playa** beach
**playa nudista** nudist beach
**policía** police (station)
**policía de caminos** highway police
**policía vial** traffic police
**poliéster** polyester
**pomada** ointment
**ponga su boleto en un lugar visible** place ticket on windshield [windscreen]
**por... (pesos) extra ...** extra charge/supplement

**por favor conserve su boleto** please retain your ticket
**por favor espere su turno** please wait your turn
**por única ocasión/noche** for 1 night only
**portero** night porter
**portilla** porthole
**pósters** posters
**pozo** well
**precaución** caution; drive carefully
**precaución, escuela** caution, school
**precio por litro** price per liter
**pregunte sin compromiso** please ask for assistance
**premier** premier
**preparado sobre pedido** made to order
**preservativos** preservatives
**primavera** spring
**primer piso** second [first (U.K.)] floor
**primera** first class
**primera presentación/noche** first night
**privado** private
**probadores** fitting rooms
**productos lácteos** dairy products
**programa** program
**prohibida la entrada a niños menores de... años** no children under ...
**prohibida la entrada a personas ajenas a este lugar** staff only
**prohibida la entrada después de iniciada la función** no entry once the performance has begun
**prohibida la entrada durante la misa/la ceremonia/el servicio** no entry during services
**prohibido ...** forbidden
**prohibido bañarse** bathing prohibited
**prohibido estacionarse sin permiso autorizado** unauthorized parking prohibited
**prohibido hacer fogatas** no fires/barbeques
**prohibido jugar con pelota** no ball games

**prohibido nadar** no swimming/bathing
**prohibido pescar** no fishing
**próxima entrada o salida** highway [motorway] entrance/exit
**próximo entronque** highway [motorway] intersection [junction]
**próxima recolección a las** next collection at …
**psiquiatra** psychiatrist
**puede hacerse en microondas** microwaveable
**puente** bridge
**puente angosto** narrow bridge
**puente levadizo** drawbridge
**puerta** door, gate
**puerta automática** automatic door
**puerta de abordar** (boarding) gate
**puerta de emergencia** fire door
**puertas automáticas** automatic doors
**puerto** port/harbor
**puesto de periódicos** newspaper stand
**punto de embarco** embarkation point
**punto de encuentro** meeting place [point]; muster station

## Q

**queso** cheese
**quirófano** operating room
**quiropráctico** chiropractic

## R

**rampa** ramp
**rancho** farm
**rápidos** rapids
**rappelear** rapelling [abseiling]
**raqueta** racket/raquet
**rayos X (equis)** x-ray
**recepción** reception
**reciclado de vidrio** bottle recycling [bank]
**recital** recital
**referencia** reference
**regadera** shower
**regaderas públicas** public showers
**regalos** gift shop
**registro** check-in counter

**remo** rowing
**renta de coches** car rental
**renta de vestidos** dress hire
**renta de videos** video rental
**reparaciones** repairs
**reparación de calzado** shoe repairs
**reparación de coches** car repairs
**represa** reservoir
**reserva ecológica** nature reserve
**reservaciones** (ticket) reservations
**reservado** reserved
**retiros** withdrawals
**retornable** returnable
**revelado en 1 hora/4 horas/un día** one-hour/4-hour/overnight developing service
**revisado(-a)** revised
**revisión de pasaportes** passport check/control
**revista** review
**río** river
**rompa este vidrio en caso de emergencia** break glass in case of emergency
**ropa para caballeros** menswear
**ropa para damas** ladieswear
**ropa para niños(-as)** childrenswear
**ruinas** ruins
**ruta** bus route
**ruta de transbordador/ferry** ferry route
**ruta de tranvía** tramway

## S

**sábado** Saturday
**saborizantes** flavorings
**sal** salt
**sala** lounge
**sala de conciertos** concert hall
**sala de consulta/tratamiento** treatment room
**sala de convenciones** convention hall
**sala de espera** waiting room
**sala de pasajeros** passenger lounge
**sala de T.V.** television room
**sala/salón de eventos** conference room

**sala/salón de juegos** game room
**salida** exit/way out; gate *(airport)*
**salida de camiones** truck exit
**salida de emergencia** emergency exit/fire door
**salidas** departures
**salvavidas** life preserver [life jacket]
**salón de belleza** hairdresser
**sanitarios** toilets/restrooms
**sastre** tailor
**se alza el telón** curtain up
**se compra y vende** we buy and sell
**se consignará a las autoridades a la persona que sea sorprendida robando** shoplifting will be prosecuted
**se habla inglés** English spoken
**se multará a la persona que se sorprenda tirando basura** no littering: fine …
**se prohíbe …** … forbidden
**se prohíbe la entrada de niños sin la compañía de un adulto** no unaccompanied children
**se prohíbe el acceso a cubierta durante el transbordo** no access to car decks during crossing
**se prohíbe fumar en cubierta** no smoking on car decks
**se rentan cuartos** rooms to let
**se sancionará a la persona que se sorprenda viajando sin boleto** penalty for traveling without ticket
**se venden tarjetas de teléfono aquí** phone cards on sale here
**secador(a) de pelo** hairdryer
**sección de fumar** smoking
**sección de no fumar** non-smoking
**seda** silk
**segunda** second class
**segundo piso** second floor
**segundos** seconds
**seguridad** security
**semáforo temporal** temporary traffic lights
**sendero** footpath
**septiembre** September
**servicio a clientes** customer service

**servicio a cuartos** room service
**servicio incluido** service included
**servicio las 24 horas** 24-hour service
**servicio mecánico/eléctrico** breakdown services
**servicio nocturno** night service
**servicios de emergencia** emergency services
**si persisten las molestias, consulte a su médico** if symptoms persist, consult your doctor
**si rompe algo, debe pagarlo** all broken items must be paid for
**silencio** silence
**silla en cubierta** deck chair
**sin azúcar** sugar-free
**sin grasa** fat-free
**sin intermedios** no intermission
**sin plomo** unleaded
**sírvase helado** best served chilled
**sistema de seguridad activado/en operación** surveillance system in operation
**sitio de taxis** taxi stand [rank]
**solista** soloist
**sólo autobuses** buses only
**sólo carga** freight only
**sólo ciclistas** cyclists only
**sólo descarga** deliveries only
**sólo domingos** Sundays only
**sólo efectivo** cash only
**sólo entrada** entrance only
**sólo hombres** men only
**sólo mujeres** women only
**sólo mujeres y niños** women and children only
**sólo para uso externo** for external use only
**sólo peatones** pedestrians only
**sólo periódicos** newspapers only
**sólo personas con boleto de temporada** season ticketholders only
**sólo personas con permiso/autorizadas** permit holders only
**sólo residentes** residents only
**sólo tránsito local** no thru traffic [throughway]

**sólo turistas** tourists only
**soluble** dissolve in water
**sombra** shade
**subtitulada** subtitled
**sugerencia del chef** the chef suggests
**supercarretera** highway [motorway]
**superficie helada** icy road
**superficie irregular** uneven road surface
**supermercado** supermarket
**suplemento** supplement

## T

**tabaquería** tobacconist
**tabla de surfeo** surfboard
**tabla de windsurf** sailboard
**tabletas** tablets
**taquilla** box/ticket office
**tarifa** rate/admission charge/fee
**tarifa de cambio** exchange rate
**tarifa exacta** exact fare
**tarifa por cuarto/por noche** room rate
**tarjeta de embarco** embarkation card
**tarjeta de teléfono** phone card
**tarjetas de teléfono de venta aquí** phone cards on sale here
**teatro** movie theater [cinema]
**teatro infantil** children's theater
**teleférico** cable car/gondola
**teléfono** telephone
**teléfono de emergencia** emergency telephone
**teléfono público** public telephone
**telegramas** telegrams
**telesilla** chairlift
**televisión (vía satélite) en cada cuarto** with (satellite) TV in every room
**tenis de mesa** table tennis
**termina desviación** end of detour [diversion]
**terminal** terminus/station
**terraza** terrace
**tetera** kettle
**tienda** general store
**tienda de abarrotes** produce store [grocer]
**tienda de antigüedades** antiques store

**tienda de arte** art store
**tienda de deportes** sporting goods store
**tienda de discos** music store
**tienda de electrónica** electrical store
**tienda de fotografía** photography store
**tienda de instrumentos** music store
**tienda departamental** department store
**tienda duty-free** duty-free store
**timbres postales** stamps
**tinaco** water tank
**tintorería** dry cleaner
**toca** play
**todas las transacciones** all transactions
**todos estos platillos acompañados de ...** all the above are served with ...
**tolerancia de peso** luggage allowance
**tome su boleto** take ticket
**toque el timbre** please ring the bell
**torre** tower
**tours guiados** guided tours
**tours por el río** river trips
**trabajos concluidos** end of construction [roadworks]
**tráfico en dirección opuesta** traffic from the opposite direction
**tráfico lento** slow traffic
**tráfico/tránsito en un solo sentido** one-way street
**trailer** trailer [caravan]
**tramo angosto** road narrows
**trampolín** diving board
**transbordador** passenger ferry
**transborde en...** change at ...
**tránsito** one way
**tranvía** tram
**trasborde a...** change *(to other line)*
**tren** local train
**tren expreso** express train
**trolebús** trolleybus
**trolley** cart [trolley]
**tumba** tomb
**túnel** tunnel
**turistas** non-residents

**té** tea
**tóxico** toxic

## U

**última entrada a las ...** last entry at ... pm
**únicamente rastrillos** razors [shavers] only
**unidades** units
**unitalla** one size fits all
**universidad** university
**usted está aquí** you are here

## V

**vacantes** vacancies
**vajilla** china
**válido hasta...** valid until ...
**válido para las siguientes zonas ...** valid for zones ...
**valle** valley
**vapor** stream
**... veces al día** ... times a day
**vehículos pesados** heavy/slow vehicles
**velador** night porter
**velero** sailboat
**velocidad máxima** maximum speed
**veneno(so)** poison(ous)
**venta de divisa:** currency sold at
**venta de fin de temporada** clearance sale
**venta de liquidación** closing down sale
**ventanilla de apuestas** bookmaker
**verano** summer
**verdulería** greengrocer
**verduras** vegetables
**verifique su cambio/vuelto** please check your change
**vestidores** changing rooms
**veterinaria** veterinarian
**vía** track
**vía alternativa** alternative route
**vía alternativa de autobuses/camiones** alternative bus/truck route
**vía cerrada** road closed

**vía de alta velocidad** highway [motorway]
**vía de tren** railroad/railway
**vía para ciclistas** cycle track
**viaje** trip [journey]
**vidrio** glass
**viernes** Friday
**villa** village/town
**viñedo** vineyard/winery
**vino** wine
**vista panorámica** panoramic view
**vuelo número...** flight number
**vuelos internacionales** international flights
**vuelos nacionales** domestic flights

## YZ

**yate** yacht
**zona de obra** construction [roadworks]
**zapatero** shoemaker [cobbler]
**zapatos** shoes
**zona comercial** shopping area
**zona de campamento** campsite
**zona de estacionamiento restringida** limited parking zone
**zona de paisaje** scenic route
**zona de picnic** picnic area
**zona deportina** sports gound
**zona exclusiva para peatones** pedestrian zone [precinct]
**zona libre de tráfico** traffic-free zone
**zona residencial** residential zone
**zoológico** zoo

# REFERENCE

## GRAMMAR

### Regular verbs and their tenses

There are three verb types which follow a regular pattern, their infinitives ending in **-ar**, **-er**, and **-ir**, e.g. *to speak* **hablar**, *to eat* **comer**, *to live* **vivir**. Here are the most commonly used present, past and future forms.

|  | PRESENT | PAST | FUTURE |
|---|---|---|---|
| **yo** *I* | habl**o** | habl**é** | hablar**é** |
| **tú** *you* (informal) | habl**as** | habl**aste** | hablar**ás** |
| **él/ella/Ud.** *he/she/you* (form.) | habl**a** | habl**ó** | hablar**á** |
| **nosotros** *we* | habl**amos** | habl**amos** | hablar**emos** |
| **ellos/ellas/Uds.** *they/you* (form.) | habl**an** | habl**aron** | hablar**án** |
| **yo** *I* | com**o** | com**í** | comer**é** |
| **tú** *you* (informal) | com**es** | com**iste** | comer**ás** |
| **él/ella/Ud.** *he/she/you* (form.) | com**e** | com**ió** | comer**á** |
| **nosotros** *we* | com**emos** | com**imos** | comer**emos** |
| **ellos/ellas/Uds.** *they/you* (form.) | com**en** | com**ieron** | comer**án** |
| **yo** *I* | viv**o** | viv**í** | vivir**é** |
| **tú** *you* (informal) | viv**es** | viv**iste** | vivir**ás** |
| **él/ella/Ud.** *he/she/you* (form.) | viv**e** | viv**ió** | vivir**á** |
| **nosotros** *we* | viv**imos** | viv**imos** | vivir**emos** |
| **ellos/ellas/Uds.** *they/you* (form.) | viv**en** | viv**ieron** | vivir**án** |

Very often, people omit the pronoun, using only the verb form.

Examples: **Vivo en México.** *I live in México.*
**¿Habla español?** *Do you speak Spanish?*

There are many irregular verbs whose forms differ considerably.

### To be – ser and estar

Spanish has two verbs for *to be*, **ser** and **estar**. Their usage is complex, and we can give you only some general guidelines.

|  | PRESENT | PAST | FUTURE |
|---|---|---|---|
| **yo** | soy/estoy | fui/estuve | seré/estaré |
| **tú** | eres/estás | fuiste/estuviste | serás/estarás |
| **él/ella/Ud.** | es/está | fue/estuvo | será/estará |
| **nosotros** | somos/estamos | fuimos/estuvimos | seremos/estaramos |
| **ellos/as/Uds.** | son/están | fueron/estuvieron | serán/estarán |

**Ser** is used to identify people or objects, to <u>describe their basic and natural characteristics</u>, also to <u>tell time and dates.</u>

Examples:  **Fue caro!**  *That was expensive!*
**Somos médicos.**  *We're doctors.*
**Son las dos.**  *It's 2 o'clock.*
**Erá de Roma.**  *He was from Rome.*

**Estar** is used when the <u>state of a person or object is changeable</u> and to <u>indicate locations.</u>

Examples:  **Estoy cansado.**  *I'm tired.*
**¿Dónde estuvo?**  *Where was he?*
**¿Cómo está?**  *How are you?*
**Estarán en Roma.**  *They'll be in Rome.*

## Nouns and articles

Generally nouns ending in **-o** are masculine, those ending in **-a** are feminine. Their indefinite articles are **el** (masc) and **la** (fem). In the plural (**los/las**) the endings are **-s** or **-es** when the singular form ends with a consonant.

Examples:

| SINGULAR | PLURAL |
|---|---|
| **el tren** *the train* | **los trenes** *the trains* |
| **la mesa** *the table* | **las mesas** *the tables* |

The definite articles also indicate their gender: **un** (masculine), **una** (feminine), **unos** (plural masculine), **unas** (plural feminine).

Examples:

| SINGULAR | PLURAL |
|---|---|
| **un libro** *a book* | **unos libros** *books* |
| **una casa** *a house* | **unas casas** *houses* |

Possessive articles relate to the gender of the noun that follows:

|  | SINGULAR | PLURAL |
|---|---|---|
| *my* | **mi** | **mis** |
| *your* (informal) | **tu** | **tus** |
| *his/her/its/your* (formal) | **su** | **sus** |
| *our* | **nuestro/a** | **nuestros/as** |
| *their/your* (plural, formal) | **su** | **sus** |

Examples:  **¿Dónde está <u>su</u> billete?**  *Where is your ticket?*
**<u>Nuestro</u> tren sale a las 8.**  *Our train leaves at 8.*
**Busco <u>mis</u> maletas.**  *I'm looking for my suitcases.*

## Word order

The conjugated verb comes after the subject.

Example: **Yo trabajo en Madrid.** *I work in Madrid.*

Questions are formed by reversing the order of subject and verb or using key question words like *when* **cuándo**.

Examples: **¿Tiene Ud. mapas?** *Do you have maps?*
**¿Cuándo cerrará el banco?** *When will the bank close?*

## Negations

Negative sentences are formed by adding *not* **no** to that part of the sentence which is to be negated.

Examples: **No fumamos.** *We don't smoke.*
**No es nuevo.** *It's not new.*
**El autobús no va a ...** *The bus doesn't go to ...*
**¿Por qué no escuches?** *Why don't you listen?*

## Imperatives (command form)

Imperative sentences are formed by using the stem of the verb with the appropriate ending.
Example:

| | | |
|---|---|---|
| **tú** *you* (informal) | **¡Habla!** *Speak!* | [no habl<u>es</u>] |
| **Ud.** *you* (formal) | **¡Hable!** *Speak!* | |
| **nosotros** *we* | **¡Hablemos!** *Let's speak!* | |
| **vosotros** *you* (inf. pl.) | **¡Hablad!** *Speak!* | [no habl<u>éis</u>] |
| **Uds.** *you* (form. pl.) | **¡Hablen!** *Speak!* | |

## Comparative and superlative

Comparative and superlative are formed by adding *more* **más**/*the most* **lo más**, or *less* **menos**/*the least* **lo menos** before the adjective or noun.

| ADJECTIVE | COMPARATIVE | SUPERLATIVE |
|---|---|---|
| **grande** | **más grande** | **lo más grande** |
| *big, large* | *bigger* | *the biggest* |
| **costoso** | **menos costoso** | **lo menos costoso** |
| *expensive* | *less expensive* | *the least expensive* |

Example: **Estas tarjetas son las más baratas.**
*These postcards are the cheapest.*
**Pepe tiene menos dinero que Juan.**
*Pepe has less money than Juan.*

## Possessive pronouns

Pronouns serve as substitutes and relate to the gender of the noun.

|  | SINGULAR | PLURAL |
|---|---|---|
| *mine* | **mío/a** | **míos/as** |
| *yours* (informal singular) | **tuyo/a** | **tuyos/as** |
| *yours* (formal) | **suyo/a** | **suyos/as** |
| *his/her/its* | **suyo/a** | **suyos/as** |
| *ours* | **nuestro/a** | **nuestros/as** |
| *theirs* | **suyo/a** | **suyos/as** |

Examples:  **Sus hijos y los míos.**  *Your children and mine.*
**¿Es tuyo este café?**  *Is this coffee yours?*

## Adjectives

Adjectives describe nouns. They agree with the noun in gender and number. In general, masculine forms end in **-o**, feminine forms end in **-a** and they usually come after the noun. The feminine form is the same if the masculine form ends in **-e** or with a consonant.

Examples:  **Tenemos un coche viejo.**  *We have an old car.*
**Mi jefa es simpática .**  *My boss is nice.*
**El mar / La flor es azul.**  *The ocean / The flower is blue.*

Most adjectives form their plurals the same way as nouns:

Example:  **una casa roja**  **unas casas rojas**
*a red house*  *red houses*

## Adverbs and adverbial expressions

Adverbs describe verbs. They are formed by adding **-mente** to the feminine form of the adjective if it differs from the masculine. Otherwise add **-mente** to the masculine form.

Examples:  **María conduce lentamente.**  *María drives very slowly.*
**Roberto conduce rápidamente.**  *Robert drives fast.*
**Ud. habla español bien.**  *You speak Spanish well.*

Some common adverbial time expressions:

**actualmente**  *presently*
**todavía**  *still*
**todavía no**  *not yet*
**ya no**  *not anymore*

## NUMBERS

Larger numbers are built up using the components below:

e.g. 3,456,789 = **tres millones, cuatrocientos cincuenta y seis mil, setecientos ochenta y nueve**

Note that from 31 to 99, **y** (and) is used between tens and units, but never between hundreds and tens.

| | | | | | |
|---|---|---|---|---|---|
| 0 | **cero** _sero_ | | 31 | **treinta y uno** _treynta ee oono_ | |
| 1 | **uno** _oono_ | | 40 | **cuarenta** _kwarenta_ | |
| 2 | **dos** _dos_ | | 50 | **cincuenta** _seenkwenta_ | |
| 3 | **tres** _tres_ | | 60 | **sesenta** _sesenta_ | |
| 4 | **cuatro** _kwatro_ | | 70 | **setenta** _setenta_ | |
| 5 | **cinco** _seenko_ | | 80 | **ochenta** _ochenta_ | |
| 6 | **seis** _seys_ | | 90 | **noventa** _nobenta_ | |
| 7 | **siete** _seeyeteh_ | | 100 | **cien** _seeyen_ | |
| 8 | **ocho** _ocho_ | | 101 | **ciento uno** _seeyento oono_ | |
| 9 | **nueve** _nwebeh_ | | 102 | **ciento dos** _seeyento dos_ | |
| 10 | **diez** _deeyes_ | | 200 | **doscientos** _doseeyentos_ | |
| 11 | **once** _onseh_ | | 500 | **quinientos** _keeneeyentos_ | |
| 12 | **doce** _doseh_ | | 1,000 | **mil** _meel_ | |
| 13 | **trece** _treseh_ | | 10,000 | **diez mil** _deeyes meel_ | |
| 14 | **catorce** _katorseh_ | | 1,000,000 | **un millón** _oon meel-yon_ | |
| 15 | **quince** _keenseh_ | | first | **primero(-a)** _preemero(-a)_ | |
| 16 | **dieciséis** _deeyes-ee-seys_ | | second | **segundo(-a)** _segoondo(-a)_ | |
| 17 | **diecisiete** _deeyes-ee-seeyeteh_ | | third | **tercero(-a)** _tersero(-a)_ | |
| 18 | **dieciocho** _deeyes-ee-ocho_ | | fourth | **cuarto(-a)** _kwarto(-a)_ | |
| 19 | **diecinueve** _deeyes-ee-nwebeh_ | | fifth | **quinto(-a)** _keento(-a)_ | |
| 20 | **veinte** _beynteh_ | | once | **una vez** _oona bes_ | |
| 21 | **veintiuno** _beyntee-oono_ | | twice | **dos veces** _dos beses_ | |
| 30 | **treinta** _treynta_ | | | | |

| | |
|---|---|
| three times | **tres veces** _tres beses_ |
| a half | **una mitad** _oona meetath_ |
| half a(n) hour | **media hora** _medeea ora_ |
| a quarter | **un cuarto** _oon kwarto_ |
| a third | **un tercio [una tercera parte de]** _oon terseeo [oona tersera parteh deh]_ |
| a pair of ... | **un par de ...** _oon par deh_ |
| a dozen ... | **una docena ...** _oona dosena_ |

## DAYS

| | |
|---|---|
| Monday | **lunes** _loo_nes |
| Tuesday | **martes** _martes_ |
| Wednesday | **miércoles** mee_yer_koles |
| Thursday | **jueves** _khwe_ves |
| Friday | **viernes** vee_yer_nes |
| Saturday | **sábado** _sa_bado |
| Sunday | **domingo** do_meen_go |

## MONTHS

| | |
|---|---|
| January | **enero** e_ne_ro |
| February | **febrero** fe_bre_ro |
| March | **marzo** _mar_so |
| April | **abril** a_breel_ |
| May | **mayo** _ma_yo |
| June | **junio** _khoo_neeo |
| July | **julio** _khoo_leeo |
| August | **agosto** a_gos_to |
| September | **septiembre** septee_yem_breh |
| October | **octubre** ok_too_breh |
| November | **noviembre** nobee_yem_breh |
| December | **diciembre** deesee_yem_breh |

## DATES

| | |
|---|---|
| It's … | **Hoy es …** oy es… |
| July 10 | **10 de julio** dee_yes_ deh _khoo_leeyo |
| Tuesday, March 1 | **martes, primero de marzo** _martes_, pree_me_ro deh _mar_so |
| yesterday/today/tomorrow | **ayer/hoy/mañana** a_yer_/oy/ma_ña_na |
| this | **este/esta** _este_/_esta_ |
| next | **el próximo/la próxima** el _prok_seemo/la _prok_seema |
| every | **cada** _kada_ |
| … month/… year | **… mes/… año** mes/_año_ |
| last week/month | **la semana pasada/el mes pasado** la se_ma_na pa_sa_da/el mes pa_sa_do |
| on [at] the weekend | **el fin de semana** el feen deh se_ma_na |

## Seasons

| | | |
|---|---|---|
| spring | **la primavera** | *la preema<u>be</u>ra* |
| summer | **el verano** | *el be<u>ra</u>no* |
| fall [autumn] | **el otoño** | *el o<u>to</u>ño* |
| winter | **el invierno** | *el eenbee<u>ye</u>rno* |
| in spring | **en primavera** | *en preema<u>be</u>ra* |
| during the summer | **durante el verano** | *doo<u>ra</u>nteh el be<u>ra</u>no* |

## Greetings

| | | |
|---|---|---|
| Happy birthday! | **¡Feliz cumpleaños!** | *fe<u>lees</u> koompleyaños* |
| Merry Christmas! | **¡Feliz Navidad!** | *fe<u>lees</u> nabee<u>dath</u>* |
| Happy New Year! | **¡Feliz Año Nuevo!** | *fe<u>lees</u> año <u>nwe</u>bo* |
| Happy Easter! | **¡Feliz Semana Santa!** | *fe<u>lees</u> se<u>ma</u>na <u>san</u>ta* |
| Best wishes! *(my/our)* | **¡Mis/Nuestros mejores deseos!** | *mees/<u>nwes</u>tros me<u>kho</u>res de<u>se</u>yos* |
| Congratulations! | **¡Felicitaciones!** | *feleeseetasee<u>ey</u>ones* |
| Good luck!/All the best! | **¡Buena suerte! ¡Que todo salga bien!** | *<u>bwe</u>na <u>swe</u>rteh. keh <u>to</u>do <u>sal</u>ga bee<u>yen</u>* |
| Have a good trip! | **¡Buen viaje!** | *bwen bee<u>ya</u>kheh* |

## Public holidays

National holidays observed in all Latin-American countries:

| | | |
|---|---|---|
| January 1 | **Año Nuevo** | New Year's Day |
| May 1 | **Día del trabajo** | Labor Day |
| October 12 | **Día de la Raza** | Columbus Day |
| December 25 | **Navidad** | Christmas |
| Moveable dates: | **Viernes Santo** | Good Friday |

*Others (Mexico)*:

**Día de la Constitución** (Feb 5)
**Natalicio de Benito Juárez** (Mar 21)
**Aniversario de la Batalla de Puebla** (May 5)
**Día de la Independencia** (Sept 16)
**Día de todos los Santos** (Nov 1)
**Día de los Muertos** (Nov 2)
**Día de la Revolución** (Nov 20)
**Día de la Virgen de Guadalupe** (Dec 12)

| | |
|---|---|
| Excuse me. Can you tell me the time? | **Disculpe. ¿Puede decirme la hora?** _dees<u>kool</u>peh. <u>pwe</u>deh de<u>seer</u>meh la <u>o</u>ra_ |
| It's five past one. | **Es la una y cinco.** _es la <u>oo</u>na ee <u>seen</u>ko_ |
| It's … | **Son las …** _son las_ |
| ten past two | **dos y diez** _dos y dee<u>yes</u>_ |
| a quarter past three | **tres y cuarto** _tres ee <u>kwar</u>to_ |
| twenty past four | **cuatro y veinte** _<u>kwa</u>tro ee <u>beyn</u>teh_ |
| twenty-five past five | **cinco y veinticinco** _<u>seen</u>ko ee <u>beyn</u>tee-<u>seen</u>ko_ |
| half past six | **seis y media** _seys ee <u>me</u>deea_ |
| It's … | **Faltan …** _<u>fal</u>tan_ |
| twenty-five to seven | **veinticinco para las siete** _<u>beyn</u>tee-<u>seen</u>ko <u>pa</u>ra las see<u>ye</u>teh_ |
| twenty to eight | **veinte para las ocho** _<u>beyn</u>teh <u>pa</u>ra las <u>o</u>cho_ |
| a quarter to nine | **un cuarto para las nueve** _oon <u>kwar</u>to <u>pa</u>ra las <u>nwe</u>beh_ |
| ten to ten | **diez para las diez** _dee<u>yes</u> <u>pa</u>ra las dee<u>yes</u>_ |
| five to eleven | **cinco para las once** _<u>seen</u>ko <u>pa</u>ra las <u>on</u>seh_ |
| It's twelve o'clock (noon/midnight). | **Son las doce en punto (mediodía/ medianoche).** _son las <u>do</u>seh en <u>poon</u>to (<u>me</u>deeo-<u>dee</u>ya/<u>me</u>deea-<u>no</u>cheh)_ |
| at dawn | **al amanecer** _al ama<u>ne</u>ser_ |

| | |
|---|---|
| in the morning | **por la mañana** *por la mañana* |
| during the day | **durante el día** *dooranteh el deeya* |
| before lunch | **antes de la comida** *antes deh la komeeda* |
| after lunch | **después de la comida** *despwes deh la komeeda* |
| in the afternoon/evening | **por la tarde** *por la tardeh* |
| at night | **por la noche** *por la nocheh* |
| I'll be ready in five minutes. | **Estaré listo(-a) en cinco minutos.** *estareh leesto(-a) en seenko meenootos* |
| He'll be back in a quarter of an hour. | **Él volverá en un cuarto de hora.** *el volbera en oon kwarto deh ora* |
| She arrived half an hour ago. | **Ella llegó hace media hora.** *el-ya l-yego ase medeea ora* |
| The train leaves at … | **El tren sale a …** *el tren saleh a* |
| 13:04 | **la una y cuatro minutos** *la oona ee kwatro meenootos* |
| 0:40 | **doce y cuarenta** *dose ee kwarenta* |
| The train is 10 minutes late/early. | **El tren está retrasado/adelantado diez minutos.** *el tren esta retrasado/adelantado deeyes meenootos* |
| Your watch is five minutes fast/slow. | **Su reloj está adelantado/atrasado cinco minutos.** *soo relokh esta adelantado/ atrasado seenko meenootos* |
| from 9 a.m. to 5 p.m. | **de las nueve de la mañana a las cinco de la tarde** *de las nwebeh deh la mañana a las seenko deh la tardeh* |
| between 8:00 and 2:00 | **entre las ocho y las dos** *entre las ocho y las dos* |
| I'll be leaving by … | **Saldré alrededor de la(s) …** *saldreh alrededor deh la(s)* |
| Will you be back before …? | **¿Volverá antes de la/las …?** *bolbera antes deh la/las* |
| We'll be here until … | **Estaremos aquí hasta la/las …** *estaremos akee asta la/lasr* |

UNITED STATES

Océano Atlantico

México

Cuba

República Dominicana

Puerto Rico

Honduras

Guatemala

El Salvador

Nicaragua

Venezuela

Costa Rica

GUYANA

Panama

SURINAM

Colombia

FRENCH GUYAN

Ecuador

BRASIL

Perú

Océano Pacífico

Bolivia

Paraguay

Chile

Uruguay

Argentina

**AMÉRICA LATINA**